Metaphors o

Jonathan Charteris-Black

Metaphors of Brexit

No Cherries on the Cake?

Jonathan Charteris-Black
Faculty of Arts, Creative Industries
and Education
University of the West of England
Bristol, UK

ISBN 978-3-030-28767-2   ISBN 978-3-030-28768-9   (eBook)
https://doi.org/10.1007/978-3-030-28768-9

Cover illustration: Harry J Milburn

This Palgrave Macmillan imprint is published by the registered company Springer Nature Switzerland AG
The registered company address is: Gewerbestrasse 11, 6330 Cham, Switzerland

Preface

For many Brexit is equated with division, contention and discord—yet it can also tell us a great deal about human nature and human morality. For 'Leavers' and 'Remainers' alike a study of the metaphors of Brexit may contribute to a better understanding of the language and moral thought of British people in the earlier part of the twenty-first century. The outcome of the 2016 Referendum shocked most commentators since economists and other experts had warned against leaving the European Union after 43 years of membership and very few pollsters had predicted that they would. The decision to leave originated in a gut reaction against 'Brussels' among a majority rather than, perhaps, in a fully rounded assessment of the national interest.

Yet should we have been so surprised? There is an increasing amount of research that shows that human decisions are often not rational and are made on the basis of moral and emotional judgements rooted in intuition: in 'heart' rather than 'head'. In this book, I explore the insights offered by metaphors, and related aspects of language, into why the case to Leave the European Union proved more convincing to a majority of voters than the case to Remain. I suggest that 'Leavers' framed their arguments using symbols, allegories and metaphors that aroused deeper emotional responses and moral judgements.

Drawing on ideas developed in cognitive linguistics, metaphor theory, classical rhetoric and moral psychology this book examines Brexit-related metaphors occurring in press articles, political speeches and Tweets during the period 2016–2018. Although the patterns of metaphor described offer glimpses into British moral codes, I hope they will also contribute to an understanding of moral thought, language and persuasion that is not necessarily limited to a particular time and place.

Bristol, UK   Jonathan Charteris-Black

Contents

List of Figures

List of Tables

1

Cherries on the Cake?

Introduction: Metaphor and Brexit

In some pubs the word 'Brexit' is treated as a swear word and you have
to buy a round of drinks every time the word is mentioned because of
its potential to initiate conflict. The topic invites positions to be taken,
makes people angry and turns them away from reason. Some are annoyed
by the very word 'Brexit' itself: the media driven blend of 'Britain' and
'exit' to produce the simple, croaked, bi-syllabic sound conceals a reality that leaving the European Union is the most complex international
negotiation on which the United Kingdom has ever embarked. The word
'exit' is found in public building such as a cinema or a hotel and implies
there is a simple choice between being 'in' or 'out' of something but the
reality is different. Metaphors have dominated thought about 'Brexit' in
the deliberations of politicians and media discussions and they have influenced the private reflections of individuals. Supporters of Leave found
evidence of 'collaborators', 'saboteurs' or 'traitors' who were committing
'treason' while the Remain 'side' referred to their opponents as 'wolves
in sheeps clothing'. But in their urge to persuade, advocates of both
sides commonly forgot that these were metaphors at all, so that political

© The Author(s) 2019
J. Charteris-Black, *Metaphors of Brexit*,
https://doi.org/10.1007/978-3-030-28768-9_1

positions ended up in a linguistic maze—few even understood the meaning of the endlessly repeated 'Backstop'—a maze without an 'exit'. Is it any wonder that 'Brexit' became a taboo word?

In this book I illustrate how metaphor was 'weaponised' in discussions surrounding Britain's decision to leave the European Union and how it contributed to the tone of the Brexit debate. Sometimes this tone has been savage with medieval words such as 'betrayal' and 'traitor' becoming everyday vocabulary. But once we look under the surface we find that understanding the metaphors of the Brexit debate provides rich insight into the profoundly moral outlooks that influenced both those who sought to leave the European Union and those who wished to remain in it. Members of the public, opinion formers and politicians relied on metaphor as a way of framing political issues and creating persuasive stories and allegories. Understanding these better helps us to understand not only what divided the two sides but also what both sides held in common: a belief and desire that they could improve their country.

In this opening chapter I illustrate *how* metaphors influenced the Brexit debate in various ways. When Boris Johnson claimed "My policy on cake is pro having it and pro eating it" he was combining moral reasoning with humour. When political cartoonists represented Britain or the European Union as the 'titanic' they were contesting allegories in which the same symbols expressed opposing perspectives. When Theresa May insisted on her 'red lines' she was using a familiar idiom to mean: 'I am not prepared to negotiate on these issues'—strong language that was not reflected in the strength of her political position. In the second half of the chapter I introduce various linguistic and psychological concepts that contribute to an understanding of the pervasive and persuasive role of metaphor in the discourse of Brexit.

Reasoning Through Humour: "Having Your Cake and Eating It"

When asked in an interview in April 2019 about being accused of wanting 'to have his cake and eat it' Boris Johnson said: "Well, I still am. Let's not beat about the bush here. My policy on cake is still pro having it and pro eating it."[1] This metaphor expressed an argument that on withdrawing from the European Union Britain would still be able to retain many of the benefits that it had enjoyed as a member. But its morality was contested through different interpretations of the metaphor. Belgian MEP Philippe Lamberts told Theresa May: "I think it will be interesting to see how things develop but *you cannot have your cake and eat it*".[2] In the following month an eagle-eyed reporter photographed a handwritten note, carried by Julia Dockerill, an aide to the Tory vice-chair Mark Field stating: "What's the model? *Have your cake and eat it*". To pro-Europeans this implied that the UK wanted to retain all the main benefits that came from being a member of the European Union (henceforth the EU). It sought to restrict EU immigration and leave the Single Market, while ensuring that frictionless trade with the EU would continue after Brexit: but this appeared to the EU negotiators as wanting to 'have it both ways'.[3] The idiomatic proverb therefore pointed to a moral dilemma that was familiar to other Europeans; in French the proverb took the form: "Wanting to have the butter and the money from the butter, and the milkmaid's ass", suggesting that the moral dilemma was not an especially British one.

The moral contest was reasoned through other 'food' metaphors, such as when a German political thinker, Ulrike Guérot, wrote on *Politico*:

> Yes, we indulged you while you were part of the European Union. We gave you your rebate. We allowed you to sit on the sidelines of Schengen and the euro. But those days are over, now that you've decided to go. It's time for you to stop acting *like a spoiled child* and accept that you can't have everything both ways - departure from the EU but membership in programmes like Galileo and Erasmus; an Irish border that's both closed but somehow open; access to the single market without its most important conditions; the freedom of movement and no oversight by the European Court of Justice; *your pick of the European cherry tree, without bothering to water the soil or tend to its branches.*[4]

Here after likening Britain to a 'spoilt child', she introduced the idea that Britain was 'cherry picking' by wanting to select only beneficial aspects of EU membership. She extends the cherry tree metaphor to take into account the necessary preconditions for growing the 'European cherry tree'. In this regard she was framing the EU as an essentially productive enterprise nurtured with love and care. These two different metaphors—'having cake' and 'cherry picking'—offer the similar moral argument that choosing *only* pleasurable actions while avoiding the painful ones is morally naive. The metaphors allude to each other and create an intertextual relationship precisely because they share the same moral reasoning: they accuse the person who is 'cherry picking' or trying to 'have their cake and eat it' of being selfish by putting their own interests before those of others. They are both usually indicative of an EU perspective on the British position on Brexit, as shown in the 'Metaphor Brexicon' at the end of this book.

Like many fixed expressions taken from popular culture it is often their traditional sense that may be played with for rhetorical effect. The meaning of the proverb is not clear because it would seem quite logical to 'have your cake and eat it'—until we realise that the phrase was originally in reverse order: "Wolde ye bothe eate your cake, and haue your cake?"[5] This meant that you could no longer have your cake *after* you have eaten it because there would no longer be any cake left to eat. Normally speakers accuse *others* of 'cherry picking' or 'wanting to have their cake and eat it' but sometimes if they were being self-ironic they could represent *their own* actions and positions in this way. Boris Johnson is the most notable political exponent of the art of metaphor and his image is constructed partly through humour and embodied forms of persuasion. He reversed the moral judgement implied in the idiom with his version: "My policy on cake is pro having it and pro eating it" and this worked well because food is a topic that he has a reputation for exploiting humourously. He rejected the bias implied by the original proverb by expressing it in terms of rational self interest: it is quite logical to want to possess cake and to eat it. His version of the proverb came to symbolise a defiant and unyielding position associated with supporters of a so-called 'hard' Brexit.

The 'cake' metaphor was taken further by the British Chancellor of the Exchequer Philip Hammond, who, while speaking at the annual conference of the Christian Democrats Economic Council, quoted the economist and finance minister Ludwig Erhard, that:

…a compromise is the art of dividing a cake in such a way that everyone believes he has the biggest piece.[6]

Hammond went on to argue that there is "some applicability to the Brexit negotiations, although I try to discourage talk of 'cake' amongst my colleagues" and went on to say that he was hopeful that "we can maximise the size of the cake and each enjoy a bigger piece". Indirectly, Hammond was arguing for a much 'softer' type of Brexit than the 'hard' one proposed by Boris Johnson. Both speakers were using 'cake' metaphors to outline political positions by finding the right tone for different audiences and Hammond was alluding to Johnson, but he wanted to alter the moral argument from that implied by Johnson. He shifted the reasoning with the idea that a division of the cake that appears fair keeps everyone happy and implied that both the EU and the UK would benefit from a negotiated settlement.

The cake metaphor became so well established that it created a new word to describe a morally ambiguous position: 'cakeism'—the word was first used in the press by the strongly pro-Remain Guardian:

Not so the foreign secretary, whose doctrine of *cakeism* (having baked goods and eating them) is familiar from his Brexit prospectus.[7]

Often the new word was accompanied by brief explanation indicating its origin:

The approach has become known as "*cakeism*" over claims the Government is trying to "have its cake and eat it".[8]

In the three-year period covered by this book 'cakeism' was used 63 times in the British press, of which 7 were in headlines. The word even developed an adjective 'cakeist':

May's *cakeist approach* to Brexit (as in, having it and eating it) is beginning to find its limits. Yet it still appears that May believes, or needs to appear to believe, that it is possible *to have most of the cake* - even though the EU27 have *already taken a bite*.[9]

Realising the argumentative potential of the metaphor, after the Salzburg meeting of Theresa May with EU negotiators, Donald Tusk posted on Instagram a picture of showing himself and May looking at a tray of small cakes with the ironic caption:

A piece of cake, perhaps? Sorry, no cherries.

Here Tusk blended the two food metaphors discussed above—'having cakes' and 'picking cherries' with a third one a 'piece of cake'; when something is very easy to do it can referred to as a 'piece of cake'. Tusk's post was intended ironically as negotiating the Brexit agreement was not in the least 'easy'. It caused a mixed response on social media—some finding it 'savage', others 'brilliant'—depending on their political stance. Theresa May reacted with an official statement demanding that Britain be treated with respect: the cake without cherries post had caused sufficient hurt to elicit a frosty and formal response. Some tweets were more humorous:

It is very unfair of the #EU to keep talking about cherry picking when we are about to run out of agricultural workers.[10]

Others followed by mixing food metaphors; the strong Brexiteer John Redwood posted on Twitter:

It's because the EU is no bowl of cherries many of us wish to go. There are no cherries to pick. Now we pay for our own cake & for other countries' cake too. I look forward to paying just for our own cake, making more of it at home. Then we can have better cake & more prosperity.[11]

Redwood was elaborating and mixing the metaphors to develop an argument about finance and the British net contribution to the EU budget. Others also sought to entertain the Twittersphere through humorous elaboration of the metaphor:

Leavers were never realistic about the Irish border, citizens rights or trade. Now the UK is being held hostage by the DUP. The Tories will be eating #Brexit humble pie rather than having their cake and eating it.[12]

Such tweets illustrate how metaphor combined humour with moral reasoning. Although I have argued that the primary role of 'cake' metaphors was moral reasoning, it is equally clear that the media echoed the metaphor for its entertainment value. For example, between January 2016 and December 2018, there were 1237 press articles that had 'Brexit' in their title and both 'eat' and 'cake' in the text. As well as adding vigour and humour to lighten the cut and thrust of conventional political debate, metaphor has the potential for activating visual imagery—either humorous posts on social media, or political cartoons. In this respect metaphors are integral to the negotiation of power relationships between competing agents—and the side that wins the argument employs moral reasoning most effectively by finding the best metaphor. Also essential to winning the argument is the telling of stories, and this often required an allegory, a sort of cautionary tale, in which the moral reasoning was favourable to the speaker's argument—let's see how this works.

Contested Allegories: Sinking Ships and Getting Divorced

When speaking to students in Luxembourg University on the amount the UK would have to pay for leaving the EU, its President, Jeane-Claude Juncker, described a scenario: "If you are sitting in the bar and you are ordering 28 beers and then suddenly some of your colleagues [are leaving without] paying, that is not feasible. They have to pay. They have to pay"; the metaphor raises an ethical issue by drawing attention to what constitutes right action in a situation that would be familiar to his student audience: buying a round of drinks. It framed the ethical question by two different scenarios: one where the customer leaves without paying and the other where he pays. But because the audience understood that he was really cautioning Britain about their financial obligations on withdrawal from the EU it became an allegory that evoked laughter from the students suggesting that they had understood its hidden meaning and it became widely circulated. However, a critic might have observed that 28 is an unusually large round, particularly if some of these had not even been in the bar when the round was first offered. Because the meaning of an allegory is oblique it can be contested.

In another allegory, or cautionary tale, Leavers referred to the EU as a 'sinking ship'. The sinking ship symbol engages audiences by arousing fear and activating memories of the Titanic. Allegories invite symbols and soon the titanic became a symbol for self-inflicted disaster. In this allegory a huge, prestigious ship struck an iceberg forcing the crew to abandon ship. Those who could, climbed on to one of the very few lifeboats, but most were abandoned to their fate in a cold and lonely ocean. It is a cautionary tale about hubris with two distinct roles: one for the Titanic and one for the heroic lifeboat; but the identity of the victim depended on how each side used the allegory. Before the referendum supporters of Leave gave the EU the role of the sinking ship and Britain the role of the lifeboat. A sense of immanent disaster was stimulated by the rise of right wing populism in Europe, and in this version of the allegory leaving the EU was the final opportunity to escape before disaster struck. Nigel Farage observed that: "Europe is in one hell of a mess – thank goodness we got onto a lifeboat off the Titanic and I can't think of a better time for us to have done it".[13] Remain supporters generally avoided the titanic allegory. However, when the House of Commons voted against withdrawing without a deal in March 2019 a senior European negotiator described is as 'The Titanic voting for the iceberg to get out of the way'.[14] The roles had become reversed: Britain was no longer symbolised by the lifeboat but by the Titanic: the Titanic was a contested image through which each side cautioned the other about the dangers of hubris. It was the metaphors, political allegories and contested symbolism that communicated a moral vision of Britain's political situation in the world.

A number of tweets were accompanied by some form of image of a sinking ship—capsized at 45 degrees. Some included the phrase 'Abandon Ship'—yet there was still just time to disembark. This reminds us that metaphor encourages visual images that have long been used by cartoonists to frame political situations by drawing on the stereotypical associations of nations, politicians or other actors and entities.

A cartoon published by the British European Revue in 1915 represents Germany as an eagle about to pounce on France depicted as a female wearing revolutionary colours while Austria, dressed as a clown, clings on desperately onto the German eagle. Heroic Britain—a large powerful John Bull like character—wraps his sleeves up and, clutching a sabre, prepares to stride across the channel to sort out the mess, with the Empire, represented by small figures, in support. By contrast, a French cartoon map of Europe drawn by Paul Hadol in 1870 shows a brave France fending off Prussia while Britain is depicted as an old crotchety granny facing towards the Atlantic and walking away with its back towards Europe. Clearly, these two cartoons framed Britain's relationship with Europe in two contrasting cautionary tales offering moral comment. Some satirical cartoons of this period depict Russia as a large octopus with its tentacles spreading across Europe and strangling its neighbours. Satirical images symbolising the European nations engaged audiences by offering contested moral visions.

Britain's withdrawal from the EU was commonly referred to as a 'divorce' and there was talk from the start of the financial obligations that Britain had incurred as a result of its historic commitments; these were framed as a 'divorce' bill. There were no less than 1108 newspapers articles in the period January 2016 to December 2018 that included the words 'Brexit' and 'Divorce' in their headlines. Around half of these included reference to a 'divorce bill'. Given that over 4 in 10 marriages in the UK end in divorce, framing Brexit as a 'divorce' was a way of engaging readers by drawing on a familiar scenario with allegorical potential. The allegory had different scenarios: for many British people membership of the EU had always been a 'marriage of convenience', and for many Europeans the UK was always a difficult marriage partner. Marriage metaphors in which the relationships between nation states are conceptualised as if they were relationships between individual people have *always* been an attractive rhetorical strategy for contesting allegorical scenarios. This is because they are the most familiar arena for working out how moral beliefs, interpersonal relationships and behaviours cumulatively tie society together.

Naming Concepts—The 'Backstop' and the 'Emergency Brake'

Metaphor also offers a language for simplifying complex political concepts: reference to the 'backstop' and 'red lines' came to be shorthand terms for very complex political positions. 'A backstop' is a thing that is placed at the rear of something to form a barrier behind it. The 'backstop' served as a crucial concept in the debates between the UK and EU governments because both sides wanted to avoid there being an actual physical border between Northern Ireland and Ireland. Although neither side wanted a land border there would need to be a means of monitoring trade between Northern Ireland and the Republic of Ireland if they were no longer in the same Customs Union. Both the UK and the EU sought to avoid a so-called 'hard' barrier—customs posts with systematic checking of vehicles and people crossing between the north and south of Ireland. The 'backstop' became shorthand for the requirement for the UK to remain within a Customs Union until a solution was found to this Irish border problem.

The 'backstop' was a fallback position for dealing with the trade across the border and meant that if there were no agreement by the end of the transition period (December 2020) then the whole of Britain would remain in the Customs Union—which would restrict its ability to trade outside the EU. The British plan to monitor traffic across the border using either technology or by collecting tariffs on behalf of the EU was unlikely to be accepted by the EU, while the EU preference for the whole island of Ireland to come within the single market and customs union was felt to challenge the integrity and jurisdiction of the UK government—which depended on the Democratic Unionist Party—and so challenged one of Theresa May's so-called, 'red lines'. Because of the fear of there not being an agreement concerning the border the EU negotiators insisted the UK sign up to a legally binding 'backstop' clause. The very length and detail of this explanation shows why a word like 'backstop' was necessary!

The 'backstop' metaphor is rather different from some of the metaphors that I have discussed above because it was a metaphor that has a specific legal meaning of remaining in a Customs Union. It therefore summarised and simplified a legal and regulatory concept. The primary sense of 'backstop' is spatial, in sports such as baseball and rounders 'backstop' refers to a fielding position located behind the batter where the fielder should stop the ball in the event of the batter missing it. But in the withdrawal negotiations it referred to abstract financial arrangements concerning the collection of import duties, which makes it a metaphor. The similarity with the 'cherry picking' and 'having cake' metaphors is that 'backstop' serves as shorthand by encapsulating complex political positions succinctly; but it is different because, although it concerns a moral issue, it does not have offer a moral argument. Any reference to a political concept also needs to be intelligible, at least to politicians—and although not precise—at least unambiguous. When negotiating parties can use the same linguistic terms with a similar, if not necessarily identical, inter-pretation they need to rely on metaphor as it offers a sufficiently loose but well understood concept. However nobody I asked could offer me a clear explanation of what 'backstop' meant—so, while intelligible to politicians, it was not so for the general public; for this reason many news reports followed mention of the 'backstop' with a lengthy paraphrase!

There is no doubt that concern about immigration was a major issue regarding support for Brexit. Britain had been one of only three states to grant immediate free movement citizens from Eastern Europe states that joined the EU in 2004. Between May 2004 and September 2009, 1.5 million workers migrated from the new EU member states to the UK, although around half of these returned home. On announcing a referendum David Cameron sought to renegotiate the conditions sur-rounding one of the so-called 'four freedoms' of EU membership: the right of workers to move anywhere within the EU. He was offered what became known as an 'emergency brake' which was an arrange-ment by which the EU deal would allow any member country to limit access to in-work benefits for new EU immigrants for up to 7 years with the agreement of the European Parliament. The official name of the arrangement was 'an alert and safeguard' mechanism; this had a highly technocratic ring to it and so it became known in the media as an 'emergency brake'. An emergency brake is a brake (on a car or train) that can be used for stopping in the event of failure of the main brakes. The reason why the metaphor was probably so attractive was because it acknowledged that immigration to the EU had reached a crisis point: there was some form of emergency. This implied a moral duty to undertake action. This metaphor shows how technical language has to be translated by metaphor into language that is intelligible because of its implied moral meaning.

Purpose and Approach

The purpose of this book is to explain how, why, and with what effect, metaphor was employed by the two sides in the Brexit debate. This purpose is part of Critical Metaphor Analysis[15]—an approach that explores how metaphors are used to create rival, contested views of the world, ideologies. Given the complexity, seriousness and emotion surrounding the question of EU membership—and its very high political stakes—it is hardly surprising that metaphors have coloured the discourse. Whether in official statements of political position, press articles, social media posts or in the more formal arguments developed in debating chambers, metaphors were used in the telling of moral stories that resonated with audiences. This is because they echoed the essentially popular language of so-called 'ordinary' people many of whom are not experts and are not well versed in the discourse of trade agreements or international law. Not only do metaphors serve up 'palatable' ideas that seek out their own audiences on social media, they are ways of bringing moral issues into the domain of popular experience. Drawing on the proverbs and idioms to which people respond translates professional registers into a language that is more familiar for average people: the eating of cakes, the picking of cherries and emergency brakes.

My method was to identify, analyse and compare metaphors relating to Brexit from three data sources. Wherever I found a metaphor in one of the sources I hunted around to see if it also occurred in one of the others. From this process I was able to identify patterns of metaphor common to all three sources and identify the underlying meaning frames that are presented in this book. The sources were:

1. **Social Media** I read many of the postings from Twitter during the period 1st January 2016–31st December 2018 using the following hashtags: #Brexit, #VoteLeave and #VoteRemain—and all of the postings with these hashtags in the week prior to the UK Referendum (June 16th–June 23rd 2016). The personal nature of Twitter, entering into the privacy of the home, enhanced its potential as a source of personal and cognitive insight. A study of metaphors on Twitter provides a snapshot view into the social cognition of voters. During the Referendum campaign the use of marketing experts by politically interested groups has demonstrated that Twitter and other social media platforms were available for propaganda purposes.

2. **Political Communication** I read the scripted text versions of many speeches and all press articles authored by politicians with a focus on Boris Johnson and Jacob Rees-Mogg. For Boris Johnson I assembled 40,000 words of his speeches and 82,000 words of his press articles and for Jacob Rees-Mogg I assembled 16,300 words of speeches and 46,000 words of his press articles. In both cases these were taken from the 3-year period 2016 to 2018 (inclusive). As well as reading these language samples, identification of metaphor was assisted by electronic techniques such as the creation of wordlists and keyword lists. For this purpose I used a sample corpus of 500,000 words of texts authored by British politicians.

3. **Press Media** I examined all newspapers during the period January 2016 to December 2018, using the Nexis database. Because of the volume of data it was necessary to take a qualitative analysis of a representative sample of texts with balanced attention to the views of both sides in the campaign. I searched for articles with 'Brexit' in the headline field. This allowed me to confirm and find further examples of the frames, metaphors, allegories and scenarios that I had identified in the other two data sources as well to identify new metaphors. The press were divided over their position during the referendum and Table 1.1 summarises their positions and approximate readership in 2018.

The number of newspaper types were evenly divided between the two referendum 'sides', however, once circulation is taken into account,

Table 1.1 British national press circulation and affiliation (2016)[a]

Pro-Remain		Pro-Leave	
The Mail on Sunday	1,388,059	The Sun	1,787,096
The Daily Mirror	809,147	Daily Mail	1,589,471
The Sunday Mirror	749,061	The Sun on Sunday	1,487,301
The Times	404,155	The Sunday Times	770,370
The Sunday People	279,837	The Daily Telegraph	472,033
The i	271,859	Daily Star	470,369
The Financial Times	198,237	Daily Express	408,700
The Observer	183,210	The Sunday Express	369,666
The Guardian	164,163	The Sunday Telegraph	355,044
The Independent	55,193	The Daily Star Sunday	299,146
Total	4,502,921		8,009,196

[a]https://en.wikipedia.org/wiki/List_of_newspapers_in_the_United_Kingdom_by_
circulation· (The figures are based on the Audit Bureau of Circulation)

the readership of newspapers advocating leaving the EU was approximately twice that of newspapers advocating remaining in the EU. The 3 newspapers with the highest circulation—*The Sun*, *The Daily Mail* and *The Sun on Sunday*—all supported Brexit. Though this is an over-simplification as many newspapers published opinion articles on both sides of the debate, it gives a general idea of press bias. When ranked in terms of their editorial positioning the three most pro-Leave newspapers were *The Daily Express*, *The Daily Mail* and *the Sun*, while the three most pro-Remain newspapers were *The Financial Times*, *The Guardian* and *The Daily Mirror*; the most neutral were *The i* and *The Times*. A report by the University of Loughborough Centre for Research in Communication and Culture of the content of articles summarised the position as follows:

> Our analysis reveals five national newspapers are backing REMAIN and five, including The Sun, are backing LEAVE. But if you factor in the strength of papers' endorsements and the size of their circulation, LEAVE has an 82% to 18% advantage over REMAIN.[16]

This survey only included the daily press, which explains the total of 10 newspapers whereas my overview of circulation includes additional Sunday papers taking the total number of papers to 20. Overall, both in terms of the strengths of the endorsements, as well as the circulation numbers, the British media presented a pro-Brexit position.[17]

By identifying the frames, metaphors, allegories and scenarios of each side in the debate I hope to demonstrate how political opinions are contested through metaphor and how metaphors provide the raw material for both political manipulation and moral communication. Awareness of the relationship between metaphors, cognitive frames and political intentions by the general public should reduce vulnerability to external sources of manipulation—something which has been of growing concern since the Cambridge Analytica scandal revealed the selling of personal data for the purposes of propaganda and political marketing.

The referendum offered the perfect opportunity for identity formation by providing a framework for side-taking as 'them' and 'us' tribes formed around the 'in' and 'out' sides of the Referendum debate. Metaphors contribute to public debate since the metaphors of one group may be contested in a number of different ways: for example, by reversing the same metaphor, by adapting an existing metaphor, or by introducing an alternative metaphor frame. Metaphors become ideological when they express a set of beliefs and values that are shared by a particular social group and contribute to a worldview that unites and defines this group. Ideology is 'the basis of the social representation shared by members of a group'.[18] In the case of the UK referendum two different ideologies emerged: one of a global world based on interdependence and internationalism and the other of a world of separate national states with competing interests. But before seeing how this happened let's consider some linguistic essential concepts for understanding what is going on: a warning the next section explores the theory and if you are not a linguist you may prefer to go directly to Chapter 2—and then refer back to this section as necessary.

Critical Metaphor Analysis—Some Concepts

In this section I explain how Critical Metaphor Analysis[19] relies on a set of linguistic concepts that allows us to identify how language exerts a subtle influence over thought and opinion, and which eventually creates myths and ideologies: whole ways of viewing the world. I would like to explain a set of terms that are crucial in this book including frames, allegories, scenarios and scripts and indicate how these all contribute to the approach that I have named 'Critical Metaphor Analysis'.

Framing and Frames

I would like to emphasise that to 'frame' something is an action, a verb that creates subjective representations. When something is continually represented in the same way so that it becomes the established way of thinking about something it creates a frame, a noun: a socially shared perspective on something. The action of framing repeatedly creates frames that then form ideologies—socially shared representations. 'Framing' means drawing attention to, or raising awareness of, selective aspects of a particular entity or situation thereby introducing some form of cognitive bias. Entman offers a fuller definition of framing as:

> ...select[ing] some aspects of a perceived reality and mak[ing] them more salient in a communicating text, in such a way as to promote a particular problem definition, causal interpretation, moral evaluation, and/or treatment recommendation for the item described.[20]

In political contexts framing represents a social situation as problematic, conveys a moral perspective and offers arguments for solutions to that problem. For example, studies by Thibodeau and Broditsky (2011,[21] 2015[22]) conducted empirical research into a fictional city that was undergoing a crime wave. When crime was framed by using 'beast' metaphors, participants in their experiment, advocated that the 'beast' should be captured and controlled, but when it was framed by 'virus' metaphors, the same participants thought that the 'virus' should be diagnosed and treated. Though it seems that nowadays it is rather more likely that a threatening virus might break out than a beast might go on a rampage—most researchers agrees that the frames activated by metaphor influence interpretation (though they differ in how they do this) and can influence the way that people think and act in the world. It is important to note two things: first the metaphors that activate the frames have to be introduced early on in a text and second that these metaphors do not act alone: frames are *not* activated by mentions of just *single* nouns like 'beast' or 'virus' but when these are followed up by related metaphors such as "in good shape" and "no obvious vulnerabilities".

Frames are not triggered by metaphors that come screaming at you in the face. They are encrypted in patterns of extended metaphors that narrate allegories and scenarios. Nor are metaphors are the *only* way of framing: sometimes frames are created by the assumptions they make: for example the phrases 'Take back Control' (Vote Leave 2016 Campaign) and 'Make America Great Again' (Trump 2016 Candidacy Campaign) both implied that in the past the British people had been in 'control', and now no longer were in control, and that America had been 'great' but no longer was. The use of 'back' and 'again' framed the historical status of these nations; framing historically implied that at an unspecified time in the past the nation was succeeding more than at present, so they framed a situation in terms of nostalgia for the past through the hidden logic of what linguists call 'implicature'. Both phrases were systematically repeated so that they became the slogans of their respective campaigns. Trump also repeated phrases such as 'crooked Hillary', 'The Queen of Corruption' and 'drain the swamp' to frame his opponent as dishonest.[23] We are not sure that voters really thought Hillary Clinton should be 'locked up', as Trump urged, but the frame created an element of doubt in some people's minds about her trustworthiness. This frame was then developed with claims about deleted emails from her home email server. Metaphor, repetition and, claims (true or false) provide the frames that form the basis of what were essentially moral arguments.

Over time the action of framing produces a result, a frame i.e. a noun (also known as a schema) that is a perspective that arises when things are constantly described in the same way. A frame arises from past experience on which participants rely when understanding situations. It is a conceptual structure derived from previous representations that allows us to understand a present situation better and serves as a filter for future interpretation of similar situations. Burgers et al. (2016,

p. 410[24]) propose two elements in such frames: framing devices—those elements that draw our attention, and reasoning devices that provide the conceptual content of a frame and through which 'the problem, cause, evaluation, and/or treatment is implied'. I am going to argue that in political language it is initially metaphors that draw our attention and then the allegories, symbols and scenarios through which these metaphor frames are developed that—along with reasoned arguments—provide moral reasoning devices.

'Framing' refers to something that we are cognitively engaged in: appraising and judging that is best articulated by verbs. Since nations are often discussed as if in a set of family relationships, I will use 'the family frame' as a general term to include everything we know about the family; but when applied to Brexit in expressions such as 'the European family', or the 'divorce bill' I will show how metaphor provides the conceptual material for allegories and reasoning about alternative positions in scenarios (see below). The concept of 'frame' overcomes the problem of one person's metaphor being another's literal statement and is therefore a broader concept that includes all forms of referential and associative meaning that influence political decision-making. Once frames are identified I describe whether Leave and Remain supporters used the same frames, and, if they did, how they reasoned about a situation in different ways so as to articulate their different ideologies. I am especially interesting in explaining how frames assist in establishing 'Self' and 'Other' identities.

Allegory and Myth

An allegory is a brief story that offers some form of covert ethical comment that cautions the reader or listener indirectly on how to behave when faced with some form of moral question. As we have seen on Twitter Britain was often represented by the Titanic. Attention was drawn and interest aroused by the metaphor, but the reasoning of these metaphors depended on which scenarios developed from the allegory. While it is not restricted to any particular scenario, the Titanic became an allegory for *any* serious but avoidable disaster arising from the human flaw of hubris. It symbolised *any* subsequent instance of avoidable disaster by serving as a specific, well known and prototypical example for hubris. It was this allegorical status that gave it the potential for use in the Brexit debate. The symbolic meaning derived from knowledge about the dangers of the sea, of lifeboats and of the Titanic itself. The point about allegory is that it attains its cautionary purpose by generalising from a specific case to other instances that are claimed to be morally similar. Because allegory can 'misdirect',[25] its meaning is indirect, it is contested and this is why the interpretation of the allegory depends on *which* scenario is adopted by a particular discourse community. This in turn will depend on the way that moral reasoning is employed. So metaphor and allegory provide the raw material for framing, but framing then works cognitively by creating specific scenarios. Critical Metaphor Analysis describes the contestation between alternative allegories and how these are shaped by competing scenarios drawing on moral reasoning to communicate conflicting ideologies.

Why might allegory be a term that is preferable to 'myth'? I think it is because of the cautionary comment that is implied by allegory. The growth of 'fake news' has led to 'myth' developing a sense in opposition to 'truth', so 'myth' has become a general term for misrepresentation. While politicians are often involved in myth-making the characteristic of the narratives of Brexit was their highly moral tone: after all leaving Europe had more to do with ethical perspectives on the European Union, such as how democratic it was, rather than on any calculation of economic self-interest. This concern with ethical comment is implied by allegory since allegorical narratives have the cautionary role of offering covert advice on right behaviour. The titanic frame was about hubris and advised leaving the ship, while judgements about the 'divorce settlement' that Britain should pay the EU was based on moral accounting as to what was 'owed'. So 'allegory' offers a richer ethical framing of a situation than is provided by 'myth' alone.

Scenario

To illustrate scenarios let's return to the allegory of the Titanic; this I suggest created two scenarios, both cautionary, but with opposing arguments. One had Britain in the role of the titanic and argued for the considerable dangers arising from Brexit, whereas the other had Britain in the role of a lifeboat and argued that Britain outside was safer than it was inside the EU. The *same allegory* therefore activated *two different scenarios* depending on the way that moral reasoning was applied. Allegory is the general term for the heuristic or reasoning devices for creating these two alternative scenarios: so allegories are 'contested' to create opposing scenarios. In this case the moral reasoning of those with a pro- or anti- Brexit position determined whether it was Britain or the EU that was framed as the titanic. So how does a 'scenario' differ from an 'allegory'?

> A scenario is a set of assumptions made by competent members of a discourse community about the prototypical elements of a concept, that is, participants, 'dramatic' story lines and default outcomes, as well as ethical evaluation of these elements, which are connected to the social attitudes and emotional stances that are prevalent in the respective discourse community....The emphatic 'framing' effect that metaphors can achieve ..is attained when a discourse community decides to settle on a particular scenario as their dominant (or even exclusive) perspective on reality.[26]

In Brexit there were two different discourse communities that created two 'particular scenarios': this is why in contested political events such as Brexit we need to distinguish between scenario and allegory: because the same allegory, or cautionary tale, was contested this gave rise to two alternative scenarios.

To summarise: both 'allegories' and 'scenarios' have a fixed and stable structure: there are people who act (or 'agents', 'participants'), actions they undertake ('story lines', or 'scripts') and some form of evaluations of these people and their actions. But a scenario achieves a framing effect by drawing on an allegory in a way that *is specific to the moral intuitions of a particular discourse community*. Moral reasoning requires matching up allegorical elements so that they correspond with real world targets. In the Leave scenario Britain was a lifeboat whereas in the Remain scenario, Britain was the Titanic: both scenarios reasoned about Brexit according to each group's moral appraisal of a political situation.

To illustrate this, from dry land this time—the semantic field of the family has a set of kinship terms: mother, father, son, daughter etc. but our knowledge of the family goes beyond just biological relationships such as 'A is the father/mother of B' because it also includes other aspects of human experience. These include emotions and notions of right and wrong behaviour. Typically, a frame for the 'family' entails emotional proximity arising from joint care and nurturance of children and sharing 'brothers' and 'sisters'. Of course, sadly, this does not always take place—some children are abandoned and others may have no contact with their syblings. As well as love and support, there may also be opposite feelings deriving from insufficiency of love or estrangement and separation, so one could frame a situation drawing on less ideal alternative scenarios. The family 'frame' therefore has a complex structure, but is relatively stable and has the power to evoke moral intuitions that serve as a basis for making moral judgements.[27]

Script

Another valuable concept when focusing especially on a familiar and predictable sequence of actions is 'script'. Originally Roger Schank and Robert Abelson proposed the term 'script' to describe a pattern inferred from multiple instances of the same sequence of events; the resulting script would then influence how we experience future events. When eating at a restaurant, we know that we enter, are shown to a seat, receive a menu, place an order, receive the food, consume the food and pay the bill. The events necessarily occur in this order and some events do not occur—such as cooking the food or doing the washing up. Like 'scenario' scripts have the potential to realise allegories:

> A script is a structure that describes appropriate sequences of events in a particular context. A script is made up of slots and requirements about

what can fill these slots. The structure is an interconnected whole, and what is in one slot affects what can be another. Scripts handle stylized everyday situations. They are not subject to much change, not do they provide the apparatus for handling totally novel situations. Thus, a script is a predetermined, stereotypical sequence of actions that defines a well-known situation.[28]

I will suggest that the marriage and divorce frame offered precisely such well-known scripts because there is a predictable sequence of events in married relationships of meeting, getting engaged, encountering difficulties and separating or divorcing. I will suggest that this script was especially important in the period when the UK was negotiating its withdrawal when concepts such as 'a divorce settlement' became so important. The difference between 'allegory' and 'script' is that 'script' lacks the cautionary role of moral judgement offered by 'allegory'. So the events in a marriage offer a script, a predictable sequence of events, but what is advised in the event of divorce may be allegorical. Allegories and scenarios necessarily frame situations using moral reasoning and moral intuitions that correspond with a certain ideology.

Keywords

'Keyword' means any word that occurs with a high level of frequency in a particular discourse. For example, earlier in this chapter I illustrated just how often the expressions 'divorce settlement', and 'cake' occurred in the headlines of newspapers reports on Brexit. Using this definition they are therefore Brexit 'keywords'. Ideas of co-operation between political units are contextualised within the frame of a divorce and so the keyword phrase 'divorce settlement' occurred regularly in headlines and prepared the way for relations between nations to be thought about as if they were relations between a couple negotiating their divorce, where goodwill may be lacking. The phrase instantly triggers moral intuitions that form the basis for judgement. As previously mentioned, metaphor is a powerful means for creating frames, allegories and scenarios by first engaging attention and then developing a storyline.

When ways of talking and thinking about international relations are repeated this shows in keywords that offer insight into storylines. Keywords are especially valuable in naming frames but the name of a frame is not dependent on any single keyword but seeks to generalise from a number of keywords, metaphors and allegories.

Embodied Simulation

A final question Critical Metaphor Analysis seeks to answer is: How do the metaphors, frames, allegories and scenarios achieve their powerful persuasive effects? One answer convincingly argued by theorists such as Ray Gibbs is through the concept of the embodied simulations that they arouse. An example of this is that many metaphors related to Brexit are closely related to images of physical entrapment and ensnarement. They have a visceral nature and just reading them can make you physically wince—consider the following, referring to Boris Johnson:

> The Foreign Secretary has for days been the target of *barbed* jibes from colleagues for what they see as his destabilising Brexit interventions. Speculation was rife that fans among the party's rank-and-file would have been *infected* by the irritation and give him the *cold-shoulder* treatment.[29]

Note the words in italics. Some researchers argue that the use of metaphor facilitates an embodied simulation, a neurologically triggered physical response.[30] Barsalou (2008) offers the following definition of simulation:

> Simulation is the re-enactment of perceptual, motor, and introspective states acquired during experience with the world, body, and mind. As an experience occurs (e.g., easing into a chair), the brain captures states across the modalities and integrates them with a multimodal representation stored in memory (e.g., how a chair looks and feels, the action of sitting, introspections of comfort and relaxation). Later, when knowledge is needed to represent a category (e.g. chair), multimodal representations captured during experiences with its instances are reactivated to simulate

how the brain represented perception, action, and introspection associated with it.[31]

Boris Johnson's 'barbed jibes' and 'infected' may evoke a memory of pain caused by language; and 'cold-shoulder' may recall experiences of rejection. Building on this work a number of experts have argued that the use of metaphor facilitates an embodied simulation by people who listen to or read such metaphors.[32] It may be that rich and complex, even mixed, metaphors trigger a more intense empathic response because they evoke highly detailed scenarios. Visceral metaphors such as 'barbed jibes' may trigger an empathic response because they evoke a highly resonant pain-inducing scenario—just as when we see others experiencing pain. We may share that experience, for example by wincing, when we read or listen to these visceral metaphors because they may stimulate an empathetic reaction, so simulation may form the basis of human empathy:

> Following this perspective, empathy is to be conceived as the outcome of our natural tendency to experience our interpersonal relations first and foremost at the implicit level of intercorporeity, that is, the mutual resonance of intentionally meaningful sensory-motor behaviors.[33]

I will argue that some of the more visceral metaphors in the Brexit debates such as those by Boris Johnson create the potential for embodied simulation on the part of the hearer. For example, he contrasts the pain and loss of control that arises from EU membership with the healing and therapeutic effects that taking back control will have for Britain. In September 2019 he went as far as to say that he would "rather be dead in a ditch" than agree to a further Brexit extension. We can see the potential this had for triggering moral intuitions. However, it may be that the very word 'Brexit' has the embodied effect of raising your blood pressure? Or conversely perhaps it leaves you feeling tired and your mind in total confusion: if so this book tries to offer a form of the therapy: once you focus on the language, the metaphors and allegories create a certain cognitive distance that allows us to better understand the political issues. Language can be our guide in solving problems—even if it was language that created them in the first place! With this in mind I will consider in the next chapter the actual language of Brexit and in particular the wording of the ballot paper.

Outline of Chapters

In Chapter 2 I explore some of the lexicon of Brexit, I consider the various words that were developed in the press media to refer to those advocating Leave and their opponents. I then consider the wording of the ballot paper used in the Referendum and suggest that the questions framed the choice in a way that favoured a vote to Leave. I discuss how media advocates of Leave developed innovative words such as 'Remoaners' more creatively than those who sought to maintain the status quo. In the last part of the chapter I discuss concepts from moral foundations developed in moral psychology that help understand the metaphor frames discussed in the following chapters; I also discuss the concepts of moral intuition and moral reasoning that help explain how and why the metaphors of politicians and members of the public achieved their effects in the various texts I examined.

In Chapter 3 entitled 'I Love my Country', I explore two predominant frames for Brexit: one I call the 'Patriotism and the Nation' frame and the other the frame of 'Distrust and Betrayal'. These frames are closely related since one is the corollary of the other: the 'Patriotism and the Nation' frame strengthens the identities of belonging to a group that is defined through shared love of the homeland, while the 'Distrust and Betrayal' frame strengthens identities through common opposition to those who are represented as betraying the nation. The naming, hunting down and exacting retribution on those defined as 'traitors' contributed to solidarity among the in-group through shared involvement in claiming to do what was necessary to protect the homeland. Taken together these complementary frames offer profoundly moral worldviews. There are other less intense forms for expressing the same contrast between and 'Us' and 'Them' groups such as 'flag', trust' and 'nation' and negative forms such as 'not trust' and 'not be patriots' that contribute to a less intense framing of 'Them' and 'Us' groups. I illustrate these frames with reference to the speeches and articles authored by Jacob

Rees-Mogg and more generally how they on these contrasting frames characterise the discourse of the press and Twitter. Together they interacted with argument structures to create moral intuitions and moral reasoning. I argue that it was the Leave campaign that was most persuasive in triggering moral intuitions with these frames partly because politicians such as Rees-Mogg had developed them in the first place.

In Chapter 4 I take this argument further by showing how Leave discourse framed the Referendum in terms of a 'War and Invasion' and developed two alternative scenarios one based primarily on moral reasoning and the other on moral intuition. The 'Sovereign Nation' scenario provided the moral argument that as a democracy the UK should be free from the constraining force of Brussels bureaucracy, while the other 'Invaded Nation' scenario was based in moral intuitions in which an in-group was endangered by external threats such as immigration—especially by culturally alien groups. These two scenarios each appealed to different audiences and permitted the Leave campaign a choice of rhetorical strategies for the framing of Brexit—one based on moral reasoning and the other on moral intuition—a choice that was not available for advocates of Remain. Innovation in language corresponded with the political ideology that claimed to offer a change from the status quo. In Chapter 5 I explain some insight that can be offered by conceptual metaphor theory and use this a starting point for the explanation stage of Critical Metaphor Analysis that can supplement other concepts such as allegories and scenarios to understand moral reasoning. I explore the 'Container' Metaphor by proposed conceptual metaphors such as: BOUNDARIES ARE CONTAINERS; SUPPORTERS ARE THOSE IN THE CONTAINER and OPPONENTS ARE THOSE OUTSIDE THE CONTAINER. I also suggest an alternative framing that depends on CONTAINERS ARE BOUNDED SPACES in metaphors that viewed Britain as imprisoned within the EU. I then explore a conceptual metaphor POLITICS IS A GAME with reference in particular to hard Brexiteers who viewed Brexit rather like a public school debating society.

Having identified these core frames initiated by Leave, in Chapter 6 I undertake a case study of Boris Johnson's metaphors. I demonstrate how he deployed each of the frames previously identified in developing his own style. I argue that he represented the EU as an external constraint on the United Kingdom and he conveyed this through scenarios based on an allegory of 'Unjust Entrapment' in which the UK is wrongly ensnared by a deceitful and alien source of authority. I illustrate how the corporeal nature of his metaphors aroused simulation in his audience to recreate an embodied experience of constraint heavily reliant on moral intuition. I also illustrate how the Nation-as-Body frame underlies his use of competitive race and illness metaphors—such as descriptions of the EU as 'sclerotic'. This is a pivotal chapter because it also provides an introduction to an important frame that is developed in Chapter 7: the Family and Relationships frame. I explain how his moral reasoning depended on whether other nations were construed as 'friends', 'family', 'playground bullies' or other types of relationship such as club membership. I explore these relationships in terms of two major frames for international affairs: the 'Nation as Family' and the 'Nation as Person'.

Chapter 8 takes this line of thinking further by discussing the frame of 'Marriage and Divorce'. I illustrate how the press had long framed the United Kingdom's relationship with the EU in terms of a 'marriage of convenience' and how this morally intuitive frame sowed the seeds for later dissolution of the relationship. I also illustrate how those who supported the EU project still often fell into the trap of using a largely negative framing of the relationship as implied by metaphors such as the 'divorce bill'. I consider the history of the framing international relationships in terms of personal ones and the type of semantic prosodies that arise when words such as 'marriage' and 'divorce' are used as metaphors.

In Chapter 9 I show how animal metaphors offer a suitable vehicle for moral reasoning about political issues—one that is especially preferred on Twitter. I elaborate further on the distinction between moral reasoning and moral intuition and discuss the cultural basis for animal metaphors and idioms. I also develop the notion of allegory since many animal metaphors are allegorical in character and offer users of social media an appropriate style for rhetorical framing. I explore the motivation for such metaphors in a cultural model known as 'The Great Chain of Being' and show how this traditional model commonly occurs in popular animal idioms on Twitter. These offer a framing of people with reference to the stereotypical frames for different animals but also include allegorical elements because of their orientation to strong forms of appraisal. Finally, in Chapter 10 I suggest some general metaphors for the whole experience of Brexit.

Notes

1. Gimson, A. "Has Boris Johnson Left the Buffoon Behind?" *The Telegraph*, 10 April 2009.
2. 20 October 2017.
3. See O'Rourke, K. (2018), p. 21.
4. *Politico*, 29 May 2018
5. Heywood, J. (1546). *Dialogue of Proverbs.*
6. https://www.politico.eu/article/philip-hammond-mocks-boris-johnson-during-visit-to-germany/.
7. *The Guardian*, 26 June 2018.
8. *The Express*, 26 March 2018.
9. *The Guardian*, 22 September 2017.
10. Christian Cummins, 23 September 2018.
11. John Redwood, 21 September 2018.
12. Diccon Bewes, 4 December 2017.
13. *Daily Express*, 19 December 2016.
14. One senior EU negotiator described a vote by UK MPs to block a no-deal Brexit in any circumstances as meaningless and like "the Titanic voting for the iceberg to get out of the way". https://www.irish-times.com/news/world/uk/eu-on-no-deal-brexit-vote-like-titanic-voting-for-the-iceberg-to-move-1.3825638.
15. Charteris-Black (2004).
16. https://blog.lboro.ac.uk/crcc/eu-referendum/sun-no-longer-hedging-bets-brexit/.
17. A similar conclusion was reached by the independent Reuters Institute, for example: "• After factoring in the reach of different newspapers the pro Brexit bias is further accentuated, with 48% of all referendum focused articles pro Leave and just 22% Remain". The report is available at https://reutersinstitute.politics.ox.ac.uk/sites/default/files/2018-11/UK_Press_Coverage_of_the_%20EU_Referendum.pdf.
18. van Dijk, T. (1998), p. 8
19. See Charteris-Black (2018) part III for a more recent account of Critical Metaphor Analysis.

20. Entman, R.M. (1993).
21. Thibodeau, P.H. & Boroditsky, L. (2011).
22. Thibodeau, P.H. & Boroditsky, L. (2015).
23. See Chapter 7 of Charteris-Black (2018).
24. Burgers et al. (2016).
25. Gibbs (2015, p. 271) notes: 'Allegory adopts a "misdirection" strategy of forcing people to draw inferences about some underlying symbolic theme, which may prompt them to think of an implied topic in a new way'.
26. Musolff (2016), pp. 30–31.
27. Moral intuitions are discussed further in Chapter 2.
28. Schank, R. & Abelson, R. (1977), p. 41.
29. *Express Online*, 3 October 2017.
30. See for example Charteris-Black (2016), Gibbs (2006a, b), Semino (2010).
31. Barsalou (2008), pp. 618–19.
32. Gibbs (2006a, b), Semino (2010), Charteris-Black (2016).
33. In Semino (2010), p. 213.

References

Barsalou, L.W. (2008). Grounded Cognition. *Annual Review of Psychology* 59: 617–45.

Burgers, C., Konijn, E.A., and Steen, G.J. (2016). Figurative Framing: Shaping Public Discourse Through Metaphor, Hyperbole, and Irony. *Communication Theory* 26, 4: 410–30.

Charteris-Black, J. (2004). *Corpus Approaches to Critical Metaphor Analysis.* Basingstoke and New York: Palgrave Macmillan.

Charteris-Black, J. (2016). The 'Dull Roar' and the 'Burning Barbed Wire Pantyhose: Complex Metaphor in Accounts of Chronic Pain'. In R. Gibbs (Ed.), *Mixing Metaphor* (pp. 155–178). Amsterdam: Benjamins.

Charteris-Black, J. (2018). *Analysing Political Speeches: Rhetoric, Discourse and Metaphor*, 2nd edn. London: Palgrave.

Entman, R.M. (1993). Framing: Toward Clarification of a Fractured Paradigm. *Journal of Communication* 43, 4: 51–58.

Gibbs, R.W.J. (2006a). *Embodiment and Cognitive Science.* New York: Cambridge University Press.

Gibbs, R.W.J. (2006b). Metaphor Interpretation as Embodied Simulation. *Mind & Language* 21: 434–58.

Gibbs, R.W. (2015). The Allegorical Characters of Political Metaphors in Discourse. *Metaphor and the Social World* 5, 2: 264–82.

Heywood. (1546). *Dialogue of Proverbs.*

Musolff, A. (2016). *Political Metaphor Analysis: Discourse and Scenarios.* London: Bloomsbury Academic.

O'Rourke, K. (2018). *A Short History of Brexit.* London: Pelican.

Schank, R. and Abelson, R. (1977). *Scripts, Plans, Goals and Understanding.* Hillsdale, NJ: Lawrence Erlbaum.

Semino, E. (2010). Descriptions of Pain, Metaphor, and Embodied Simulation. *Metaphor and Symbol* 25, 4: 205–26.

Thibodeau, P.H. and Boroditsky, L. (2011). Metaphors We Think with: The Role of Metaphor in Reasoning. *PLoS One* 6: e16782. https://doi.org/10.1371/journal.pone.0016782 [PMC free article] [PubMed].

Thibodeau, P.H. and Boroditsky, L. (2015). Measuring Effects of Metaphor. *PLoS One* 10, 7: e0133939. https://www.ncbi.nlm.nih.gov/pmc/articles/PMC4517745/.

van Dijk, T. (1998). *Ideology.* London: Sage.

2

The Lexicon of the Referendum

If language influences thought, then the actual vocabulary, or lexicon, of the referendum campaign surely influenced how people voted. In this chapter I discuss this lexicon from three different perspectives. First I consider the word coinages that were developed during the UK Referendum campaign—including the word 'Brexit' itself—illustrating how new words, or 'neologisms', often have concealed and unconscious meanings that influence both how we think and our moral judgements. I then evaluate how the wording of the ballot paper might have affected the outcome of the referendum by inadvertently triggering moral intuitions. In the third section I compare the 'foundations' for moral judgements identified in previous moral psychology research with the frames that I identify by metaphor analysis in this book. I also compare moral Intuition and moral reasoning and illustrate how moral reasoning can be understood by using two concepts originating in classical rhetoric: the enthymeme and the syllogism.

© The Author(s) 2019
J. Charteris-Black, *Metaphors of Brexit*,
https://doi.org/10.1007/978-3-030-28768-9_2

Brexit Neologisms

The most common neologisms that developed in relation to 'Brexit' illustrate some of the processes of English word formation. The first of these is 'blending' where a new word is formed through the combination of the component parts of two existing words to produce a 'portmanteau' word (also known as a 'blend'); the most significant blend in the UK referendum was the word 'Brexit' itself. The next process is morphological derivation where new words are derived from existing ones by the addition of a suffix (or prefix), so from 'Brexit', 'Brexiteer' developed in which the suffix '-eer' is added to the root form 'Brexit'. This process has a history in the reporting of political affairs, for example the addition of '-gate' to indicate a scandal; this originated in 'Watergate' and lead, via 'Irangate', to 'Pussygate' (referring to a leud comment by Donald Trump) and 'Russiagate' (referring to the allegations of Russian interference in the 2016 US elections). These neologisms convey a strong evaluation, as was the case with Brexit: for example the suffix –iac was added to the root 'Remain' to produce 'Remainiac'. The third word formation process is creative exploitation of a word through the use of half (or slant) rhyme, so from 'Remain', we have 'Remoan' to refer to the dissatisfaction of those who had voted to remain in the EU—once again with a strong negative evaluation. Sometimes these word formation processes were combined, so 'remoan' (half rhyme) was combined with suffix addition to produce 'Remoaner'. Such variations and elaborations of names conveyed a strongly negative attitude towards a group that contributed to identifying them as 'Other' and contributed to a form of cultural identity politics.[1]

A final process I discuss is compounding; this is when two existing words are joined, so the campaign for a Second Referendum was referred to by its supporters as the 'People's Vote'. This sought to capture the populist mood to compensate for the failure of the Remain campaign to arouse populist sentiment during the referendum campaign. Of course, opponents of a second vote argued that the Referendum *was* a 'people's vote' and that the campaign for a second referendum was a campaign to overturn the result of a 'people's vote'. Other examples of compounding in the development of political terms are 'grass roots', 'lame duck' and 'swing vote'. I will now explore each of these processes in a little more detail.

Portmanteau Words and Blends: 'Brexit'

It could be argued that Britain would never have left the EU if the word 'Brexit' hadn't been invented. The word combines 'Britain' with 'exit' and shows some of the characteristics of a successful neologism: the meaning is readily accessible from the parts that are blended together and provokes thought as to the contribution of each of the parts to the overall meaning: with 'Brexit' we know that it relates to Britain leaving, or exiting the EU. Successful blends also sound attractive and have a relatively simple structure. 'Brexit' has two syllables in the first 'e' contains what is called an open vowel (the tongue goes down making the mouth more open) and the second syllable has 'i' which is a closed vowel (the tongue goes up making the mouth more closed) so it rolls off the tongue in a satisfying way. 'Brexit' is relatively easy to pronounce—although there are two variations: in the more common pronunciation the second consonant sound is pronounced 'ks' (known to linguists as an unvoiced velar plosive) but in the alternative version this consonant is pronounced 'ggx' (a voiced velar plosive) to produce 'Breggxit'. Before the referendum commentators sometimes hesitated while considering the correct pronunciation. Since it was a new word there was not an established pronunciation so either can be considered acceptable.

Other successful portmanteau words that were also easy to pronounce and had some aesthetically satisfying qualities include 'Eurosceptic' and 'meritocracy'. It is quite common for political portmanteau words to include a proper noun as the first element (in 'Brexit'—'Britain' is a proper noun) and other examples include 'Reaganomics' and 'Trumponomics' that blend 'economics' with 'Reagan' and 'Trump' respectively. Another example is 'gerrymandering' which refers to the practice of reorganising voting areas to gain more votes and originated in blending the surname of Governor Elbridge Gerry (who first practised this) with 'salamander'—because the shape of the new voting district on a map (it looked like a salamander).

'Brexit' was formed by analogy with 'Grexit', first used on 7th February 2012 by *The Guardian* newspaper in a headline: "Greek impasse raise fears of 'Grexit'". However, in the 3-year period covered by this book 'Grexit' was only used 29 times in press headlines, making it much less common than 'Brexit', which soon became an established word as people forgot its origins. But as recently as 2012 the word needed explanation as in this newspaper article:

> Now's the time for Britain to make an exit from the EU
>
> THERE'S a new word on the lips of Eurocrats at the moment: Brexit, short for British exit. While on the one hand it's just another piece of EU-insider jargon, the fact that it exists at all is hugely significant. When it started to look inevitable that Greece would leave the euro, politicians, economists and commentators started to refer to it as "Grexit". The word was coined because the once unthinkable had started to become reality - and it needed a name. So you can see why the emergence of Brexit is important.[2]

The author gives an indication of its origin by analogy with the blend of 'Greece' and 'exit'. This implies that the origins of 'Brexit' were in the inability of the EU to deal effectively with the financial crisis in Greece. But once the word had developed so did the concept, and, like Pandora's box, once created it could never be uncreated—so the concept and the word both gathered momentum simultaneously.

'Brexit' was first coined by Alastair Newton while working as a senior policy analyst for a large Japanese bank; he had previously been a British diplomat and served as an advisor to Tony Blair. The original form was 'Brixit' as in this media report:

> You've heard of the 'Grexit', the ugly market term for a Greek departure from the single currency - now here comes the *'Brixit'*, Nomura's coinage for the possibility Britain will quit the European Union.[3]

Since this is 'Brixit' rather than 'Brexit' it is debatable whether this is the origin of 'Brexit', since the former sounds like 'bricks' rather than 'exit'. The first use I have found of 'Brexit' was in *The Express*:

Across the European Union a new buzz word is on the lips of the political elite: "*Brexit*". This is shorthand for the likelihood of a British exit from the EU. (23 October 2012)

And the first use in a press headline was:

The main argument against an EU *Brexit* is full of holes.[4]

I examined neologisms that were modelled on 'Brexit' and referred to the possibility of other countries leaving the EU. Table 2.1 shows various neologisms (based on a previous study[5]) that occurred anywhere in press articles for the period 2016–2018. It also compares these neologisms in the pro-Leave and pro-Remain press by looking at how often they occurred in headlines.

It is very clear that, with the exception of 'Bexit', the pro-Leave press used these neologisms much more than the pro-Remain press. This is not surprising as the pro-Leave press considered their readership more interested in the possibility of other countries leaving the EU and were keen to encourage this process. The same preference by the pro-Leave press for lexical innovation was also found in related blends such as 'Grexodus'. Even neologisms that expressed remorse about leaving the EU were used more by the pro-Leave press, for example 15 out of 29 uses of 'Bregret' in headlines were by pro-Leave newspapers. The pro-Remain press only innovated when a concept was strongly

Table 2.1   Frequency of 'exit' neologisms in press headlines 2016–2018

	Total uses	Pro-Leave press headlines	Pro-Remain press headlines
Auxit (Austria)	24	2	0
Bexit (Belgium)	84	3	4
Dexit (Germany)	79	7	1
Frexit (France)	663	96	11
Grexit (Greece)	263	27	3
Irexit	219	38	13
Italexit	220	31	2
Nexit	183	14	1
Swexit	108	19	0
Total	1843	237	35

pro-Remain for example 75% instances of 'Regrexit' were by the pro-Remain press. Generally, the pro-Remain press followed linguistic trends that were initiated by the pro-Leave press.

Let's consider the implications of a possible influence of language on thought. 'Exit' originated from a late sixteenth century stage direction from the Latin *exit* 'he or she goes out', so we have expressions such as 'exit stage left'. This is significant since the dramatic origins of 'exit' suggest that it activates a more theatrical frame than the word 'leave'. A feature of new words is that they don't necessarily have a stable pronunciation, as we have seen there were two possible pronunciations of 'Brexit': 'Breksit' or 'Breggxit'—depending on whether or not the vocal chords are vibrating on the middle consonant sound. In 'Breggxit' the vocal chords are vibrating to produce what is known as a 'voiced' sound. The availability of two alternatives offers a speaker the opportunity to mark their identity by showing the influence of local dialect or personal style in their choice of pronunciation, we will also see that suffixation of the verb 'leave' created a third option: 'Leaver'. The availability of various pronunciations and a choice from a range of terms draws attention to the concept of 'Brexit'—an option that was not present for 'remain', but more importantly it marked out a political and cultural identity. For some mainly male, mainly older and often working class voters who may otherwise have lacked a strong positive identity, the word 'Brexit' contributed to the creation of a new one as a 'Brexiteer'. But how aware are we of these processes?

What are the deeper meanings of 'exit'? When used in social contexts it implies termination, end or even death. If we look at words that commonly occur immediately before 'exit' in a large sample of language (the British National Corpus[6]) we find the following associations. Among the most frequent collocations, those occurring more than 10 times are: 'fire exit' (21); and 'emergency exit' (14). Both these compound nouns carry associations of danger and are not the preferred ways of departing from a building. This is also the case with another frequent collocation 'cup exit' (17) meaning 'defeat in a football match'. These largely negative connotations continue with other collocations such as 'exit charge' and 'rear exit' as well as the more metaphoric 'final exit' meaning 'death'. The concept of 'exit' is part of a metaphor frame that models human experiences on the basis of spatial motion according to what is known by cognitive linguists as the SOURCE-PATH-GOAL frame. But words referring to end points can also have positive associations, for example 'goal' as in phrases such as 'achieving ones goals', 'attaining goals', or 'destination' as in 'safe arrival at a destination'. But profiling the end stage of a series of activities by using the word 'exit', substituted the negative associations deriving from its typical contexts with a clear sense of purpose, a clear and definitive outcome as in the much quoted phrase 'Brexit means Brexit'. The goal focus brings about a reversal of semantic prosody as when the normal use of 'wicked' meaning 'evil' is reversed to mean somethink like 'cool' or 'amazing'. So the goal focus of 'Brexit' combined with its innovative word form shifts the negative connotations of 'exit' to the positive ones that 'Brexit' had for its supporters.

Derivation in Group Identities: 'Brexiteer' and 'Remainiac'

An example of derivation was the word 'Brexiteer' that was derived from 'Brexit'. Although some words with this suffix are negative, as in 'profiteer', or 'mutineer', others have strongly positive connotations such as 'volunteer' or 'charioteer' and imply a dynamic human subject, often with romantic associations, as noted by Michael Gove:

> 'Brexiteer brings to mind buccaneer, pioneer, musketeer,' says Michael Gove. 'It lends a sense of panache (= the quality of being able to do things in a confident and elegant way that other people find attractive) and romance to the argument.'[7]

This may be one reason why for a long period after the referendum result the term 'Brexiteer' took on increasing importance and gradually replaced its more neutral rivals 'Leaver' and 'Brexiter'. This is because the potentially negative associations of 'exit' disappear once '-exit' becomes '-exiteer'—it changes from referring to an impersonal end point to a human agent. 'Brexiteer' gradually replaced its alternatives 'Leaver' and

'Brexiter' so that between December 2016 and December 2017 its use in headlines had more than doubled and continued to grow. The opposite happened with the less romantic 'Brexiter': In June 2016 it occurred in 70 press headlines, but there was only a single 'Brexiter' headline by December 2016, although it increased again once the difficulties of the 'hard' Brexit emerged in 2018 it was always a much less preferred term than 'Brexiteer'. The contribution of press dramatisation significantly assisted the Leave cause, as one observer noted:

> Put Brexiters in their place might you consider, please, referring to Brexiters, rather than Brexiteers? The latter, with its obvious rhymes with "musketeer" and "buccaneer", bestows incongruous connotations of gallantry, courage and generosity of spirit upon Boris Johnson, Jacob Rees-Mogg (a person so patriotic he has stated his principal allegiance is with an Italian religion, not Britain), John Redwood and the rest. "Brexiter" avoids this.[8]

The innovative nature of the 'Leave' position was created through language: while 'Remainers' could only be referred to neutrally using a single group identity name, there were at least three group identity names available for those wanting to leave the EU. Moreover, when an additional name was developed for those supporting Remain, the suffix –iac was added to produce the derogatory 'Remainiac'. Table 2.2 summarises changes in the frequency of these words in newspaper headlines over the period covered by this book; I searched for each group identity name in newspaper headlines in the months of June and December at six monthly intervals.

The table shows large variations. 'Brexiteer' was very common in the period before the Referendum and regained its dominance in the period of the Withdrawal negotiations. 'Remainer' was less common in headlines especially before the Referendum. Another unconscious influence is that of an initial capital letter because it adds the status of properhood: in June 2016 around 20% of both 'leaver' and 'remainer' avoided an initial capital whereas 'Brexiteer' and 'Brexiter' were *always capitalised* from the start. The use of a capital letter raises the importance of an entity by making it into a proper noun: this was much more readily

Table 2.2 Naming and group identities in press headlines: change in use

	December 2015	June 2016	December 2016	June 2017	December 2017	June 2018	December 2018
Brexiteer(s)	867	115	76	52	168	188	263
Brexiter(s)	0	70	1	3	14	15	14
Leaver(s)[a]	0	38	11	9	20	24	43
Remainer(s)	0	65	95	104	114	207	182
Remainiac(s)	0	2	2	1	1	0	0

[a] I excluded references to 'school leavers'

available for a neologism because there was no established word as there was with 'leave' or 'remain'. Also since 'Britain' commences with a capital letter, the status of its properhood carried over to 'Brexiteer' making the identity appear more patriotic. 'Leaver' and 'remainer' only became capitalised once they had become established concepts. By September 2018 there were only 6 instances of avoiding the initial capital as in 'remainer' and only 2 instances of 'leaver': once again it was 'Brexit' that set the agenda to which other words adapted.

The first use of 'Remainers' was in a press article was in *The Daily Telegraph*:

> If polls continue to show a trend of "leavers" edging ahead of "remainers", I think the Prime Minister will concede that the intransigence of the EU has led him to recommend withdrawal. (4 October 2015)

The first use without speech marks was in *The Guardian* on 9 October 2015. The table above shows that 'remainer' quickly caught on and at times was used more frequently in press headlines than 'Brexiteer'. However, 'remainer' does not have a strong brand identity because of its negative associations: it sounds similar to 'remainder'—that which is left over, as in the phrase 'the remainder of his life'. It is also not far phonetically from 'remains'—the parts left over after something has been destroyed—as in 'human remains', 'charred remains', 'mortal remains' or 'mangled remains', all phrases that occur commonly in English. Once we introduce the idea that meaning of a word is influenced by the common contexts in which it occurs and can have an unconscious influence on its 'real' meaning we need to consider the implications for the wording of the referendum ballot paper and I do this later in the chapter.

Half Rhyme: 'Remoaners'

After the referendum result became known, those who supported the decision to Leave the EU, shifted the diphthong vowel in the second syllable of 'remain' from /ei/ to /ou/ to shift the pronunciation and

Table 2.3 'Remainer' and 'Remoaner' in press headlines: change in use

	December 2015	June 2016	December 2016	June 2017	December 2017	June 2018	December 2018
Remoaner	0	0	75	20	28	31	2
Remainer	0	65	95	104	114	207	182

meaning of 'Remainer' to 'Remoaner'. This had the same ridiculing effect as 'Remainiac' and was employed widely by the Leave supporting press to comment negatively on those who complained about the result. 'Remoaner' was used in the context of arguing against those who could not accept the referendum result and who, eventually, campaigned for a second ballot. Table 2.3 compares how the the press used the terms 'Remoaner' and 'Remainer' in British press headlines.

'Remoaner' was not used at all prior to the Referendum but by December 2016 it had become nearly as frequent as 'Remainer'. Through 2017 'Remainer' became the dominant term and by December 2018 'Remoaner' had faded away. 'Remoaner' was always given an initial capital giving it the status of a proper noun. Its first use was in *The Express*:

> But Bryant's bizarre comment is all too typical of the embittered world now inhabited by the *Remoaners*. Lacking a genuine sense of patriotism, they want to turn their forecasts of doom into a grim reality. Yet doom-mongering hardly matches events. Contrary to the *Remoaners'* predictions, there has been no emergency Budget. …With smug sarcasm, the *Remoaners* continually speak of the task that ministers face in "clearing up the mess" from European withdrawal. But there is no "mess", just an exciting opportunity to embrace national liberation.[9]

The writer emphasises the negativity surrounding those who were upset about the result with words such as 'embittered', 'doom', 'grim', 'dangers', 'ludicrous', 'lies' and 'clearing up the mess': the negative appraisal is unmitigated and sustained and 'Remoaner' spread even to newspapers that opposed Brexit, while Brexit supporting newspapers ensured the currency of the term. On July 29th *The Daily Telegraph* ran a headline 'Remoaners are determined to find bad news'. 'Remoaner Steve Coogan

Table 2.4 'Remoaner' in pro-Brexit press headlines December 2016 and December 2017

	December 2016	December 2017
Daily Express+Express Online	48	23
Daily Mail + MailOnline	25	3
The Daily Telegraph	1	0
Daily Star	1	0
The Sunday Express	0	1
The Sun	0	1
Total	75	28

SLAMS Brexiteers as 'DINOSAURS like Alan Partridge" shouted the *Express Online* on 11 December 2017. 'Remoaner' was used exclusively by the pro-Brexit press as shown in Table 2.4 that analyses the word in headlines in December 2016 and December 2017:

'Remoaner' was a name used almost entirely by *The Daily Express* and *The Daily Mail* and their online versions; it is not surprising that the pro-Remain press—*The Guardian, The Observer, The Independent* and *The Daily Mirror*—avoided the word in their headlines. Such creative exploitation of a word representing a valid political opinion—one that lead to a demonstration of more than 100,000 people who sought a 'People's Vote'—suggests that the pro-Brexit press was aware of the propaganda potential of neologisms and word coinages.

Compound Words: 'Independence Day'

Compounding—that is joining two words together to produce a new word—is an important method for creating new words by bringing together two existing words, but rather than blending them together in compounds each word retains its separate word-like status. Compound words can be created by linking together different word classes; for example 'cherry picking' combines a noun with a verb; 'hard Brexit' combines an adjective with a noun and 'cliff edge' combines two nouns. Each word of the compound contributes equally to the meaning, and the meaning is more readily accessible than is the case with blends, so 'vasal state' retains the sense of both 'slavery' and 'nation' whereas in 'remoaner'—we may forget the core meaning of 'moan', or in 'Brexiteer' we may no longer think especially of the word 'exit'. The following table shows some of the most common compound noun forms relating to Brexit; I was interested in establishing whether compound neologisms were used more by the pro-Leave or pro-Remain press. I searched for 10 different compound words that, although they had meanings in senses other than Brexit, had a Brexit-specific meaning. I did this by searching for press articles with the word 'Brexit' alongside another compound form—both somewhere in the headline. I then allocated the compound words to two groups according to whether the term was employed more by newspapers that supported Leave or those supporting Remain; the findings are shown in Table 2.5.

What emerges from the compound word analysis is that while in general the pro-Leave and pro-Remain press used them with equal frequency, there were three exceptions all of which were words that occurred significantly more often in the headlines of pro-Leave newspapers. These were 'divorce bill' and 'Independence day' that was used three times more frequently by the pro-Leave press, and 'Project fear' that was used over ten times more frequently in pro-Leave press headlines. These slogans were ones that were developed for propaganda purposes and which newspaper editors who supported Leave saw as highly appealing to their readers. Evidence of the status attached to them by these newspapers is that these phrases usually commenced with a capital letter. For example, out of the 57 instances of 'Independence Day' around 30 used a capital letter for both words. The first word in 'Project Fear' was nearly always capitalised

Table 2.5 British press 2016–2018: 'Brexit' + compound noun in press headlines

Compound	Pro-Leave press	Pro-Remain press	Total
Breaking point	11	9	20
Cherry picking	20	23	43
Cliff edge	73	97	170
Divorce bill	310	242	552
Fat cat	14	16	30
Independence day	43	14	57
Project fear	578	47	625
Red lines	114	81	195
Sunlit uplands	6	2	8
Vassal state	15	14	29

and 'Project Fear' was much more common than 'Project fear'. It is through these markers of status and importance that—intentionally or otherwise—typographic considerations have an unconscious influence on the value attached to these concepts. The Leave campaign was always the linguistic innovator creating more interesting neologisms that gained more attention, were quickly adopted and widely diffused—even if this was only on a temporary basis.

The Wording of the Ballot Paper

The Electoral Commission report has the following guidelines:

> Our guidelines say that a question should be clear and simple, that is, easy to understand; to the point; and not ambiguous. It should also be neutral, which means it should not encourage voters to consider one response more favourably than another or mislead voters.[10]

The major considerations that they explored were:

> Should there be a 'yes/no' question or some other question format?
> What words should be used in asking the question in such a way that it did not bias voters?
> Should the word 'remain' or 'stay' be used?
> Should the option of 'leave' be mentioned?

The Electoral Commission used a combination of one-to-one in-depth interviews and focus groups to test various question formats, they also consulted members of campaign groups and language experts. I will develop a discussion of these topics offering an evaluation as well as an alternative method to exploring these answers.

The original question proposed was:

1. Should the United Kingdom remain a member of the European Union?
Yes/No.

A variation that avoided the word 'remain' but retained the yes/no format was:

2. Do you think that the United Kingdom should be a member of the European Union?
Yes/No.

Both these were designed as similar to the question that had been asked in the Scottish referendum:

3. Should Scotland be an independent country?

However, a major difference between 'remain a member of'/'be a member of' and 'be an independent country' is that the polarity is reversed, so that answering 'yes' to either questions 1 or 2 implies that there will be NO change to the status quo, whereas answering 'yes' to number 3 implies there will be a change.

However, there is an underlying problem with the 'yes/no' question format; this is the psychological argument that respondents prefer to give answers that they believe are preferred by the questioner, so since 'yes' is more commonly preferred to 'no', there will be an unconscious bias towards answering 'yes' over 'no' since it implies an affirmative and positive meaning—irrespective of the question that is asked. This issue, along with the decision as to the order in which questions are presented was raised by the Plain English society:

> It may be argued that putting 'Yes' first invites people to think this is the answer the questioner wants to hear and thus introduces a bias towards 'yes'. The Government is likely to recommend a 'yes' vote, so any assumed bias towards 'yes' may skew the results in the Government's favoured direction....There is also the question of possible bias in that 'yes' will probably be the positive or status quo response, which will allow the 'yes' campaign to paint itself as the positive or conservative option.

This claim assumes a rather obedient electorate who like to go along with government recommendations—perhaps a rather outmoded assumption in contemporary democracies? However, after consultation with political parties and campaigners and other interested parties the electoral commission rejected the notion of a 'yes' or 'no' question format:

> ... because of what we heard through the consultation and research about the perception that the question encourages voters to consider one response more favourably than the other. These views raise concerns about the potential legitimacy, in the eyes of those campaigning to leave and some members of the public, of the referendum result – particularly if there was a vote to remain a member of the European Union.

This conclusion is curious because it implies that the perspective of perceptions about what was viewed as 'fair' was that of those who were seeking to leave the EU; the viewpoint of Brexit supporters was apparently more salient to the electoral commission. It is almost as if the electoral commission were imagining itself needing to defend accusations of a 'stitch-up' in a scenario in which Leave lost the ballot, rather than a scenario in which Remain/Stay had lost. The Remain position was taken as the default option. This concern about the perception of legitimacy by leavers lead to the decision to include the word 'leave' on the ballot paper.

The ballot paper for the UK Referendum put the 'Remain' option first (see Fig. 2.1).

The question format avoided a yes/no question and included both the words 'Remain' and 'Leave'. So the reason for the inclusion of 'Leave' was to avoid a 'yes' 'no' format, but why was 'remain' chosen (as in number 1 above) rather than 'be' as in number 2 above? The Electoral Commission argued that

> ...although the question used brief and straightforward language, the phrase 'be a member of the European Union' to describe the referendum choice was not sufficiently clear to ensure a full understanding of the referendum as a whole. *This was because some participants in our research did not know that the United Kingdom is currently a member of the European Union while others who did know thought the question suggested the United Kingdom was not a member.* (my italics)

Referendum on the United Kingdom's Membership of the European Union

---

Vote only once by putting a cross X in the box next to your choice

---

Should the United Kingdom remain a member of the European Union or leave the Eureopean Union?

Remain a member of the European Union

Leave the European Union

Fig. 2.1   Format of the UK referendum ballot paper

I found it astonishing that the Electoral Commission should be designing a ballot paper for a crucial political decision on the basis of the assumed level of knowledge of a minority of the population. How many voters did not know that the UK was already in the European Union? And if they did not know this, why were they voting at all—let alone determining the wording of the ballot paper? Why should the needs of *those who did not know whether the UK was actually in the EU* be considered capable of making an informed decision in a referendum? However, the Electoral Commission accepted the view of its informants who 'strongly agreed overall that the question should convey current membership status in order to avoid misleading voters'—it was this that lead to the inclusion of 'remain' in the final wording- even though out of 1000 respondents, 850 had preferred 'be' over 'remain'. They found from their research that 'some people will perceive either positive or negative associations with the phrase 'remain a member of the EU'. It was at this point that the 'Leave' option was added to produce the phrase: 'Leave the European Union' as one of the choices. There was awareness of the novelty in moving away from 'yes/no' question:

As we indicated that this highlighted an important decision for Parliament about retaining or moving away from the UK's recent experience of referendum questions using 'Yes' and 'No' as response options.

'Stay' or 'Remain'

Once the Electoral Commission had rejected a 'yes/no' question format the actual words used in the question became all the more important. As we have seen above, a major question was whether or not the word 'remain' should be used: the alternative 'stay' was considered as one of four possibilities that were tested in 2015:

> Should the United Kingdom stay a member of the European Union or leave the European Union?

The Electoral Commission commented that:

> It appeared from the research, therefore, that the reason some people preferred 'stay' (less formal, more everyday language) was the same reason that others preferred 'remain' (more formal, more suitable for a referendum question). Overall, participants agreed that whether the word was 'remain' or 'stay', it was important to include one of these options in the question in order to clarify current UK membership of the EU.

So let us consider how 'stay' might have influenced voters differently from 'remain'. A method of evaluating unconscious meaning is to look at the sort of words and contexts where each word is used, and to do this I had a look at the British National Corpus to compare common expressions that include the words 'remain' and 'stay' to see if they might be considered as having any cognitive bias. These words that commonly occur near to a particular word of interest are known as its 'collocates'. So let us compare the collocates of 'stay' with the collocates of 'remain'. I did this by looking at the most common words that occur up to 3 words after 'stay' (used as a verb) and 'remain'.

Generally, collocates for 'stay' were much more positive than 'remain'; for example, the most frequent expressions were 'stay at home' (284);

'stay the night' (154), 'stay in bed' (88), 'stay together' (86), 'stay over-night' (76), all of which have ideas of security and comfort. Other positive collocations were 'stay alive' (56); 'stay healthy' (27); 'stay dry' (25) and 'stay cool' (19). The use of 'stay' on the ballot paper also carries associations with closely related words such as 'stayer'—this implies a tenacious person (or horse) that has staying power to complete whatever tasks they have been set. This is rather different from 'remainer' that sounds more like the left over drunk in the living room after the party. Indeed the Electoral Commission had itself found preference for 'stay' over 'remain':

> Separately, we heard via our consultation that some people such as those with learning disabilities may find 'stay' a more accessible word than 'remain'.

However they continued: 'although this was not found in our research and the advice we received from the Plain Language Commission said that 'the crucial word 'remain' is shown in vocabulary lists as being familiar to the average nine-year-old'". Now of course people need to understand something as important as a ballot paper but why should the needs of children determine a text designed for adults? If you don't understand what 'remain' means you shouldn't be voting. However, words to have unconscious associations and I decided to explore the unconscious associations of 'remain' (arising from previous uses of the word) by examining the words that commonly follow 'remain''. Within a 3-word span I found that among the most frequent 60 words were 10 words that had a negative prefix as illustrated in Table 2.6, with totals from the British National Corpus[11] in the second column and from the Corpus of Contemporary American English[12] in the third column and an example in the fourth column.

In all these instances 'remain' refers to a mental state that is in some sense problematic. The fact that a problem continues to be a problem is indicated by the negative prefix 'un' on the following verb or adjective. In a world of *solutions* it is preferable for questions to be answered, but the phrase 'remain + negative past verb participle/adjective' implies that this is not the case: we don't really want things to remain 'unknown', 'unclear' or 'unanswered'.

Table 2.6 'Remain'+x in British and American English (0,3)

	BNC	COCA	Examples from BNC
Unchanged	103	251	After a meeting with Mr. Major last November, Mr. Kohl said: 'What is decisive for us is that the Maastricht treaty should <u>remain unchanged</u> and should be ratified as such by all states within the Community so that it can come into force in 1993.' (Scotsman)
Unconvinced	24	62	The most spectacular mock accident was in 1984, when a nuclear flask was virtually undamaged after a 100 mph rail crash. But opponents of nuclear power <u>remain unconvinced</u>. (News)
Unanswered	22	170	We are therefore talking about more than a thousand deaths from the Windscale accident. Three questions <u>remain unanswered</u>: was all the area of radioactive fall-out monitored? (New Scientist)
Unresolved	20	96	Thirdly, equal treatment between domestic nationals and citizens of other member states. But some problems <u>remain unresolved</u> or unaddressed. (Social Policy)
Unknown	20	167	The specific carcinogens, however, that cause the colorectal cancers in humans <u>remain unknown</u>. (Academic journal)
Unclear	19	166	It must be accepted that at the end of the interview the child may have given no information to support the suspicion of sexual abuse and the position will <u>remain unclear</u>. (Child protection law)
Unaffected	17	49	It was a strange unsettling atmosphere. No one could <u>remain unaffected</u> by it. Some were hardened by it. (Fiction)
Unaware	16	63	An obvious major difference between corporate and conventional crime is that the former's victims often <u>remain unaware</u>. This has considerable implications for regulating and controlling corporate crime. (Social science)
Untouched	14	72	What is evident from the women studied is that they wanted and needed paid work for economic, social, psychological and personal reasons. These wider, non-material aspects of unemployment and poverty <u>remain untouched</u> by any legislative provision. (Social science)

(continued)

Table 2.6 (continued)

	BNC	COCA	Examples from BNC
Uncertain	13	98	The truth was fearsome and unavoidable. She remains uncertain still what was to be done with it, though she consoled herself with the thought that in entering the court of Le Grand Jeu and submitting to its verdict, she had already taken the first tentative steps. (Fiction)

Other words following 'remain' also had negative associations; for example in 5th place was 'anonymous': someone who is anonymous is someone whose name is not known. In 6th place in the frequency list was 'silent'; to 'remain silent' implies a negative context where someone who would like to speak knows that it is preferable not to do so. Other words that were among the 50 most common after 'remain' included 'obscure', 'hidden', 'empty', and 'aloof'. There were some more positive context of the word such as 'constant', 'calm', 'independent', 'strong'; however, on closer examination this was often not the case. For example, typical contexts of 'remaining calm' are in situations that would *normally arouse a negative emotion* such as anger. The collocation 'remain strong' which again appears positive is actually used in contexts where there is some form of threat or danger:

> However all is not gloom as in many cases the revenue reserves *remain strong*.
> They were haunted by the fear of another Dunkirk and were anxious to *remain strong* in the Middle East.

So what I am suggesting is that '**remain' has a much higher potential to arouse negative responses**, ones which the Electoral Commission's informants may not have been consciously aware of because of the method they were using (a sample of informants). In fact in their own research the Electoral Commission had identified doubts about the word 'remain':

.. some participants perceived either positive or negative associations with the phrase 'remain a member of the European Union' and this could potentially introduce some risk of perceived bias. With this in mind, overall, participants preferred a question that paired both options of 'remain' and 'leave'.

However, there was another word that been put forward in their 2013 research, and this was 'continue' as in:

4. Should the United Kingdom continue to be a member of the European Union?
Yes/No.

By not using the more neutral verb 'continue' they were setting 'remain' in opposition to 'leave', so let's consider the unconscious meanings of 'leave'.

'Leave'

The Electoral Commission quoted some doubt about 'leave':

> Some noted that not mentioning the word 'leave' was a positive element of the proposed question, as they felt that 'leave' was a strong word with potentially negative connotations and therefore including this word (instead of remain) could influence the voter decision (in favour of remaining).

What evidence does corpus linguistics offer to explore the associations and deeper meanings of 'leave'? Well the first finding is that there is not a single negative prefixed word directly following 'leave' (as we found in 'remain unchanged', 'unconvinced' etc.)—this is because it is a verb that takes an object, so it is commonly followed by pronouns such as 'them', 'me', 'her', 'he', 'their' and 'his' followed by a noun. Even when we extend the search range to three words after 'leave' we still only find 4 negative prefixed words that occur more than 10 times, as illustrated in Table 2.7.

In all these cases a material object follows the verb. What are the implications for meaning? Well 'remain' is a verb that *does not take an object* (known as 'intransitive') and it is a mental state verb—all the

Table 2.7 'Leave' + x in the British National Corpus (0,3)

Unattended	18	There is no legal minimum at which you can <u>leave</u> your child <u>unattended</u>
Unlocked	12	Yet back in the 1950s there was the 'Teddy Boy' to alarm the public and to set against the allegedly poor but honest inter-war years when people could <u>leave</u> their doors <u>unlocked</u>. (Book)
Untouched	12	Pleas from the MCofS for climbers to send objections seems to have worked and Wimpey have amended their expansion plans to <u>leave</u> the quarry <u>untouched</u>. (Book)
Unturned	10	He pledged the Movement 'to investigate any individual case referred to them' and promised 'to <u>leave</u> no stone <u>unturned</u> to make the most satisfactory arrangements possible'

examples or 'remain' above are some form of mental state of knowing: this is quite different from the material verb 'leave' followed by a concrete noun. Therefore, *there is linguistic evidence that 'remain' is a much more abstract concept than 'leave'*. Unconsciously, on linguistic grounds, 'leave' is connected with *more tangible* and hence *less uncertain* meanings than 'remain'. These meanings could have overriden the advice offered by the Remain campaign when people were told that the outcome was uncertain if people voted to 'leave' because it was a type of uncertainty that could be considered cognitively accessible. We know more about what it is like to leave a room, because it entails a spatial change rather than we do if we 'remain' in an abstract entity such as the EU.

The corpus search has shown that generally, 'leave' is followed by a material object, in cases where this is not the case, an abstract noun is typically a positive one, so for example there was a pattern 'leave + positive adjective (good, optimistic etc.)'. 'Leave' also has a positive connotation when used as a noun in patterns such as 'maternity/paternity leave' and 'paid leave', 'sick leave' and 'annual leave' all of which imply that someone is being paid while not working. There was therefore little evidence of why it was that people should have believed that 'leave had potentially negative connotations'. Unfortunately the methodology employed by the Electoral Commission did not explore the issue of cognitive and usually unconscious associations of mental state verbs that I have explored above. These clearly indicate that 'remain' is more negative and more abstract because it typically refers to mental states rather than material events. In summary, the methodology of the Electoral Commission might have benefited from identifying unconscious word associations—something for which their informant based approach only provided limited access as compared with the methodology that I have demonstrated in this section. The methodology of the Electoral Commission was qualitative and they admitted this in their report:

> It should be noted that whilst qualitative research can identify participant reported views regarding neutrality of question wording based on participant perceptions, the approach does not capture any unconscious impact of question wording and structure. It is thus possible that questions might influence participants to answer in a particular way without them being aware of it.

What I have sort to demonstrate in this section is how a quantitative, numbers based approach using a corpus of language provides insight into the unconscious influences that derive from experience of how words are typically used. In linguistics findings from large corpora of language are know as 'semantic prosody'. It seems that language may have influenced thought after all: the words used on the ballot paper influenced the outcome. Most of the focus on Brexit literature to date has been on other variables established by political scientists—variations between age groups, social classes or between regions, rather than on the language choices offered in the ballot paper. These unconscious influences continued in the development of new words during the Withdrawal period. In the last part of this chapter I would like to discuss the foundations of moral psychology that may underlie the frames identified in the following chapters.

Moral Thinking

In *The Righteous Mind*, the social and cultural psychologist Jonathan Haidt provides insight into the moral foundations of politics. Although his model of the righteous mind is developed primarily in relation to the United States, and he employed a completely different method, it corresponds closely with my own findings that the moral arguments of the Leave campaign appeared to be more persuasive than those of the Remain campaign. I will therefore refer to it the discussion of the various metaphors and frames that I describe in the following chapters.

In providing an account of human motivation Haidt agrees with the view of the eighteenth century philosopher David Hume who argued that people made moral judgements quickly and intuitively and that their moral reasoning was usually just a post hoc justification. The metaphor that Haidt uses to describe this is that of a rider and an elephant: the rider (reason) is small and has only limited control over the elephant (intuition) which is large: he develops the image as a theme in his book along the lines that the rider can only direct the elephant by leaning in the direction that it is already going. Morally intuitive responses are innate senses of moral approval or disapproval. For example, the desire to protect offspring from harm is a moral intuition as is a strong judgement of moral disapproval towards incest and both have an evolutionary basis. Through the method of creating short stories in which a moral principle might appear to be violated and then collecting informants' reactions to these stories, he was able to propose a set of moral foundations that provide the basis for these moral intuitions. My view is that a distinction between moral reasoning and moral intuition concerns the degree of conscious reflection involved. Moral intuition occurs without conscious deliberation, while moral reasoning requires deliberation. Moral intuition is a judgement or solution that appears suddenly and effortlessly without awareness of the mental processes that lead to it, whereas moral reasoning occurs more slowly and with some effort.[13] This is rather like the two different ways of learning a language: either by listening and absorbing it (acquisition) or actually studying its patterns (learning): a lot of our learning of language occurs through the gradual absorption processes that occur from being surrounded by it which is why it is always easier to learn a language when living in the place where it is spoken. Following the elephant and rider metaphor, moral reasoning provides a retrospective justification of a decision or judgement that was originally made on the basis of moral intuition.

Moral Intuition and Moral Reasoning in Brexit

In relation to Brexit many voters report having made judgements on the basis of 'instinct' rather than 'reason'. Many people described voting with their 'heart' rather than their 'head'—and some may have regretted that thereafter. Frames and scenarios often arise from moral reasoning, while allegories more commonly rely on intuitive forms of moral appraisal. If we think of the origin of moral intuition, it is often in childhood experience of fairy tales and fables that caution as regards the outcomes of certain types of behaviour. Allegories based on the family frame often incorporate moral appraisals based on intuitions about what a good or bad parent should do, or how a good or bad child should behave towards others in their family. The allegory offers a set of emotive responses and ideas concerning moral obligation and cautions by drawing on a rich and dense network of knowledge derived from experience, often of language itself, as in the messages of fairy tales. But when framing takes place, *any* aspect of the family can be drawn on as a cognitive device to create different scenarios. So an opponent of Brexit could develop a scenario in which Britain was isolated from Europe by representing it as a single mother, or, even worse, as an abandoned orphan. Conversely, a supporter of Brexit might develop a scenario for Britain as a jilted partner who deserved a decent divorce settlement having honourably paid the family bills over a period of 43 years. So the same allegory exploits both moral intuitions offered by the frame to create different scenarios through which participants articulate their ideological positions with reference to stable frames deriving from experience.

To analyse moral reasoning I rely on the classical rhetorical notion of logos. According to classical rhetoric the most persuasive means of proving an argument was by a syllogism; this is a pattern in which there is a major premise, a minor premise and a conclusion. For a conclusion to be accepted, both premises need to be accepted by the audience, on the basis of contextual knowledge. Classical rhetoricians often preferred an incomplete syllogism known as an enthymeme where part of the argument is left unstated.[14] This can be illustrated with reference to a tweet as follows:

> Who do you trust? Leading UK manufacturers or the bankers who crashed out economy? #VoteLeave #c4debate (352 retweets)[15]

I will analyse this first as two separate arguments because there are two topics: manufacturers and bankers. The structure of the syllogism for each can be summarised:

Bankers
[**Major premise**]. Bankers cannot be trusted.
[**Minor premise**]. Bankers support Remain.
[**Conclusion**] You should vote to Leave.

Manufactures
[**Major premise**] Manufacturers can be trusted.
[**Minor premise**] Manufacturers support Brexit
[**Conclusion**] You should vote to Leave.

The rhetorical question at the start of the tweet introduces the idea of trust; it relies on the reader to have pre-existing views on the trustworthiness of each of the two social groups that supply the major premises. There is an assumption in the minor premise that manufacturers supported Brexit. This assumption is hidden by contrasting bankers, who most people knew were opposed to Brexit, with manufacturers who had mixed opinions. Larger companies generally preferred Remain while some smaller ones saw advantages in Brexit.

Importantly from a rhetorical point of view the question is asked but NOT answered: it relies on the reader to supply the answer through moral reasoning. The reader has to fill in the minor premises by using contextual knowledge drawing on his or her frames for the relative trustworthiness of the two groups. The reliance on inferencing in enthymemes is effective because the audience believes they have arrived at the conclusion on their own, rather than because they have been told what to think. Shared interpretations of social categories, such as bankers, contribute to psycho-emotional bonding and this helps explain why it was retweeted 352 times on the crucial day before the referendum. But the real point is that Vote Leave, who authored the tweet, were influencing on the basis of a moral intuition that Brexit was somehow the right policy; they drew on their expertise in manipulating the moral intuitions of their readership as regards their expected beliefs about the relative trustworthiness of bankers and manufacturers and about their political positions. So moral reasoning follows moral intuitions.

Consider the following from an acccount that Twitter has now deleted and relied on the inferential power of the enthymeme:

A vote for the declining #EU is like buying a ticket for The Titanic - after it hit the iceberg #VoteLeave #Brexit[16]

[**Major premise**] It was certain the Titanic would sink after it hit the iceberg.

[**Minor premise**] The EU is the Titanic.

[**Conclusion**] It is as dangerous to vote Remain as it was to buy a ticket for the Titanic.

In this tweet a metaphor is implied by the word 'like' and forms a minor premise that requires the reader to interpret the sense in which the EU is like the Titanic; this interpretation relies on there being a 'crisis frame' for the EU—with contextual knowledge of serious problems concerning immigration and the economy. So the moral reasoning of the enthymeme relies on metaphor and a pre-existing 'crisis' frame for the EU to invite an interpretation that supports Brexit. But the intuition about the catastrophic nature of the EU preceded the moral reasoning of the analogy. Most successful tweets rely on creating arguments through moral reasoning by the use of frames, allegories and metaphors. Quite a number of the tweets included in the book were deleted after I collected them at the time of the Referendum, and in some cases accounts no longer exists. For example, Vote Leave deleted some of their tweets from the week immediately before the Referendum and the account 'Defiant Lion UK' no longer exists. I can only leave the reader to infer possible reasons for such deletions. Perhaps it reveals beliefs about how important framing and metaphor were in the minds of those who deleted these tweets and accounts? Analysis of moral reasoning provides insight into the competing worldviews through which Brexit was framed.

Moral Foundations and the Righteous Mind

On the basis of his analysis of people's judgements on the morality of actions outlined in his short scenarios, Haidt argues that the elephant of intuition has six 'taste receptors'; these are the six different 'foundations' for moral judgements:

1. Care/Harm; this is the desire to protect others—especially vulnerable groups, such as children or the elderly, cute animals or endangered species.
2. Fairness/Cheating; this is grounded in altruistic feelings towards unknown others, for example insisting on their right to free education and healthcare with expectations of reciprocal altruism—i.e. that these others will act in equally altruistic fashion towards you and your group in the future.
3. Loyalty/Betrayal; this is tribal loyalty towards a social group or team with which individuals identify.
4. Authority/Subversion; this is the view that a society requires hierarchies so that those who do not follow the rules are reprimanded by those responsible for enforcing these rules.
5. Sanctity/Degradation; this is based on emotions such as disgust towards dead or decaying matters or towards behaviours such as incest that seem to challenge basic rules of morality. These may have their origin in resisting the spread of microbes, or genetic deformity. He later added a sixth foundation:
6. Liberty/Oppression; this prevents attempts by one group to dominate another and is the basis for freedom fighters everywhere but is in tension with the Authority foundation: it is what pushes people to unite together against bullies and tyrants.[17]

Haidt proposes that each of these foundations offers some form of evolutionary advantage to humans by addressing adaptive challenges. He uses them to distinguish between American Democrats and Republicans. Both the political left and political right subscribe to the Liberty/Oppression foundation. But Democrats (the political left) base their moral judgements *only* on the Care/Harm and Fairness/Cheating foundations because their overriding concern is with social justice. By contrast, in addition to these two foundations, Republicans (the political right) base their moral judgements on three additional foundations: Loyalty/Betrayal, Authority/Subversion and Sanctity/Degradation. This access to six rather than three foundations gives Conservatives a considerable advantage in terms of the range of moral arguments they can make. Further research confirmed that liberals (in the American sense) made greater use of the Care/Harm and Fairness/Cheating moral foundations, whereas Conservatives endorsed all the foundations more equally.[18]

After I had analysed the frames of the Brexit debate I found that Haidt's moral foundations corresponded closely with the frames that I identified through the analysis of Brexit-related metaphors and which I discuss in the following chapters. One of the features that struck commentators who analysed the UK Referendum result was that voting behaviour did not correspond with the traditional political right and left but followed other divides. A YouGov survey of June 2016 showed Leavers to be distinguished from Remainers by the following characteristics: regions (Midlands versus London); social class (C/D/E versus A/B); educational level (graduates versus non-graduates) age (older versus younger) and ethnicity (White British versus Minority).[19]

I found that Haidt's six foundations corresponded well with my frames—although his foundations were identified by reactions to invented stories in which an aspect of morality was violated, for example through an act of incest, rather than by language analysis. Metaphor analysis shows that a much wider range of frames were employed on Twitter by Leave; these reflected and reinforced those used by Leave leaders such as Boris Johnson and Jacob Rees-Mogg and the Leave supporting press shown in Table 1.1.[20] Remain supporters relied on only two moral foundations: the Care/Harm and Fairness/Cheating paradigms but Leave supporters used metaphor frames for Patriotism and the Nation, Distrust and Betrayal, 'divorce' scripts and **all six of the moral foundations**. Table 2.8 gives an overview of how the moral foundations identified through moral psychology correspond with the metaphor based frames described in the following chapters.

Table 2.8 Leave metaphor frames and their moral foundations

Leave moral foundations (Haidt 2012)	Leave frames
1. Care/Harm	Patriotism and the Nation (Chapter 3)
	War and Invasion scenario (Chapter 4)
	Boris Johnson (Chapter 6)
	Relationship metaphors (Chapter 7)
	Animal-as-Human (Chapter 9)
2. Fairness/Cheating	POLITICS IS A GAME (Chapter 5)
	Jacob Rees-Mogg (Chapter 5)
	Boris Johnson (Chapter 6)
	Relationship metaphors (Chapter 7)
	Marriage of convenience and divorce scripts (Chapter 8)
	'fat cats' metaphor (Chapter 9)
3. Loyalty/Betrayal	Distrust and Betrayal (Chapter 3)
	BOUNDARIES ARE CONTAINERS (Chapter 5)
	Boris Johnson (Chapter 6)
	Jacob Rees-Mogg & Relationship metaphors (Chapter 7)
	Allegorical Frame for Deception and Disloyalty (Chapter 9)
4. Authority/Subversion	Jacob Rees-Mogg (Chapter 3)
	Sovereign Nation scenario (Chapter 4)
	Boris Johnson (Chapter 6)
5. Sanctity/Degradation	Memories of war heroes/ancestors and Jacob Rees-Mogg's view of the nation as sacrosanct (Chapter 3)
	Take Back Control (Chapter 4)
	Boris Johnson (Chapter 6)
	'Smell a Rat' & 'Rats Leaving a Sinking Ship' and other allegorical animal idioms (chapter 9)
6. Liberty/Oppression	Jacob Rees-Mogg (Chapter 3)
	CONTAINERS ARE BOUNDED SPACES (Chapter 5)
	Boris Johnson (Chapter 6)

Haidt goes on to illustrate the strong human tendencies towards group formation and how humans could share their intentions through language and shared symbolic meanings. The argument of this book is that the frames, metaphors and scenarios that I illustrate in the following chapters show how the intentions of Leavers were communicated more persuasively, and more in line with many voters underlying moral judgements, because they were expressed in a richer set of allegories and symbols that triggered their moral intuitions. This was especially the case in the language of Boris Johnson and Jacob Rees-Mogg, though certain moral foundations such as Liberty/Oppression also featured in Nigel Farage's language. Although this suggests that Leave supporters were more successful in communicating their arguments, it does not, of course, necessarily imply that they were right.

Notes

1. 'Identity politics' refers to the forming of exclusive political alliances on the basis of a shared racial, religious, ethnic, social, or cultural identity. This is in contrast to traditional party politics, where allegiances are on the basis of a set of abstract values such as belief in equality or in freedom.
2. Stephen Pollard, *The Express*, 26 October 2012.
3. *MailOnline*, 9 August 2012.
4. *The Telegraph*, 10 January 2013.
5. Lalic-Krstin & Silaski, N. (2019).
6. https://www.english-corpora.org/bnc/.
7. *The Spectator*, 24 September 2016.
8. Michael Rosenthal, Banbury, Oxfordshire.
9. *The Express*, 18 July 2016.
10. This is available at https://studylib.net/doc/18642364/question-assessment-report.
11. This is known as the 'BNC' and is 100 million words in size.
12. This is known as 'COCA' and is 520 million words in size.
13. The contrast between moral intuition and moral reasoning was made in Haidt (2001).
14. A more detailed account of syllogisms and enthymemes is given in Charteris-Black (2018), Section 1.3.2 entitled 'Logos'.
15. Vote Leave @vote_leave, 22 Jun 2016.
16. Defiant Lion UK@DefiantLionUK, Jun 22 2016.
17. Based on Haidt (2012), Chapter 7.
18. Graham et al. (2009).
19. See Clarke et al. (2017), Chapter 7 'Voting to Leave'.
20. Based on Haidt (2012), Chapter 7.

References

Charteris-Black, J. (2018). *Analysing Political Speeches: Rhetoric, Discourse and Metaphor*, 2nd edn. London: Palgrave.

Clarke, H.D., Goodwin, M., and Whiteley, P. (2017). *Brexit: Why Britian Voted to Leave the European Union*. Cambridge: Cambridge University Press.

Graham, J., Haidt, J., and Nosek, B.A. (2009). Liberals and Conservatives Rely on Different Sets of Moral Foundations. *Journal of Personal and Social Pyschology* 96, 5: 1029–1046.

Haidt, J. (2001). The Emotional Dog and Its Rational Tail: A Social Intuitionist Approach to Moral Judgment. *Psychological Review* 108, 4: 814–34.

Haidt, J. (2012). *The Righteous Mind: Why Good People are Divided by Politics and Religion*. London: Penguin.

Lalic-Krstin, G. and Silaski, N. (2019). 'Don't Go Brexin' My Heart: The Ludic Aspects of Brexit-Induced Neologisms. In V. Koller, S. Kopf, and M. Miglbauer (Eds.), *Discourses of Brexit* (pp. 222–36). London and New York: Routledge.

3

I Love My Country

The Patriotism and the Nation Frame

Patriotism is an intense sense of belonging characterised by feelings for an ancestral homeland based on shared cultural practice and common historical memory. It finds its voice through patriotic songs and memories of the sounds or colours of a familiar landscape or cityscape. There are many different levels at which patriotism can be displayed ranging from the public display of symbols to knowledge of a shared literature. Though patriotism implies geographical boundedness it is different from nationalism because its allegories, though intense, have a veiled meaning that is only accessible to those who share the same patriotic feeling: it is intuitive rather than reasoned, as Orwell put it: "By 'patriotism' I mean devotion to a particular place and a particular way of life, which one believes to be the best in the world but has no wish to force on other people".[1] I would consider the following tweet as illustrating the appeal of patriotic feeling:

> Fellow Brexiteers I thank you.
> Your optimism, passion, resilience and patriotism make me so proud to be British. It's time. #VoteLeave (+ image of Union Jack)[2]

© The Author(s) 2019
J. Charteris-Black, *Metaphors of Brexit*,
https://doi.org/10.1007/978-3-030-28768-9_3

The appeal is to emotion rather than reason as the tweeter thanks others for sharing her feelings of patriotism and solidarity: she refers to 'you' and then talks about the effect of 'you' on 'me'. Clearly, what the tweeter cares about most is her own group: those who are supporting Brexit. It is based on the Loyalty/Betrayal moral foundation.

Nationalism has a political meaning about social identities linked to beliefs about the political autonomy of the nation state that is defined in contrast to foreign states. Henry VIII encouraged a belief in the English nation when he dissolved the monasteries because this symbolised an end to the authority of the Catholic Pope. Orwell stated that nationalism "…is inseparable from the desire for power. The abiding purpose of every nationalist is to secure more power and more prestige, *not* for himself but for the nation or other unit in which he has chosen to sink his own individuality".[3] The new form of national sentiment that developed in the UK referendum was characterised both by patriotism and nationalism. The Leave campaign framed their argument in terms of a shared identity of 'us':

> Let's #VoteLeave and take back control of the money we send to the EU. (148 retweets; 146 likes)[4]

This tweet does not distinguish between 'you' and 'me' but appeals on the basis of a common and unspecified 'we' that is defined in opposition to the EU.

Individual views on the balance between patriotism and nationalism depend on geographical and historical circumstances, and on personal experience of power through invasion or colonial domination. Many people living in the Baltic States, and in the nations of Eastern European have different allegories of nation from those living in countries that have less experience of foreign domination. The Eastern European desire to break away from the former Soviet Union was driven by liberal notions of self-determination rather than xenophobic nationalism. There is a difference between patriotism rooted in a sense of identity arising from shared social practices and cultural values and a view of nationhood that assumes the supremacy of one nation over other nations. Heroic, patriotic allegories originate in the search for a collective identity arising from a common history and shared memories that stretch across generations. By contrast jingoistic, xenophobic, nationalist frames originate in the assertion of identity through the subjugation of an enemy identified through racial, ethnic or linguistic difference. However, both patriotism and nationalism derive from the moral foundation of Loyalty/Betrayal, which may be why they are sometimes conflated.

British nationalism derives from a narrative of resistance to overseas sources of authority that are associated with foreign domination—for example by a Catholic force (the Armada), Napoleonic France or the German Third Reich. So it is also grounded in the Liberty/Oppression moral foundation. In its modern form the concept of Britain as a sovereign nation commenced with the Napoleonic wars and resistance to Napoleonic expansion; the Battle of Trafalgar and later Waterloo became symbols of resistance to threats of invasion and have seeped into the 'national consciousness' through the naming of significant places such as Trafalgar Square and Waterloo Station. This frame is collectively reinforced by the practice of wearing red poppies and participating in commemorations of Armistice Day. The British allegory of nation celebrates *our own* dead rather than *all* victims of war.

Patriotism and nationalism flourished before and throughout two World Wars, and were somewhat artificially revived—probably for internal political reasons—in the Falklands War, and the two Gulf Wars and the Afghan War. These later manifestations of national identity became more patriotically inward looking so that the focus was on *British* victims of war in media campaigns such as 'Homes for Heroes'. It was hardly surprising that in the UK Referendum debate the Leave campaign sought to re-activate nationalist frames in arguments for 'Independence' from an oppressive foreign source of authority and to guarantee national sovereignty by 'taking back control'. These were rhetorically powerful because they identified the European Union as a source of external authority, rather than with something of which we were already part and were based in the moral foundation of Sanctity/Degradation. The Remain campaign retaliated by claiming it was equally patriotic, though not nationalist. The frame of patriotism is irresistible and denied at your own cost.

An analysis of tweets in the week before the referendum shows several keywords for the frame 'Patriotism and the Nation' reflecting a cline of views from those expressing concerns about political legitimacy to mythic ideas of a heroic leader. These tweets were posted mainly by supporters of the Leave campaign and can be interpreted in terms of allegory and scenario. Many Twitter posts emphasised positive emotions associated with patriotism such as pride in being British. Although the Patriotism and the Nation frame was more naturally attuned to the mindset and rhetoric of the Leave campaign, the keyword 'patriot' was one that was contested. Interestingly, it was the Remain side that wanted to appeal most to being 'patriotic' for example a search of 'patriot', 'patriotic' and 'patriotism' under #Remain in the 24 hour period before June 23rd shows 36 posts. By contrast there were only 8 posts in this period that included any reference to these words under #Leave, of which only 3 actually supported 'Leave'. It may be that Leave supporters were fearful that the murder Jo Cox by a mentally deranged supporter of Brexit, would have a significant backlash on their cause and so deliberately avoided making excessive claims to patriotism. As he shot and stabbed the Labour MP Jo Cox one week before the Referendum, Thomas Mair had shouted "Britain first, this is for Britain, Britain will always come first", and "Make Britain independent". On his arrest he gave his name as "death to traitors, freedom for Britain". This demonstrates the contested nature of the frame for 'Patriotism and the Nation'—while naturally a frame associated with the political right, it was one that 'Remain' would not hand over lightly.

Leave developed more persuasive arguments through moral reasoning and these confirmed beliefs that had already been formed on the basis of emotional intuition. In Chapter 1 we saw that the basic structure of a syllogism was a major premise, a minor premise and a conclusion. If someone accepts both the premises then it logically follows that they will accept the conclusion. There is a distinction between the syllogism where all three elements are found, and the enthymeme where the minor premise is missing on the assumption that it could be worked out from context. Aristotle believed that the enthymeme was likely to be more persuasive and this is probably because it was better at confirming a pre-existing belief and Leave were more successful in using such confirmation bias. Let's compare the moral reasoning in the arguments of some Remain and Leave tweets on the topic of patriotism. Remain Tweeters were keen to emphasise the claim that staying in the EU was a patriotic choice and stated their belief in a syllogism; for example, the leader of the Liberal Democrats Tim Farron posted the following:

> "I am voting REMAIN because I am a patriot and a parent." Pledge to #VoteRemain: https://voteremain.win (25 retweets)[5]

Its reasoning structure is as follows:

[**Major premise**] It is patriotic to vote Remain
[**Minor premise**] It is responsible to vote Remain
[**Conclusion**] I am voting Remain

Leave tweeters often presented moral reasoning by including rhetorical questions and by enthymemes. In enthymemes the full form of the argument is not stated and so the meaning relies on implicature:

> @timfarron voting in because he's "a patriot".... do patriots sell their country out to Berlin + Brussels? No. #BBCDebate #Brexit #EURef (30 retweets)[6]

We could represent the argument like this:

[**Major premise**] Tim Farron says he is a patriot.
[**Minor premise—Implied**] Patriots do not sell their country to foreign powers.
[**Conclusion—Implied**] It is not therefore patriotic to vote Remain.

The minor premise takes the form of an ironic question—"do patriots sell their country out to Berlin + Brussels?" The question and answer pattern raises doubts about the 'patriotic' claim made in the major premise and crucially *the conclusion is not stated*, but only implied. The moral reasoning is emotional because it is directed towards a named politician using an ad hominem ('to the person') argument. It is clearly based on the Loyalty/Betrayal moral foundation as it argues that Remainers are betraying the nation and so is consistent with Leave framing of Remain supporters as unpatriotic. The same strategy of personal attack occurs here:

> Sadiq Khan claims the patriotic choice is to attach ourselves to a stagnant union which wants federalism… #BBCDebate #EUref #Brexit (106 retweets)[7]

The tweet is deliberately ambiguous as to whether the topic is Sadiq Kahn or the EU. The moral reasoning is as follows:

> [**Major premise**] Sadiq Khan claims that Remain is patriotic.
> [**Minor premise 1—Implied**] The EU is a stagnant organisation
> [**Minor premise 1—Implied**] THE EU seeks a federal Europe.
> [**Conclusion—Implied**] Sadiq Khan and other Remainers are not therefore patriotic.

The tweet only expresses the major premise and allows the reader to infer the minor premises and conclusion. The two Leave posts suggest that their authors are skilled in linguistic methods for persuasive messages: in this case engaging the hearer by implying a conclusion. Unlike Remain posts, they allow a position to be inferred and rely more on the elephant of intuition rather than the rider of reason. Although Leave Tweeters used the term 'patriot' less frequently than Remain in the week before the referendum, their tweets were retweeted much more. This is because they designed tweets based on sound rhetorical principles. By contrast, Remain tweets simply *stated* an argument in the form of syllogisms and failed to invite the cognitive engagement that arises from enthymemes. Organisations supporting Leave clearly used experts in the rhetoric of social media who could access more morally intuitive ways of reasoning.

'Honour' was a keyword for Leave supporters based on the Loyalty/Betrayal foundation and was less contested as a much larger number of Leave supporters used this keyword alongside symbols of heroic nationalism, such as images of Spitfires in the Battle of Britain, as the following:

> June 22nd (Account Subsequently Deleted)
>   Tomorrow its your turn.. make the RIGHT decision *honour* your forebares .. lets do this people.. #Voteleave #Bluehand + PICTURE OF 2ND WORLD WAR SPITFIRE (20 retweets)

There were also tweets that drew on the memory of previous left-wing opponents of the EU in order to guard against the accusation that 'Leave' was the prerogative of the poltical right:

We may miss great people such as Hugh Gaitskell, Peter Shore, Tony Benn and Barbara Castle, but we must *honour* their belief. #VoteLeave. (25 retweets)[8]

Some tweets using 'honour' implied strong emotional attachments that had formed with other activists during the referendum campaign:

REALLY PROUD TO KNOW YOU BREXIT BOYS & GIRLS. IT'S BEEN AN *HONOUR.* #VoteLeave #LeaveEU #EUref #Brexit #leave #Lexit (23 retweets)[9]

This was accompanied by a humorous image of 3 cartoon characters drawn on 3 raised fingers with the slogan 'MY BREXIT BESTIES' and 'NO REMAINERS FIND YOUR OWN MATES'. This suggests that the success of Leave campaign was because it emotionally engaged supporters and gave them a common social purpose by establishing a social identity based on membership of a group of people who shared the same moral intuitions. Efforts by Remainers to develop counter narratives of authenticity and community often backfired—for example when they appealed to the memory of Jo Cox—because this allowed Leave Twitters to construe them as propaganda:

An MP was murdered and the Establishment are expecting you to vote IN to honour her. I no longer want to live on this planet! #Brexit (37 retweets)[10]

We can represent the argument of the first sentence as follows:

[**Major premise**] An MP was murdered.
[**Minor Premise—Implied**] The Establishment say is it honourable to vote Remain.
[**Conclusion—Implied**] It is not really honourable so you should still vote Leave.

The moral reasoning relies on inferencing because neither Jo Cox nor the identity and political views of her murderer are mentioned. All this has to be supplied by context. The second sentence has the style of irony because it is exaggerated—perhaps a simulation of what a frustrated

Leave supporter might *say*—but importantly does not instruct the reader how to vote. Instead it appeals to the moral foundation of Sanctity because it implies that it is only genuinely honourable to be patriotic.

Keywords such as 'hero' and 'honour' were contested by both sides in the debate with Remainers identifying contemporary 'heroes'—in particular Jo Cox herself—but also other celebrity endorsers of their campaign, such as David Beckham. Conversely, Leave supporters drew on heroic allegories of the Second World War by arguing that the Remain position was an insult to the memory of 'war heroes' as in the following:

#EUref
91yr OLD WW11 NAVY HERO DIES
HIS DYING WISH WAS FOR #Brexit
LET US DO HIM PROUD
#Brexit (13 retweets)[11]

The tweet equates patriotism and nationalism and again seems to draw on the Sanctity/Degradation moral foundation as it suggests those who do not support Brexit are dishonouring the sacred memory of the war dead. However, supporters of Remain were not handing over heroic allegories without a struggle and referred to a Remain supporter as a 'hero' because he had financed an advertisement in the Metro of a pie chart showing that the net migration figure of 330,000 per year was only 0.5% of the British population.

In its more extreme forms the frame of patriotism manifested itself in allusions to 'Jerusalem' and reflected an idealised version of British history; the familiar refrains of 'Swing low sweet chariot' that rings from the rafters of the national rugby stadium, and 'Britains never never shall be slaves' as it has been sung over the years by voices strained to breaking point on the Last Night of the Proms have sometimes offered an irresistibly heroic narrative. Like the overpowering scent of lillies on a hot summer's evening, the extreme form of patriotism known as 'jingoism' suspends reason: the ideal of a free people, resisting all forms of oppression at home and abroad provides a morally intuitive basis for social engagement based on the moral foundation of Liberty. Typical patriotic allegories offer an idealised self-image, the 'right' morally appealing story—as one tweeter put it:

Where is Mozes to lead us out of #EU slavery into the promised #UK land of freedom!! Milk and honey after #Brexit![12]

Consider the following:

> @Arron_banks To all intents and purposes, @nigelfarage could be King Arthur, risen from his slumber at the time of greatest need #VoteLeave[13]
> Vote #Leave, if it's the King Arthur who say it... #Brexit[14]
> where's the SPIRIT of this country gone? Robin Hood would turn in his grave, and King Arthur come to that...we gotta leave the EU #Brexit[15]

The first is an allegory that refers to a historic persona—King Arthur and equates him with the leader of UKIP Nigel Farage. The allegory evokes ideas of invasion, since King Arthur became a symbol around which the Celtic tribes could merge against their invaders. It combines the Sanctity/Degradation moral foundation with Loyalty/Betrayal. There are distant evocations in historical memory of chivalry—through the revival of the romanticism of the Arthurian myth that has proved resonant to this day. Some referred to Nigel Farage as a 'legend':

> @gavthebrexit @Nigel_Farage this man is a legend. I serious hope his family member is alright. This is why we need leave eu #VoteLeave[16]
> @Nigel_Farage absolute legend #VoteLeave[17]

References to 'King Arthur' and 'legends' are patriotic allegories that assume shared cultural and historical beliefs and identities. This frame has the power to evoke long term memories—some lost in the unconscious—that still impact on current political decision-making. I have argued elsewhere (Charteris-Black 2011) of the importance of telling the right story and it seems that the Leave campaign succeeded in creating allegories that were in keeping with populist moral intuitions—especially about the Sanctity of the nation. Populist allegories have their risks:

> Populists don't just criticize elites or play on the prejudices of people using emotionally charged rhetoric. They posit that there is one true, unified people and that they alone are its legitimate representatives.[18]

In a speech by Rees-Mogg from March 2018 'people' occurs 16 times. However, it is not a word that is exclusively used by the political right as Jeremy Corbyn also frequently refers to the British people as a single unified entity:

> The British people made the decision to leave the European Union and Labour respects that decision.[19]
> We are asking the British people for their support, above all on the basis of that programme of social justice.[20]

Populism therefore cut across 'left' and 'right' divisions and created a myth of the leader as the one who has special insight into the needs of the people and who could realise their collective desires. However, it has the sort of dangers that one writer describes as 'authenticism':

> For authenticists, what matter most is not argument, but story: their 'truths' are inextricably bound up with the narratives they tell about their community. The facticity of a given claim matters less than its fit with the narrative. If something *feels* true, then in some sense it must *be* true.[21]

If we accept that reasoned arguments are post hoc rationalisations of emotional intuitions (as much research in cogntive psychology has shown) this is hardly surprising.[22] The frame for Patriotism and the Nation provided heroic narratives that took on a more covert and allegorical character in the tweets of those supporting Leave because they relied on greater inferencing by asking questions and not instructing people how to think. Remain tweets had less complex arguments that often just stated an intention to vote Remain and therefore lacked an allegory and often failed to appeal to the emotions.

Appeals for protection and defence of the nation are central to a number of frames that occur in Brexit metaphors—especially those dependent on the War and Invasion frame discussed in the next chapter. These are intended to avoid the accusation of nationalism by emphasising that beliefs are based on the positive emotion of patriotism. The semiotic form that most clearly represents the British identity as a sovereign nation is the Union Jack flag—a symbol that has become ubiquitous in the Brexit debate—adopted by Brexiteers as the symbol of their aspirations for 'independence' from the European Union. Some mythic allegories refer to the flag either in verbal or in visual form. For example:

The Union Jack is my flag the one I proudly stood for & fought for during my time in the services #Brexit, EU never[23]

Some questioned the appeal of the EU flag:

This is it Brits let's do this for democracy and for freedom. No longer will we be a star on someone else's flag! #IndependenceDay #Brexit[24]

An image showing both the Union Jack and the European Union flag alongside each other made the following offer:

Take your pick today. It's your chance for the #EU flag on the right to be lowered for good. #VoteLeave last chance[25]
Each star on that Flag represents the death of a nation. (175 retweets)[26]

The practice of evoking historical memories through the established symbols offered by flags was contested:

I will not have the flag of our country stolen by people whose aim it is to make us hate each other #VoteRemain (209 retweets)[27]

Political cartoons provide additional evidence of symbols and allegories because cartoonists are skilled in capturing ways of thinking through the visual and verbal modes or through multimodal symbols. They are a genre whose purpose is to entertain and amuse while passing some form of satirical comment on current affairs—often drawing on the cartoonists' moral intuitions. They typically depict politicians or other pre-eminent figures in public life such as royalty or celebrities. Fundamental to the interpretation of political cartoons is recognition of their authors' rhetorical purposes:

The purpose of a political cartoon is to represent an aspect of social, cultural, or political life in a way that condenses reality and transforms it in a striking, original, and/or humorous way. The field of politics is often complex and bewildering, and cartoons offer a way of explaining the significance of real life events and characters through the means of an imaginary scenario.[28]

Cartoons achieve a number of rhetorical goals simultaneously: they entertain, explain, evaluate and simplify. Metaphor offers the most effective way of combining these diverse objectives by creating imaginary worlds that reveal some aspects of reality that might be concealed by a literal rendering. Since cartoons intend to influence public opinion, politicians are typically represented by allegories implying that they are immoral, greedy, or dangerous, but occasionally they may be represented as benevolent or harmless.

Using the search terms 'Brexit' and the keyword 'flag' in cartoons from the British Cartoon Archive the depicted individuals were the Queen, Boris Johnson and Theresa May. In a cartoon published on 28 December 2016 by *The Guardian* the queen is depicted outside a polling station dressed in a Union Jack outfit wearing a badge with the caption 'Brexit Now' that commented on a popular, but unsubstantiated, claim that the Queen supported Leave.[29] In another by *The Independent* on 15 July 2016 Boris Johnson is depicted with toy pistols firing a Brexit pistol with the speech bubble "Hello foreign oiks, let's do business"; in the lower part of the image 4 different international leades are shown in horror with their backs turned towards him crying "The Boris is Coming, the Boris is Coming!" The cartoonist, Brian Adcock commenting satirically on Boris's negotiating competence by associating it with childish behaviour; it questions his ability to negotiate trade deals. In a similar vein a cartoon for *The Times* published on 6 May 2016 shows two frames: in the left hand ('before') frame Boris Johnson is shown in a suit under the caption 'Mayor', while in the right ('after') frame he is depicted wearing a massive a Union Jack flag under the caption 'Nightmare'. Some cartoons did not represent politicians at all, in one for *The Guardian* by Steve Bell on 24 August 2017 a physical bundle wrapped in a Union Jack wearing the caption 'Kick me Hard' is surrounded by the gold stars of the EU flag. Here the cartoonist is telling an allegory in which the outcome of negotiations with the EU are unpleasant and painful.

Humour is an especially important—if not defining—feature of successful political cartoons because it evokes emotionally intuitive responses. It can arise from word play, caricature or by an interaction between words and image. Although harsh, critical comment will often be more humorous when the means through which it is realised are subtle. The commentary on leading Brexit politicians often involves exaggeration of recognisable aspects of their appearance—Boris Johson's mop of hair. Depictions of Jacob Rees-Mogg show an English aristocrat wearing a suit with a waistcoat and top hat to imply that his views originate in an earlier epoch. The conventions of the genre give free reign to the imagination of the cartoonist who has the privileged status of Court Fool because he can express moral intuitions: they are allegorical in nature.

In the final Televised debate on European Union membership Boris Johnson declared in the conclusion to his brief address "I believe that this Thursday can be our country's "Independence Day"—the phrase was picked up by the popular press appearing on the cover of *The Sun* newspaper and there were over a thousand tweets that refer to 'Independence Day' on June 22nd alone. Boris Johnson here was justifying his position by drawing on an allegory that argued that Britain needed to gain its independence. The connotations of Independence draw on the allegories of patriotic struggle for national identity and relied on the Liberty/Oppression moral foundation. In many nations Independence Day is a national holiday as it symbolises heroic struggle against colonialism. By using 'Independence Day' Johnson was contributing to an allegory in which the European Union was a colonial power that was imposing its authority on Britain. This was a myth since the decision to join the European Economic Community was approved by a referendum of the British electorate in 1975. However, it was a political myth that was alive and kicking at the time of the British Referendum and the 'Independence Day' trope activated the emotionally powerful 'War and Invasion' frame.

'Patriotism and the Nation' in the Discourse of Jacob Rees-Mogg

Leading Brexiteers such as Boris Johnson and Jacob Rees-Mogg shared a worldview in which the boundaries of a nation state, especially when geographically enforced by a coastline, constitute a *natural* location of allegiance, loyalty and social identity that has moral sanctity. A nationalist viewpoint sees any other identities, such as being 'European', as in conflict with a heroic allegory of nation. This view is most clearly articulated by Jacob Rees-Mogg who believes in the manifest destiny of Britain's desire to Leave the European Union; in a significant speech that he made early in 2018 he employed many metaphors (in italics) to argue for British heroic leadership of the world as the saviour of free enterprise:

> We have reached *the portals* of tremendous possibility. If the UK is to execute an independent trade policy then it can play a role in ensuring that there is an *injection of wealth* into the global economy. This will improve the lot of all mankind and we, the British people, *will be propelled forward on this rising tide*. … …I have talked about who we can be as a nation. We must also understand our particular role in the world at this critical time. The world's *economic architecture is stuck* and the UK is expected by the rest of the world to advocate policies that *will release its energy*.. ..If the UK *is unfettered by the deadweight of the EU* then it will play a role in *jumpstarting the global economic system*. This *will unblock many initiatives that have been gummed up for too long*. We must never forget that wealth can be created or destroyed, but it is much harder to create than destroy.[30]

Here he employs metaphors of blockage 'stuck', 'gummed up' to refer to EU membership that are contrasted with those of force: 'portals', 'injection', 'propelled forward', 'jumpstarting', and 'unblock': 'release', 'unfettered' that are linked to leaving the EU. He then develops his argument for British exceptionalism with a conventional 'journey' metaphor in the choice between two 'paths':

> We are coming to a fork in the road. We can *take the familiar path* that leads to a *gradual erosion* of our wealth, our success and ultimately our

values, by staying close to the EU and aligning our regulations to theirs. We could simply manage decline. Or we *could take another road* that may look to us now like an unfamiliar one. In which case *our best days lie before us.*

A stark choice is framed by spatial metaphors that offer two contrasting scenarios: one associated with failure and the other with success. There is also a contrast between the known past (negatively appraised) and a known future (positively appraised). The metaphors emphasise the choice between these alternative scenarios and an assumed social identity for 'we'. His allegory represents Britain as a single homogeneous and exceptional entity without competing interest groups—an allegory of unity that not even the Brexit campaign had dispelled. Jacob Rees-Mogg is the leading Brexit politician who admits quite openly to the appeal of historic myths of national identity and the Sanctity of the nation. As Chairman of the European Research Group, while speaking at a 'Leave Means Leave' event in Central London he humorously quipped:

> I know that I am sometimes teased for being the 'Honourable Member for the 18th Century', but it is a badge I wear with pride because it was in the 18th Century that the seeds of our greatness, sown long before in our distinguished history, sown conceivably by Alfred the Great, began to grow and to flourish in a way that led to our extended period of good fortune and greatness.[31]

Here he shows his affinity for allegory and symbolism that combined to express his feelings of patriotism: so nationalist arguments were framed within patriotic emotions. An example of these patriotic emotions is in a set of metaphors that frame national life in homely rural metaphors:

> A report last week said that we would have a 10-page document on a political agreement saying that *motherhood and apple pie* was all fine and dandy.[32]

He was ready to consume whatever fruit metaphors the discourse of Brexit had on offer:

Just *to add a cherry to the top of the cake that we are all looking forward to eating* in due course, they have accepted a date for the implementation of article 50.[33]

In contrast to these homely rural metaphors, Jacob Rees-Mogg also has the style of an 18th patrician; this is conveyed through his display of erudition and learning drawing on classical, biblical and historical allusions that permeate his language:

I rather feel *as the diners must have felt at the Belshazzar's feast*, when the words appeared written on the wall, *"Mene, Mene, Tekel, Upharsin,"* and Daniel came and translated them and said, "You have been weighed in the balances and found wanting." After the feast they all went to bed and woke up the next morning, and instead of *Darius the Mede having taken over, Belshazzar carried on as normal.* It was business as normal, and that is what is so impressive about this Budget.[34]

His role as an MP is one whereby he is a servant of the people rather than a power-wielding aristocrat:

One of the titles of the Pope is *"servus servorum Dei":* the servant of the servants of God. That is how we should view our role —*as the servants of the people* of the United Kingdom, whom I happen to think are also the people of God. We must work to ensure that we can help them lead better, more prosperous lives.[35]

Citing the Pope indexes his Catholicism—a reserve of moral foundations related to Sanctity and Degradation—and the idea of servants is one that he later uses in the emotionally charged notion of Britain becoming a 'vassal state'. But the irony is that while he is himself an employer of servants, he puts himself forward as a representative of the people:

I confess that I have a romantic belief in both trial by jury and democratic decision-making. If not quite 'Vox Populi, Vox Dei', nonetheless the masses are more likely to be right than the elite.[36]

Ironically, here he does so using a Latin expression that would in most cases not be part of the lexicon of anyone educated outside of a public school. Whenever he talks about 'elites' it is always *as if he were not himself one of such an elite*:

> Outside the political elite, at events across the country, people tell me (quietly, as it is not the fashionable view) that they too want to leave. And in London, I get supportive shouts from people driving lorries and taxis - a somewhat unusual experience for a Conservative politician.[37]

He frames himself as a man of the people appealing to the same audience as Donald Trump:

> His election depended upon similar factors to those that led to Brexit. He appealed to voters left behind by the metropolitan elite and he exudes confidence about his own nation and a determination not to be a manager of decline, which also inspires the Brexiteers.[38]

He identifies closely with a patriotic and nationalist rhetoric that is spreading across Europe:

> Instead of fostering democracy, it is now encouraging the growth of extremist parties, with voters driven into their arms by a complacent and uncaring EU elite.[39]

Here it is the EU that is elitist while he regards himself as a friendly voice of the people:

> Across Europe the plump, self-satisfied elite is being washed away by populist movements who often encompass extreme and politically dangerous views.[40]

So Jacob Rees-Mogg is able to imagine a nation in which there is a place for learned patricians who are more aware of the needs and feelings of the people than remote Brussels bureacrats and who can communicate their sentiments in the unique, allusive style of an English country gentleman.

The Distrust and Betrayal Frame

Rather than focusing on defending an independent nation that is threatened *from without*, this frame is motivated by the idea of betrayal of the homeland *from within*. Patriotic defence of the homeland had, as its corollary, dark accusations against those *within the nation* who were intuitively felt to threaten its survival. This frame drew on scenarios in which traitors were named and, in some cases, the necessary action taken against them. The counterbalance to a nostalgic yearning for an imagined community of believers who share collective values—the sacrosanct nation—was a quest for traitors who degraded these values and threatened the unity of the people. Such traitors to the national cause intentionally sought to conspire against and corrupt the pure and sacred nation. This frame is grounded in the utter rejection of trust—whether by politicians, institutions or by the 'mainstream' media. It was therefore the frame of a so-called 'post-truth' narrative of disillusionment and betrayal. While the Patriotism and the Nation frame corresponded with the moral foundations of 'Loyalty' and Sanctity, the Distrust and Betrayal frame corresponded with the 'Betrayal' and 'Degradation' elements of these moral foundations.

Words such as 'traitor' and 'treason' aroused moral intuitions about betrayal in which dark forces degrade national unity by poisoning its wellspring. Keywords that emphasised highly negative characteristics of opponents included:

betrayal
conspiracy
collaborator
disloyalty
humiliation
hypocrisy
Judas
lies
quisling
sabotage
steal
traitor
treachery
treason

Opponents were labelled 'traitors', 'quislings' or 'Judases' who were guilty of hypocrisy, treason or treachery because they had betrayed, or might betray, the nation. Emotive names such as 'Judas' or 'traitor' rejected any form of deliberation because the trial had already taken place by an imagined voice of the people, as Müller points out:

> Populists assume that the entire people can speak with one voice and issue something like an imperative mandate. There is therefore no need for debate, let alone the messy back-and-forth of deliberation in national assemblies.[41]

In this section I argue that the Distrust and Betrayal frame—while not entirely absent from the statements of politicians—dominated the social media postings of Brexit supporters. I suggest that communication experts working for the Leave campaign set the tone for the debate on social media by negative framing of the elite and claims to authentic self-representation:

> You don't need to trust politicians to vote for Brexit. Just trust yourself writes @JuliaHB1 #Brexit #LeaveEU[42]

This tweet was retweeted 181 times and received 165 likes. Without offering proof it expresses a moral intuition in a double imperative that simultaneously invites the reader to distrust all 'politicians' and trust 'yourself'. Statements of ethical judgement are made with a very high level of certainty, as if they are neither debatable nor contentious:

> The #EU have stolen our Fish
> #WeWantOurFishBack
> #EURef #VoteLeave #Brexit #remain #INorOUT #LabourIN #No2EU
> (39 retweets)[43]

The terms 'stolen' in the major premise contains its own ethical argument and the chain of hashtags indicates that the author is familiar with the grammar of Twitter, and how the topic linking function of the hashtag contains the seed for dispersal through this social media platform.

Once social media campaigners had introduced the frame others adopted its style; here are some tweets containing semantically related keywords (in italics):

> John Major is a *traitor*. He signed the Maastricht Treaty, an act of *TREASON* against the sovereign British nation! #VoteLeave #Britannia[44]
> *Quisling* brothers have only 10 days left in office. #Brexit #Leave (+ link to a photo of Cameron and Osborne).[45]

These keywords imply an enemy within; the frame activates a number of allegories and scenarios around disloyality—either because politicians are in it for themselves or because they hold allegiance to a foreign power—'Brussels'. This frame argues that Remainers are simply not to be trusted. Words such as 'quisling' evoke a Second World War name 'Quisling' that has since become an allegory for betrayal of the nation. Just as in former periods Catholics were accused of being a threat to a nation because they were loyal to an alien source of authority—so Remainers—and their leaders—are not 'loyal':

> With more loyalty to a terrorist state outside of Europe can a *traitor* be trusted? #Cameron #Brexit #VoteLeave[46]

In the week before the Referendum there were 60 tweets that contained the words 'Cameron' and 'traitor'—ironically there would never have been the opportunity to vote on EU membership had David Cameron not made his fateful political decision to have a referendum. Having made the decision he became a prime target of Leave campaigners since he was personally campaigning to Remain. Brexiteers found Remain tendencies in their own party equally tainted:

> How about a #generalelectionnow? Too many *quisling* Conservatives at Westminster misrepresenting the wishes of their #Brexit constituents. (81 retweets)[47]

> Here's the deal. Although we voted for #Brexit the Conservative Party
> will deny us our wish by imposing the *quisling* #TheresaMay as PM. (29
> retweets)[48]

Words such as 'quisling' occurred frequently on Twitter in the
Referendum debate to create allegories of betrayal. While it was mainly
Brexit supporters who employed the emotive 'Distrust and Betrayal'
frame, the most retweeted tweet was by a Remain supporter and containing a link to an article:

> To wash its hands of Europe would be a *betrayal* of Britain's past - and
> future: (link to Economist article) #VoteRemain (65 retweets)[49]

Here the author anticipated the Brexiteer argument that staying in the
EU was a betrayal of the nation. Brexiteer tweets viewed Remainers
as 'collaborators', fear was sustained by historical imaginings of what
might have happened had the planned German invasion of Britian
succeeded:

> Is it Time For Someone To Take Nazi *Collaborator* Soros Behind the
> Wood Shed?[50]

Allegories based on historical memories of Second World War victory had been closely related to the rise of UKIP as a political force.
Similarly, in some Labour voting areas voters had shifted to UKIP
because Labour was believed to have betrayed the working class:

> @polnyypesets @CarolineLucas Labour will not be forgiven for this
> *betrayal* of the working class in support of corporate power. #VoteLeave[51]
> the working class *betrayed* by the out of touch political class will win
> the referendum for #Brexit (+ link to *Guardian* article by Lisa McKenzie)

In allegories of betrayal, Judas served as the 'traitor':

> Cameron eluded to a churchillian connection, to compare the two is to
> compare Jesus to *Judas* the great redeemer and the *traitor*. #Brexit[52]

> @UKLabour should be the UK *Judas* party *selling out* your country for a bag of silver #Traitors #EUref #VoteLeave #Democracy[53]

In rhetorical terms the Distrust and Betrayal frame contributes to what Edelman refers to as myth of the Conspiratorial Enemy.[54] In this frame there are a caucus of united interests—businessmen, politicians—who find it in their interests to betray the real needs of the nation, the homeland. True patriots support the sovereignty and sanctity of their country as symbolised by fallen ancestors by protecting themselves from shame. No doubt similar arguments were made by Protestants who resisted attempts to re-establish Catholicism as the national religion in the sixteenth and seventeenth centuries—they therefore have a pedigree in historically-based allegories of national identity: allegories in which the needs of the nation are elevated to a spiritual status and override all other forms of loyalty. However the Distrust and Betrayal frame also corresponded with the prevailing climate of conspiracy theory. This was summarised by Ryan Coatzee, the director of strategy for the Remain campaign, as follows:

> Britain got caught up in something that is sweeping the West, and that involves distrust to the point of paranoia. It involves growing fear of the other, whether that person is foreign of black or whatever it might be. It involves a turning away from reason, evidence, logic – those ideas that have built what is called the West over the past five hundred years. What the Leave campaign did was they turbocharged that lack of trust.[55]

The concept of conspiracy permeated social media throughout the period leading up to the Referendum and continued thereafter with fears that the outcome would not be respected and that somehow the nations leaders—including the new Prime Minister—would conspire with the EU to subvert the referendum result:

> Charlie Mullins: "Theresa May's government are now part of a criminal *conspiracy!*"[56]

Although predominantly a Brexiteer frame, Remain supporters also referred to 'conspiracies' after the Referendum result:

#Brexit was and is a *conspiracy* by #Russia and #NigelFarrage to break the #UK, the Western Alliance, and the #EU.[57]

#Brexit is a fraudulent *conspiracy* to deny economic and democratic rights and benefits to the British people. It was funded by Russians and foreign speculators and won through lies and mis-use of data. But @theresa_may is covering it up.[58]

Along with 'conspiracy', 'traitor' was a rhetorically powerful keyword. The concept is emotive since it implies an intense, historically rooted condemnation; it rejects feelings of trust that characterise positive human relationships and it can be applied equally to the betrayal of individuals or to principles. 'Traitor' has a declining use in official political discourse, for example in parliamentary debates it was used 4.35 times per million words in the 1810s, 1.57 times per millions words in the 1910s and only 0.24 times per million words in the 1990s. It was only recorded once in Hansard throughout the whole of 2003 and only once in 2004 and neither of these are directed to specific politicians:

Mr: Cook One of the commendable ingenuities of the hon: Gentleman is that he always manages to find a way of making his point without my having to arrange a debate: He has just done so again: I fully concur with him in the sentiment behind his point— there is nothing heroic in being a *traitor*: I think that the whole House would agree...[59]

Another girl who had won a place very nearly did not come at all because her teachers told her that she was a class *traitor*...[60]

One pro-Brexit tweeter posted the following allegory for the traitor that claims to be a quote from Cicero but is in fact a paraphrase by J.M. Caldwell:

A nation can survive its fools, and even the ambitious. But it cannot survive *treason* from within. An enemy at the gates is less formidable, for he is known and carries his banner openly. But *the traitor* moves amongst those within the gate freely, his *sly* whispers *rustling* through all the alleys, heard in the very halls of government itself. For the *traitor* appears not a *traitor*; he speaks in accents familiar to his victims, and he *wears* their face and their arguments, he appeals to the *baseness* that *lies deep in the hearts* of all men.[61]

Here the allegory is told using a triple repetition of 'traitor' combined with a set of words (in italics) relating to moral deception and personalised with the poetic quality of 'his *sly* whispers *rustling* through all the alleys' and invited embodied reactions ('in the hearts'). 'Traitor' was used in highly personalised attacks:

> What does Stephen Kinnock know about patriotism? He supports the UK to be subservient to Brussels and Berlin. *Traitor*! #VictoriaLive #Brexit[62]

'Traitor' allegories evoke a sense of moral turpitude and channel feelings of suspicion and enmity toward the political class because they are inherently deceptive. Donald Trump was surely to learn something of this in his campaign attack on the Washington 'elite'. Some Remainers picked up on the danger of the word 'traitor' as a form of ad hominem attack:

> ...And if a *'traitor'* is defined by someone who dedicated their life to bringing people together to create a better world #VoteRemain[63]
> @Brexpats If that is what Thomas Mair calls me, I'm proud to be a *traitor*. Je suis *traître*. #Iamatraitor #JoCoxMP #ThomasMair #VoteRemain[64]

Here supporters of Remain contest the traitor allegory either by using it ironically to refer to themselves, or by drawing attention to the discourse of tweets:

> It seems that all those #brexit bods who bandy around the word *traitor* about those who disagree with them .. Might like to think again.[65]

Drawing attention metalinguistically is a form of contestation enabled in social media debates.

The accusation of 'treason' is potentially even more threatening than 'traitor' since it refers to the crime of betraying the nation by seeking to overthrow the sovereign or government. 'Treason' challenges the legitimacy of the government and since it violates the moral foundation of Sanctity demands an act of retribution from the state in order to assert its legitimacy. High treason was so serious that in the Middle Ages it led to the desecration of the culprit's body by hanging, drawing and quartering. The last execution for treason in the United Kingdom was that of William Joyce (Lord Haw Haw), by hanging, in 1946. 'Treason' has also been in decline in use in parliamentary debates, for example in Hansard there has been a constant decline in its use from 67 times per million words in the 1810s to 3.92 times per million words in the 1910s and only 1.42 times per million words in the 1980s. It was—at least until Brexit—a word that was rarely used in political debate. However in the Twitter Referendum campaign frequent demands were made for retribution on the grounds of treason:

> #VoteLEAVE Hundreds of Germans Trying To Bring *Treason* Charges Against #AngelaMerkel Over #Migration Policy #LEAVE (25 retweets)[66]

The argument for direct punishment of the opposition was largely restricted to supporters of Brexit and some Remainers showed offence at this use of language:

> @montie It's not a tragedy if Brexiters announce we are at "Breaking Point" & accuse opponents of *treason* -it's vile campaigning. #VoteRemain[67]

Another word that is closely related to the Distrust and Betrayal frame that has the power to evoke allegory is the word 'treachery':

> Osborne says remain so that's my signal to do the opposite *#treachery* #Voteleave (8 retweets)[68]
> I despair at the gullibility and naivety of the general public in believing establishment and ruling elite lies n *treachery* #Brexit (6 retweets)[69]

Accusations of treachery are based on moral intuition: the more they imply punishment for those who oppose Brexit, the more they seek to influence on the basis of fear. Although supporters of Brexit would claim that fear was an emotion that Remain supporters had sought to encourage by presenting wide-ranging claims about the damaging effect that leaving the EU would have on the British economy. These claims became referred to by supporters of Brexit as 'Project Fear' thereby making explicit the emotional nature of the argument on which they were based. A possible justification for the use of emotive keywords by Leavers is that their weaponisation of words such as 'treachery', 'traitor' and 'treason' was to counter the so-called 'Project Fear' strategies of Remainers.

The Distrust and Betrayal frame is based on an absence of trust of politicians who are viewed as largely self-seeking; one of the strongest sources of anti-European sentiment in the UK is a suspicion that the EU contributes to a highly paid and corrupt 'mandarin' class; for example the following tweet was retweeted 486 times and liked 806 times:

1. "I can't trust the Tories so I'm voting remain."
2. Right, but you can trust people whose names you don't know who you didn't elect.[70]

It is framed as a two-part dialogue (I have inserted numbers to show this); each part contains two arguments and the ironical second argument points to the logical inconsistency of the first argument. The argument structure of the first part can be represented as:

Major Premise: I don't trust the Tories
Minor Premise: If we vote to leave the Tories will be stronger
Conclusion: Therefore I am voting Remain

This part is an enthymeme, as the minor premise is not stated. The second part is also an enthymeme with two minor premises:

Major Premise: You trust people you cannot name, don't know & didn't elect.
Minor Premise A: You should trust people who you can name, know & elect.
Minor Premise B: You don't know, can't name, and didn't vote for your MEP.
Conclusion (Implied): Therefore Don't trust the EU commission & Vote Leave.

In this enthymeme the reader has to supply the minor premises and the conclusion. As we saw in analysis of the Patriotism and the Nation frame, the ability to design enthymemic tweets is highly persuasive because they rely on reader inferencing. Recognition of the meaning requires a complex decoding because the reader has to supply the minor premises and the conclusion. Interpreting and, more importantly, sharing ('retweeting') implies that you too are a member of an in-group who 'gets it': social media is all about getting it, and getting it fast, and, more importantly, retweeting to others displays having got it! Social judgements are like snowballs rolling down a hill.

One reason that the Remain campaign was not trusted was because it seemed to be based on calculations of financial gain. The high frequency of 'hypocrite' in the week before the Referendum indicates the rhetorical influence of ethos. 'Hypocrite' was an accusation more commonly made by Brexiteers. There were 20 tweets in the Referendum week referring to 'Cameron' as a 'hypocrite' and another 10 referring to 'Corbyn'; other 'hypocrites' included Farage (8); Johnson (7) and Geldorf (6). Typically tweets that accused individuals or groups of hypocrisy were not extensively retweeted, with only the following receiving double figure retweets:

> Richard Branson tells us to stay in EU & he lives on Private island & isnt taxed *hypocritical* don't you think (14 retweets)[71]

Accusations of hypocrisy are interesting in so far as they contain a powerful moral condemnation and fit with the media strategy of comparing old with current film footage to reveal a shift in a politician's opinion. In 2019 a campaign called 'Led by Donkeys' posted billboards of past statements by pro-Brexit politicians that appeared to conflict with their current political position and implied hypocrisy. This is viewed as an acceptable form of entertainment since it reveals inconsistencies—although in reality most people shift their opinions over time according to changing circumstances, however it encourages moral intuitions of distrust regarding politicians.

'Distrust and Betrayal' in the Discourse of Jacob Rees-Mogg

While some politicians, such as Jacob Rees-Mogg, have been highly consistent in their views regarding EU membership, others, such as Boris Johnson, oscillated. Once Leave had won the campaign Rees-Mogg argued for a Hard Brexit that would allow Britain as much independence as possible from the EU. In a significant speech in March 2018 he argued vehemently for the need to support the outcome of the Referendum by imagining what would happen if Britain did not leave:

> What would that mean for this Nation? If we were not to leave, if we were to find a transition bound us back in? Well it would be Suez all over again. It would be the most *almighty smash to the national psyche* that could be imagined. It would be an admission of abject failure, a view of our politicians, of our leaders, of our Establishment that *we were not fit*, that we were *too craven*, that we were too weak to be able to govern ourselves and that therefore we had to go *crawling back to the mighty bastion of power that is Brussels*. .... Poor little Blighty *must shelter itself from the winds of global competition* by *hiding behind the protective, albeit crumbling, walls of Fortress Europe*. We would be saying, if we reversed this decision, particularly if we did so by subterfuge, by *prestidigitation, by legerdemain*, – we would be saying that once again not only can we not govern ourselves but we are so frightened of our electorate that we dare not tell them that that is what we believe. *As with the disaster of Suez it would end up being a national humiliation based on lies.*[72]

This extract employs multiple metaphors (in italics) to frame not leaving in terms of Distrust and Betrayal. The keyword 'humiliation' occurs towards the end and is 'based on lies'—it is an allegory that relies on post hoc moral reasoning of an imagined future of Britain remaining in the EU. This is the prophetic language that often characterises the far right—Enoch Powell had offered similar predictions of the national humiliation and disaster that awaited should immigration continue. Such appeals seem to combine the moral foundations of Authority/Subversion with Sanctity/Degradation. If the nation is sacrosanct then subverting it by relying on other sources of power such as the EU is a form of degradation because it is humiliating. The framing of relationships through allegory construes the EU as an oppressive and authoritarean power that should not be trusted:

> Anyone who had any doubts about the niceness, the kindliness, the friendliness of the European Union need only look at its approach, its *bullying approach*, to us in the negotiations: have they entered into the negotiations in the spirit of wishing everyone good will? No, not at all. They have entered it in the spirit of they know best and we must do as we are told. No wonder two thirds of British people in an opinion poll say the EU's behaviour *is bullying*.[73]

Such pronouncements convey the same narrative of Distrust and Betrayal that characterises the more vitriolic language of social media— different genres of political communication exist in different media but share common underlying moral intuitions. Eventually, Rees-Mogg's framing of the EU led to the creation of the symbol that received the most uptake among the Hard Brexiteers: the concept of the 'vassal state' which he claimed Britain would become if it accepted the terms of Theresa May's withdrawal deal. Originally the metaphor was used quite literally to refer to Iceland:

> For Iceland however, a former *vassal state* of the Danes which only gained independence at the start of the 20th century, they seemed to have accepted their place in the continent's patchwork of relationships.[74]

It was later used by *The Telegraph* to refer to Trump's attitude towards Britain:

> By proposing Mr Farage as Britain's ambassador to his court, Mr Trump seemed, in some British eyes, to be behaving with a breathtaking arrogance usually reserved for dealings with *vassal states*.[75]

It ws then picked up by President Macron to describe the same US-Britain relationship:

> But now it is becoming a *vassal state*, meaning it is becoming the junior partner of the United States.[76]

The Labour politician Barry Gardiner used it to refer to Britain's relationship with the EU:

> Mr Gardiner also claimed that being part of the single market by remaining in the European Economic Area would render the UK a *"vassal state"* and would be viewed as a "con" by the 52 per cent of Britons who voted Leave in the referendum.[77]

But the archaic phase seemed to capture the moral intuition on which so much of Rees-Mogg's discourse was based: appeals to the Sanctity of the nation and the Degradation suffered at its loss. 'vassal state' evoked conquest by the Romans, when conquered tribes were enslaved and forced to serve the Roman Empire. Rees-Mogg developed it further in February 2018:

> When we leave the EU on 29th March next year we need not continue to behave as if we were still a member. That would make us a *vassal state* and there have been no *vassals* in this country since the era of the Plantagenets.[78]

He even developed it into a previously little used abstract noun 'vassalage':

> Brexit will mean Brexit and Brexit shall be done. The alternative is defeat and *vassalage*.[79]

Later in 2018 Jacob Rees-Mogg claimed that the Government's White paper:

> …is the *greatest vassalage* since King John paid homage to Phillip II at Le Goulet in 1200.[80]

As well as erudite historical allusion, the metaphor of the vassal state was creatively elaborated by a literary metaphor alluding to Jonathan Swift's eighteenth century novel *Gulliver's Travels*:

> The answer, then, is that we are generous and say yes to people who are living here, but that *we say no to being a vassal state, no to being tied down by Lilliputians,* and no to squandering taxpayers' money.

We were lucky ...were... removed, as they would have allowed all European law *to have been brought back through the back door. It would have gone out through the front door and returned through the back door.* Now, primary legislation will be needed, but that primary legislation is dubious, because *it will produce a vassal state—Gulliver tied down by the Lilliputians*; this great nation state *tied down* by petty bureaucrats, *running all over us, tying us down with ropes*—because we will have to do whatever the European Union says during the implementation period.[81]

The visual nature of the image and the fact that it is elaborated with an image of extreme physical constraint—a powerful man being physically tied down by ropes creates the potential for embodied simulation so his audience can actually feel the pressure of the ropes 'running all over us'. This was not the only instance of visual and embodied metaphor, as he also draws on his style-marking 'apple' metaphor in developing the Distrust and Betrayal frame in relation to the EU:

The point of Brexit is that the EU i*s rotten like a fallen apple full of wasps and worms. It is rotten* in its bureaucracy and contempt for voters, *it is rotten in its ambition* to be a state but *it is also rotten* in the basic structures of the single market and customs union.[82]

An indication of the deliberate exploitation of this frame is when he combines it with literary allusion:

As Shakespeare had it, "A goodly apple *rotten at the heart*, O, what a goodly outside falsehood hath!"[83]

Images of apples from the homeland that would rot if explosed to the corruption that is the EU creates an allegory in which the England was naturally fecund until it was exposed to the lack of care of a morally corrupt and self-seeking EU: corruption evokes the moral foundation of Degradation. For Rees-Mogg the EU was no cherry tree, but rather the blight that destroyed the labours of others:

The European project is a failure, unpopular across the continent, where its economic policies have *blighted* the lives of millions, especially of young people who cannot get jobs.[84]

Distrust and Betrayal is the leitmotiv of Rees-Mogg's metaphors whose eloquence stands in contrast to cruder and less erudite renditions of the same frame. It was rooted in traditional social hierarchies arising from a projected image of aristocratic social class, with references for example to 'nanny', which he employs in a similar negative way to Boris Johnson to imply overdependence and authoritareanism:

> As with tower blocks, so with energy policy. It is striking how wrong the big state can be. It was the "*Nanny knows best*" approach that led to the scandal over diesel emissions.[85]

His background is not something that he denies, but something that he highlights as offering him priveged insight into the true nature of the British class system, as he indicated in an article published shortly before rhe referendum:

> Perhaps because I was born into the Establishment, I find its arrogance and presumption especially unattractive - and its failings obvious. Over the past 100 years alone, the Establishment has consistently picked the wrong side; favouring appeasement, supporting European integration - including membership of the disastrous Exchange Rate Mechanism - loathing Margaret Thatcher, and, for many years, adoring Tony Blair, even when he invaded Iraq. Now it assumes a nation *yellower than* a Lib Dem leaflet will be frightened into remaining in the European Union. Virgil's **'Monstrum Horrendum'** has been *conjured up to cow a people*. The **panjandrums** in the EU are even worse. The revelation that plans for a European army have been deliberately *kept under wraps* until after the referendum simply shows the ambition of those who seek a single European state, and the cunning manner in which they aim to achieve their objectives. It is not the democratic will that must prevail, but rather *the master plan*.[86]

Here he developed a historical allegory for the failings of the 'Establishment' including in his indefatigable style a classical allusion to Virgil, metaphors (in italics) and obscure words (in bold). We will see in the next chapter just how controversial the issue of the Euroepan Army was in the lead up to the Referendum and by highlighting the plans for a European Army, he draws on the frame of Distrust and Betrayal using the term 'Master plan' that alludes to Hitler. But why, as a self-confessed—if not prototypical—representative of the Establishment should Rees-Mogg be likely to betray the interests of his own social class?

Summary

In this chapter I have illustrated two complementary frames for the Brexit debate: the 'Patriotism and the Nation' frame and the 'Distrust and Betrayal' frame. I have illustrated how they served to distinguish between the positive emotional associations of the 'Us' group and powerful negative fear-based associations of a 'Them' group and demonstrated how this corresponds with Haidt's Loyalty/Betrayal moral foundation and the Sanctity/Degradation moral foundation. The 'Us' group is defined by identification with a nation state that is sacred because it rooted in shared memories arising from historical allegories and myths. The 'Them' group is defined by suspicion of an outside group and a distrust of those who do not meet the criteria for identification with the 'Us' group. Both frames were introduced by pro-Brexit politicians, and their supporters, but were also sometimes deployed by Remain supporters who sought to harness their persuasive potential.

Though these frames are manifested more explicitly on social media, in psychological terms they are not fundamentally different from the more modulated and strategically calculated language of politicians. I have illustrated how Jacob Rees-Mogg systematically employed both frames combining them with his own learned and prophetic style to make predictions of disastrous outcomes should the demands of the Hard Brexiteers not be met. He successfully combines the moral foundations of Loyalty/Betrayal, Authority/Subversion with Sanctity/Degradation based on the idea that the EU had subverted the British nation that was entirely sacrosanct. Different genres of political communication reflect orientation to different audiences. Boris Johnson employs his column in *The Telegraph* for greater elaboration of his views on Patriotism and the Nation than in his speeches, and this will be explored in more detail in Chapter 6. Jacob Rees-Mogg's social media posts show evidence of careful attention to language as compared to the other groups campaigning for a Hard Brexit; his more stylish performance of the Distrust and Betrayal frame is through historical, biblical and literary allusion and with use of archaic terms such as 'vassalage' and 'panjandrum'. Both politicians share a strong predilection for metaphor, at times combined with humour and always as a form of engaging audiences.

It is worth noting how the two complementary frames shift over the period covered by this book, for example during the Referendum, Brexiteers used the Distrust and Betrayal frame to target David Cameron and others who had campaigned against leaving the EU. But during the period of negotiations after June 2016 their target shifted either to so-called 'soft' Brexiteers, or to the EU negotiators who could not be trusted to do anything other than 'cheat' and 'bully' as they sought to reduce the UK to a 'vassal state'. While those supporting Remain employed both frames, they did so in response to their initiation by the Leave campaign and did not have access to the moral foundations of Sanctity/Degradation or Authority/Subversion, as a result were never calling the rhetorical shots in a fierce and relentless rhetorical wrestling match in which no holds were barred.

Notes

1. Orwell, George. (May 1945) *Notes on Nationalism*. Available at http://www.resort.com/~prime8/Orwell/nationalism.html.
2. Sam Swinny, 22 June 2016.
3. Orwell, George. (May 1945) *Notes on Nationalism*.
4. Vote Leaveri@vote_leave, 22 Jun 2016.
5. Liberal Democrats, 21 June 2016.
6. liarpoliticians, 21 June 2016.
7. LeaveEU, 21 June 2016.
8. Robert Kimbell, 21 June 2016.
9. The Fogeys, 20 June 2016.
10. LIAR MPs, 18 June 2016.
11. Mark C. Edwards, 21 June 2016.
12. w.a. ellende, 21 June 2016.
13. Voice of Albion, 22 June 2016.
14. Sam Sonite, 20 June 2016.
15. Inigo Sol, 21 June 2016.

16. Simon @my_red_big_end, 22 Jun 2016.
17. Notorious•Optic @WillGrigg0nFire, 22 Jun 2016.
18. Jan-Werner Müller, http://bostonreview.net/politics/jan-werner-muller-populism.
19. https://labour.org.uk/press/jeremy-corbyn-mp-leader-labour-party-closing-speech-eu-withdrawal-agreement-debate-house-commons/.
20. https://press-archive.labour.org.uk/post/161316910114/jeremy-corbyn-speech-on-brexit/amp.
21. Thompson (2016), p. 155.
22. See Haidt (2012), pp. 104–8.
23. mac-ukip-always @nufcno1fan, Jun 22.
24. silly sausage 1234 @aSillybigSausag, Jun 22.
25. EU Busters @EU_Buster, 22 Jun 2016.
26. TheOrdinaryMan@theordinaryman2, 21 Jun 2016.
27. Liberal Democrats @LibDems, 22 Jun 2016.
28. El Refaie, E. (2009) Metaphor in Political Cartoons: Exploring Audience Responses. In C. Forceville & E. Urio-Aparisis (eds.) *Multimdocal Metaphor*. The Hauge: Mouton de Gruyter, pp. 173–96.
29. These cartoons can be viewed at the British Cartoon Archive: https://www.cartoons.ac.uk.
30. Jacob Rees-Mogg Speech, 25 January 2018, https://www.tfa.net/transcript_of_speech_given_by_jacob_rees_mogg_mp.
31. Jacob Rees-Mogg Speech, 27 March 2018, https://www.leave-meansleave.eu/jacob-rees-mogg-speech-brexit-one-year-go-full-text/.
32. Jacob Rees-Mogg Speech, 10 September 2018.
33. Jacob Rees-Mogg Speech, 7 December 2016.
34. Speech, March 2017.
35. Speech, 21 June 2017.
36. *MailOnline* 29 May 2016.
37. *MailOnline*, 29 May 2016
38. *The Times*, 1 May 2018.
39. *MailOnline*, 22 September 2018.
40. *telegraph.co.uk*, 29 November 2018.
41. http://bostonreview.net/politics/jan-werner-muller-populism.
42. LEAVE.EU @LeaveEUOfficial, 22 Jun 2016.
43. TheOrdinaryMan@theordinaryman2, 16 Jun 2016.
44. JW™ @jw539, Jun 22.
45. The#Marcher @MarcherLord1, 13 Jun 2016.
46. Only 1 solution #NS @j14reb, Jun 22.

47. David Vance @DVATW, 10 July 2016.
48. David Vance @DVATW, 10 July 2016.
49. Jeremy Cliffe @JeremyCliffe, 22 Jun 2016.
50. BitByte @ByteChomper, 21 Jun 2016.
51. Chris Askew @chriskol236, 18 Jun 2016.
52. JJK @JJfanblade, 19 Jun 2016.
53. Danny C @TaxiMash, 20 Jun 2016.
54. Edelman (1988).
55. Shipman (2016), p. 581.
56. @Simplex2014, Sep 10.
57. David Romei@DavidRomeiPHD, Mar 2.
58. ketfan @batanball, Jul 2.
59. Robin Cook, House of Commons, March 2003.
60. House of Lords, May 2004.
61. https://www.researchgate.net/post/Would_Cicero_consider_Donald_Trump_a_traitor.
62. liarpoliticians @liarpoliticians, 21 Jun 2016.
63. Bex Meredith @BexMeredith, Jun 18.
64. Matthew Clarke @celestialhost, Jun 18.
65. liberalisland @LiberalIsland, 18 Jun 2016.
66. Brexit Now @BrexitNoww, 18 Jun 2016.
67. C @gibtsdes, 20 Jun 2016.
68. Blue Shell @b1ue_cow, 16 Jun 2016.
69. mr robot @winstonsmith68, 19 Jun 2016.
70. Paul Joseph Watson, Jun 22.
71. Paul addJim Kerr @JimKerr1973.
72. Jacob-Rees Mogg Speech, 27 March 2018.
73. Jacob Rees-Mogg Speech, 27 March 2018
74. *The Telegraph*, 9 March 2016.
75. *The Times*, 28 November 2016.
76. *MailOnline*, 27 January 2017.
77. *The Times*, 27 July 2017.
78. *The Telegraph*, 21 February 2018.
79. *The Telegraph*, 18 March 2018.
80. *Daily Express*, 12 July 2018.
81. Speech, 10 September 2018.
82. *ExpressOnline* 4 September 2016.
83. *telegraph,co.uk*, 13 November 2018.
84. *MailOnline*, 22 September 2018.

85. *The Telegraph*, 13 August 2017.
86. *MailOnline*, 29 May 2016.

References

Charteris-Black, J. (2011) *Politicians and Rhetoric: The Persuasive Power of Metaphor*, 2nd edn. Basingstoke and New York: Palgrave Macmillan.

Edelman, M. (1988). *Constructing the Political Spectacle*. Chicago: Chicago University Press.

El Refaie, E. (2009). Metaphor in Political Cartoons: Exploring Audience Responses. In C.J. Forceville and E. Urios-Aparisi (Eds.), *Multimodal Metaphor* (pp. 173–96). Berlin: Mouton de Gruyter.

Haidt, J. (2012). *The Righteous Mind: Why Good People are Divided by Politics and Religion*. London: Penguin.

Orwell, G. (1945). *Notes on Nationalism*. http://www.resort.com/~prime8/Orwell/nationalism.html.

Shipman, T. (2016). *All Out War*. London: Collins.

Thompson, M. (2016). *Enough Said: What's Gone Wrong with the Langauge of Politics?* London: Penguin.

References

4

'Take Back Control': Invaded Nation or Sovereign Nation?

Introduction

A primary purpose of political language is to produce collective identities that coalesce around a shared set of ideals, values and beliefs. There are two contrasting rhetorical strategies for achieving the goal of such identity formation practices: the first is to express *values that a group is positively committed to*—for example the founders of the French State shared a belief in liberty, equality and fraternity and espoused these as the ideals that defined French citizenship. The other strategy is to express *beliefs that the group is opposed to*: for example an anti-fascist and anti-sexist group defines itself through its shared opposition to fascism and sexism. By analogy with football supporters, collective identities are established *either* through praise and adulation of the team supported, *or* through shared enmity towards their most hated rivals, typically the geographically nearest team. Of course the strategies are not mutually exclusive and both may be relied on at different times. In the last chapter we looked at the linguistic realisations of these two strategies in the UK referendum by contrasting the moral reasoning and intuitions with which the 'Us' group framed its positive ideals in

© The Author(s) 2019
J. Charteris-Black, *Metaphors of Brexit*,
https://doi.org/10.1007/978-3-030-28768-9_4

the language of Patriotism and the sacrosanct character of the nation with the moral reasoning and intuitions that framed what it was opposed to in the language of Distrust and Degradation. The War frame is based on the moral foundations of Loyalty/Disloyalty, Care/Harm and Sanctity/Degradation.

In this chapter I propose that the pro-Leave campaign created group identities by framing its messages in the language of 'War and Invasion'. Everything that unified the Leave campaign was represented as preparation for war: planning, building up resources and developing strategies for defence against an external threat. In this frame it was morally justified to defend the group by taking offensive action against whatever was construed as a threat. A singleness of purpose in relation to the life and death decisions entailed by war carries the ultimate voice of legitimacy and serves to unite followers with a sense of collective identity and a common mission. The war frame creates a climate of moral exigency because our intuitions tell us that anything is permitted if it can be construed as contributing to 'victory': the shared purpose is morally grounded in Loyalty to, and Care of, the in-group and opposition to the moral Harm attributed to the out-group.

An authoritative account of the UK Referendum by Tim Shipman framed the whole campaign in terms of the 'War and Invasion' frame.[1] Consider how Chapter 6 starts:

> Steve Baker does not look like a military commander. In a decade as a Royal Air Force aerospace engineer he had never fired a shot in anger... Yet when he as first appointed commanding officer of the Conservative Eurosceptics in June 2015, it was as if Baker had been waiting for the opportunity to lead men into battle all his life. Politics is one of those arenas of conflict where armchair generals are just as effective as the physically brave...On assuming control of CfB, Baker did what any general worth their salt has done for the last millennium he read Sun Tzu's The Art of War.

Shipman frames the Referendum campaign entirely through metaphors of war. The various parts of the book are entitled: 'Skirmishes', 'Battle is joined' and 'All out War'; other headings include 'Guerilla

Warfare', 'The Coup', 'The Waterloo Strategy' and 'Fallout Friday'. War metaphors engage readers whose role is to observe titanic struggles between military generals and their armies. In a similar vein the third chapter of another Brexit book[2] is entitled 'Into Battle', referring to *The Daily Mail's* claim that Cameron would launch a '72 hour propaganda blitz' for Remain, they comment: 'in reality the so-called blitz would turn into a sustained bombing campaign that would continue for four months…'.[3] British and American political scientists who had never held a gun followed politicians and opinion formers by relying on the cultural trope of war in their framing of Brexit. It is not surprising that it became normal during the period 2016–2018 to speak of the 'weaponisation' of language. In the 520 million-word corpus of Contemporary American English all uses of the word 'weaponisation' are literal, typically referring to nuclear arms issues, as a journalist commented:

> The sudden appearance of "weaponisation" as a concept (for instance that Facebook has been "weaponised" by political campaigns) shows that once-peaceful relations are being reconceived as violent. And as the metaphor of "war" spreads (as in the "war on drugs", "culture war" or "information war"), so trust in the institutions that make up civil society deteriorates. For those intent on sabotage, this is entirely the point.[4]

The cultural trope of war is common in British media reporting partly because it is a reflection of everyday conversational language. During the Referendum campaign there were at least three separate 'wars': one between Britain and European Union; another between 'Leavers' and 'Remainers', and a further one between 'Soft' and 'Hard' Brexiteers. Once activated the War and Invasion frame would not go away: as the body politic disintegrated into factions, like a cavalry charge it was carried forwards by its own momentum.

In this chapter I outline two contrasting scenarios for the frame of War and Invasion and illustrate how these scenarios permeated the language of major actors in the campaign. I then compare how politicians employed these frames before considering how social media 'weaponised' language. I compare Leave and Remain uses of this frame and argue that—while there were rhetorical reasons for Remain to frame issues in this way—how they did so and their failure to differentiate between the two scenarios, made their campaign dependent on a frame that had been initiated by the Leave campaign. In both cases the scenarios derived from repetition of keywords and metaphors and were grounded in moral foundations.

Two Scenarios in the Referendum Campaign

To understand the role of metaphor in the framing of the UK referendum debate it is necessary to distinguish between two scenarios that I will refer to as the 'Sovereign Nation' scenario and the 'Invaded Nation' scenario. As indicated in Chapter 1, by 'scenario' I mean the 'dramatic' story lines and default outcomes, as well as the moral reasoning and moral intuitions entailed by these story lines. Many pro-Brexit supporters wanted to leave the EU because they saw the UK as symbolising freedom and democracy and the EU as symbolising authoritareanism and bureacracy. As the world's first democracy, with its free press, and relatively low level of public corruption, the UK was believed by Brexiteers to be an independent nation with a natural right to take control back from an external source of authority. The concept of sovereignty was especially important to mainstream supporters of Leave represented by the organisation 'Vote Leave' that had been designated by the Electoral Commission, in April 2016, as the official campaign. I will refer to this set of beliefs as the 'Sovereign Nation scenario' and suggest that it was based in defending democratic values. The Sovereign Nation scenario rejects accusations of racism because it is concerned with autonomy and views national identity as derived from citizenship status. It activates the moral foundation of Authority and Subversion because it argues that EU institutions subvert the authority of the British political institutions and also Sanctity because it attributes to the nation state a sacred status.

The Sovereign Nation scenario held that it was legitimate to protect the nation and identifies the groups and values that needed protection. There is a subtle difference between the words 'defend' and 'protect' in how they are typically used in British political language. I compared the words following these two words in Hansard where British parliamentary debates are recorded. Following 'Protect' we often find groups of people who are protected by government—such as 'consumers', 'children', 'citizens', 'tenants', 'women' or 'minorities'. Whereas following 'defend' we commonly find geographical spaces such as 'country', 'shores', 'territory', 'islands', 'frontier' and 'homeland'. There are none of these geographical or spatial terms in the 100 most frequent words following 'protect'. When 'protect' is used for non-human objects, these are unbounded spaces such as 'the environment', 'the countryside' or 'crops' whereas 'defend' is territorial and profiles defending a specifically defined geographical area such as the 'shores of our country', 'these islands', 'our homes', 'our frontiers' or 'these territories'. So 'protect' profiles social and abstract entities whereas 'defend' profiles spatial entities and is potentially a more emotive, tribal word because it implies something is under attack. Both words derive from the moral foundations of Sanctity and Care/Harm. Recent findings by biologists show that the behaviour of many species is to defend a nest and the food that is within foraging range from predatory intruders and parasites.[5]

The second dominant scenario is what I describe as the 'Invaded Nation scenario'; this is based on fear of an external threatening entity that is attacking honoured or sacred entities. Looking in Hansard we find that typically 'defend' is followed by 'honour' in expressions such as 'defend the honour of the nation/the Queen/the flag/the country' etc. Moral reasoning and moral intuition urges action to be taken in defence of honour. The 'Invaded Nation' scenario viewed the EU's open border policies as constituting a threat. The collapse of border controls in EU countries bordering the Mediterranean increased the threat of immigration of people from non-Christian, non-white and non-European backgrounds. This influx of people with cultural backgrounds that differed from the majority population—though Britain has a significant established Muslim population—was conceived as a form of invasion that threatened the sanctity of the nation. For nativists the effects of the political crisis in Syria was adding to an already heavy 'burden' of immigration from other failing states. In this case the out-group were male, mainly Muslim migrants. An illustration of the Invaded Nation scenario is the most controversial of the Leave EU campaign's publicity materials: a poster depicting a long winding queue of non-white, young males. Superimposed on the image itself in large red capitals was the slogan 'BREAKING POINT' with the sub text 'The EU has failed us all'. Nigel Farage was also photographed in front of the poster. This depiction was considered by many to be inflammatory and racist because it confused—asylum seekers, or refugees, with immigration.

While the picture was an authentic one of migrants crossing the Croatia-Slovenia border in 2015, some observers identified its similarities to a Nazi propaganda video, shown in the first episode of a six-part BBC documentary from 2005 called *Auschwitz: The Nazis and the Final Solution*: that was broadcast on Netflix. But the poster was equally reminiscent of one designed by Saatchi & Saatchi as an advertisement in the 1979 election campaign that had the caption 'Labour isn't Working'. In this poster an endless queue of people are depicted waiting for entrance to the 'Unemployment Office' with the slogan 'Britain is better off with the Conservatives'. The 'Breaking point' poster views the 'queue' from a front angle, whereas the Saatchi & Saatchi poster views the queue from sideways, but in both posters you *cannot see the end of the queue*—implying a limitless number of people. While both posters are fear based and derive from the moral foundation of Harm, the Saatchi & Saatchi poster activates fear of *becoming* one of the people depicted in the queue, who are the *insider* white, British 'Us' group, and conveys the idea of protecting British jobs against Labour policies: it is a Sovereign Nation appeal originating in the moral foundations of Care and Sanctity. Conversely, the 'Breaking point' poster conveys the need to defend against a large *outsider* 'Them' group—one that does not include the viewer—who are represented as 'invading' Europe and therefore contributes to the 'Invaded Nation' scenario. It is an appeal originating in the moral foundations of Harm and Degradation. The frame below the image carried the caption "We must break free of the EU and take back control of our borders".

The Invaded Nation scenario was populist in tone and saw immigration as an economic war on British jobs, and a cultural war on British values; it had a strong appeal in areas of the country that had experienced economic stagnation and cultural deterioration during a period of overall economic national growth. Many social groups in less economically privileged parts of the country felt that globalisation had prioritised the worldview of metropolitan and cosmopolitan areas that had already benefited from the growth of new technology based industries and rising house prices. In cultural terms they also felt excluded by the narrow definitions of identity that had been favoured in a period of identity politics: it was not that they did not respect the demands for equality that feminists, ethnic or religious minorities claimed as their entitlement, it was just that—because *they were not one of those groups*—their need for a sense of identity or belonging was not being satisfied and it appealed to the moral foundation of Care/Harm. The Invaded Nation scenario lay claim to a larger national identity that would bring marginal people together as members of a single nation—rather than separate them into distinct identity-based groups each with their own interests, it therefore also appealed to the Loyalty/Betrayal foundation.

The Sovereign Nation scenario was more respectable and appealed to middle class social liberals; it was of course morally justified to protect what was valued, or sacred, against threats and dangers in particular when it was democracy and the constitution that was being protected. But the advantage that the Leave campaign had when activating the War and Invasion frame was that is offered these *two alternative versions* of the national story: a scenario that appealed to groups economically affected by austerity and globalisation and another scenario with more respectable claims to be fighting for democracy and freedom: it therefore activated a wider range of moral foundations.

The War and Invasion Frame and Social Identities

The War and Invasion frame was complex because it could be used in multiple ways: the 'Sovereign Nation' scenario framed the referendum as a struggle for political control between Britain and the European Union. This was a fight for national sovereignty against an impersonal and alien supra-national body and represented the referendum as a conflict of interests between loyalty to the nation and EU membership. As Chilton notes: "Political discourse has specific connections to the emotional centres of the brain".[6] While he is unsure whether there are specific 'political' emotions, he suggests that there are politically relevant feelings related to territorial belonging and identity that include love of family and fear of intruders. The following analysis of the frame for 'War and Invasion' shows how these political emotions were triggered in the Referendum campaign. I suggest that territorial belonging and positive feelings towards the family and local community activates the 'Sovereign Nation' scenario, based on the Care, Loyalty, Authority and Sanctity/moral foundations while fear of intruders and of unknown people activates the emotionally more intense 'Invaded Nation' scenario based on Harm, Disloyalty, Subversion and Degradation moral foundations. Together the two scenarios were the wings of a rhetorical phoenix that carried the Leave campaign to 'victory'. Prononents of both scenarios emphasised sacred British institutions such as the NHS—which became a symbol of what should be defended from the threat from abroad. One of the strongest claims by the Leave campaign was the much disputed figure of £350 million per week that it was claimed the British taxpayer would save from the leaving the EU and could finance an under-resourced NHS.

The two major tropes of the campaign: 'Take back control' and 'Independence Day' were successful because they appealed respectively to the Sovereign and the Invaded Nation scenarios. These tropes gave some voters—often those who felt least in control of their lives—a scenario in which they could regain their self-respect by regaining control of their national identity. 'Take back control' implied that Britain had lost control and that a vote to leave the European Union would enable the British people to regain control over their national destiny. This was the dominant trope of the Sovereign Nation scenario.[7] However, there was a secondary meaning of the slogan which also activated the Invaded Nation scenario; a guerilla army struggles 'to take back control' over a land area that has been occupied and needs to be liberated. Perhaps the most skilled exponent of the War and Invasion frame was Nigel Farage; I will suggest that he was able to able to appeal to different audiences by drawing on either the Sovereign Nation scenario or the Invaded Nation scenario, or indeed *both* scenarios, according to which would be most persuasive for a particular audience. The covert nature of the

trope 'taking back control'—with its subtle implication of foreign occu-
pation—proved to be one of the great successes of political marketing—
partly because it resisted accusations of racism. Unlike Enoch Powell's
vivid image of a 'River of Blood', with its style of biblical prophecy, this
more apparently innocuous phrase summarised deep-seated fears of
loss of control—whether at the mercy of globalised markets, or, more
personally, in health discourse, where patients seek to regain control of
ailing bodies, or in 'life coaching' discourse where clients are exhorted
more to take control of their lives—after all, who does not want to be *in
control*?

As previously mentioned, there were several different metaphoric
wars: as well as the war of defence against immigrants, and against
'Brussels', there were various civil wars. It is these multiple 'wars',
against external and internal enemies, that accounts for the weaponisation of language during the political debate of Brexit. It might be said
that there is no better way in politics to create such a conflict-based discourse than to hold a referendum with two binary options. Whether
these are verbally phrased on the ballot paper as 'IN/OUT', 'REMAIN/
LEAVE' or 'YES/NO', the principle is the same: a referendum offered a
simple way of resolving complex disputed political questions with reference to a simple binary choice. The most basic and fundamental aspect
of human experience: a struggle to overcome a dangerous or threatening adversary offered a corresponding binary choice of identities—as
'Remainer' or 'Brexiteer'. Some people admired the bravado that the
Referendum in Scotland have given to Scottish Nationalists and saw
this as a new opportunity to construct new English identities. Unlike
elections that offer a choice from several parties, referendums have the
potential to become 'wars' because they simplify complex alternatives by
framing these in terms of 'Them' and 'Us'.

Once a Civil War frame was activated it drew on the Distrust and
Betrayal frame for identifying the enemy within as a treacherous opponent or traitor. When politicians are viewed as 'enemies' rather than
just 'opponents' there can be struggles between them and there were
vitriolic disputes among the various groups who supported Brexit as to
how their 'campaign' should be fought. At times, the two major campaigning groups, Vote Leave and Leave.EU, created social identities in

their own right and viewed each other, rather than Remainers, as the enemy. It is therefore hardly suprising that the 'War and Invasion' frame should dominate much of the language of the Referendum and nowhere more so than disputes over the 'strategy' in which 'campaigns' should be 'fought'.

As we saw in the last chapter, the frame of Patriotism, & The Nation was often supported by images of war heroes and coded references to commemoration of the sacred war dead. There is no doubt that for some areas of the Leave campaign an obsession with war and struggle was a key component of their rhetorical framing of the debate in terms of campaigns, coups, plots, strategies, generaliship, the big guns, firepower and the whole battery of military terminology that they thought would enhance their appeal. Here is an illustration from the biography of Aaron Banks (and edited by Isabel Oakeshott), who personally financed the Leave.EU campaign:

> None of this changes my basic view that being confrontational and provocative is the way ahead. We'll *take some flak*, but it will get people talking, engaging them in the campaign.[8]

For Oakeshott (and presumably Banks) aggressive physical actions are central to the framing of the message:

> Gerry has devised a brilliant *battle plan* which *hammers home t*he points the whole team needs to understand…[9]

On the resignation of Iain Duncan Smith in March 2016:

> Kapow! Cling from a former party leader, this is *weapons-grade*. Now he's liberated, he can really *hit the campaign trail.*

The high stakes of the referendum provided the moral foundation for the choice of language. The discourse of marketing takes its notion of 'strategy' (originally in Greek 'generalship') and so the closely related discourses of marketing, journalism and politics were available, depending on whether the appeal was more rational or more emotional, more inter-discursive among those who planned the political campaign or more outwardly directed towards voters. When they sought to address the logical aspects of winning, Brexit campaigners relied on targeted marketing: so that they could identify areas with a high number of swing voters—typically in the case of the Leave campaigns, Labour seats in the north and Midlands where UKIP had already built up a political infrastructure. Collection of data from social media profiles allowed analysis of the scenarios—and their corresponding moral foundations—that would be most persuasive for the target groups identified.[10]

The War and Invasion frame heightened the motivation of all those involved in the campaign. For example, according to Shipman, it was conceived in terms of an 'air war' using traditional broadcast media, a 'cyber war' employing experts in social media and a 'ground war' that required drawing on the UKIP supporters to undertake house to house leafleting and other face to face activities. Since Shipman covers many of these in his book it is unnecessary to repeat them here other than to point out that the War and Invasion frame provided a vocabulary by which activists and strategists could talk about their campaign. This then carried over into how Leave supporters framed the debate on social media.

It is well known that Leave supporters were typically older people (55+) who were often non-degree educated in less fashionable parts of the country—they were in fact probably the last generation for whom the historical memories of the Second World War were emotionally resonant in an authentic way, as part of lived experience, rather than just as history lesson facts. If there are any doubts as to the importance of the War and Invasion frame—and its ready transference from an external enemy to one within—we should recall the second most important Leave slogan 'Independence Day', as Farage put it once victory for the vote to Leave the EU had become certain:

> Dare to dream that the dawn is breaking on an *independent* United Kingdom. This, if the predictions now are right, this will be *a victory* for real people, *a victory* for ordinary people, *a victory* for decent people. We have *fought* against the multinationals, we have *fought* against the big merchant banks, we have *fought* against big politics, we have *fought*

against lies, corruption and deceit. And today honesty, decency and belief in nation, I think now is going to win. And we will have done it without having to *fight*, without *a single bullet being fired*, we'd have done it by damned hard work on the ground.[11]

Here in rational terms Farage evokes moral intuitions by confusing the metaphoric sense of battle with fighting an *actual* civil war that involves shooting life bullets. Consider the argument made by Nigel Farage when he spoke at Arron Banks Leave.EU party on referendum night:

Win or lose this battle, we will this war, we will get this country back, we will get our independence back and we will get our borders back.[12]

Deployment of the Invaded Nation and the Sovereign Nation scenarios allows multiple readings: the idea of regaining independence implied colonial invasion, while getting borders back implied loss of sovereignty: both are highly emotive because they rely on the idea of a sacred nation that risks desecration.

The distinction between the Sovereign Nation and the Invaded Nation scenarios is helpful in distinguishing between the use of the War and Invasion frames by Boris Johnson and Jacob Rees-Mogg. Rees-Mogg relied mainly on the Sovereign Nation scenario whereas Boris Johnson relied more on the Invaded Nation scenario. I consider Johnson's frames in Chapter 6 but here make some observations on Rees-Mogg's Sovereign Nation scenario. Rees-Mogg typically takes history as a conversative benchmark and frames the nation's history with reference to the Second World War:

How we came to join the European Union is an important part of understanding our Island story. *We won the war* and were full of optimism about our place in the World, but then came Suez.[13]

He views the post-war period in terms of national decline, and Brexit as an opportunity to reverse that:

And once that happened the Nation's view of itself changed and the Establishment, the Elite, decided that its job was to manage decline, that the best they could do was to *soften the blow* of descending downwards, soften the effect on the Nation of being less successful than it had been in the past, and recognise that we would not be able to keep up with other countries.[14]

Here the nation is framed metaphorically as a defeated boxer who is collapsing in the ring. In his speech delivered at a 'Leave Means Leave' event in Central London he positions his arguments primarily around sovereignty:

We are a year and two days from the witching hour, that moment when we will leave the European Union, at least legally, and will be fulfilling to some extent the promise *to take back control.*[15]

He then develops his notion of 'taking back control' with reference to sovereignty:

In truth, the vote was by people who believed in democracy. They recognised that the system that they were used to, where sending a Member of Parliament to Westminster, who would determine their laws and seek redress of grievance, was under threat because once it was EU Law it was impossible. They voted *to take back control* and, yes, they had specific concerns and some of these were over immigration and some of them were over agriculture and some over fishing and some over regulation but the fundamental underlying point was about democracy and can you change your Government?[16]

Rees-Mogg also expressed the desire to protect vulnerable groups—among whom he views nationals of EU member states:

I am glad that it is now clear that in the event of our leaving on WTO terms, *we will protect* the rights of EU member state nationals who are living in this country.[17]

In this regard, Rees-Mogg's deployment of the War and Invasion frame using the Sovereign Nation scenario appears more responsible than that of Boris Johnson; by avoiding the colourful metaphors deriving that characterise the Invaded Nation scenario, he was able to articulate more persuasive arguments based on the scenario of traditional conservativism—that of the Sovereign Nation—grounded in Care, Loyalty and Sanctity but there are also suggestions of Authority/Subversion as he expresses a patrician-like obligation to protect.

The War and Invasion Frame on Twitter

The 'Sovereign Nation' on Twitter

As with the 'Patriotism and the Nation' and 'Distrust and Betrayal' frames, the 'War and Invasion' frame was one that was taken up by pro-Brexit tweeters and then responded to by Remain supporters. Leave EU was one of the 3 competing organisations advocating the Leave position, and largely financed by the wealthy diamond mine owner Aaron Banks. Dominic Cummings, the manager of Vote Leave, launched the officially designated campaign with the slogan 'let's take back control', claiming that: 'I've done focus groups on this for years. I know this works'.[18] This central trope of the Leave campaign argued for taking back control of the legislative, financial and trading powers that had been 'conceded to' anonymous European institutions. Vote Leave reiterated the slogan throughout the Referendum campaign:

> The EU serves big corporations - not the people! #VoteLeave tomorrow and take back control. (244 retweets)[19]

'Take back control' became the refrain of supporters of a 'hard' Brexit—and a statement of tribal loyalty to which leading Brexiteers would always return in all forms of political communication, as for example by Boris Johnson writing for the Sun newspaper:

> In a heroic act of national self-belief we decided to take back control of
> our laws, borders, and all the cash we send to Brussels.[20]

Evidence from Twitter suggests that it is hard to under-estimate the
importance that 'take back control' held for the Brexit position; the
trope went viral and was circulated and retweeted many thousands of
times so that it became the battle cry of the Leave campaign. At a com-
memorative event for Jo Cox's in Trafalgar Square on the day before the
referendum a light aeroplane flew over flying a banner showing: "Take
Control: #VoteLeave". The hashtag on the banner reflects the importance of 'Twitter', but the phrase itself evoked deeper historical memories too: the small aeroplane flying over the symbol of past British
military victories evoked memories of brave spitfire pilots risking their
lives in the Battle of Britain. 'Take back control' continued to be the
defining slogan of those Brexiteers who argued most vehemently for a
'hard' Brexit. Although it had the potential to be used on Twitter for
either Leave scenario, it typically framed the Sovereign Nation scenario;
I would like to illustrate this with reference to the moral reasoning in
three tweets that were retweeted more than 100 times in the 24 hours
before the Referendum:

> And so we have it. The EU confirms that will be no reform from
> within the EU. #VoteLeave to take back control!+link to an article
> in *The Independent* with a headline quoting Jean Clause Junker saying
> 'There will be no further renegotiation of Britain's relationship with the
> European Union if we vote to leave.' (493 retweets)[21]
>   Tomorrow let's take back control of our money, economy, borders,
> security and taxes #VoteLeave #TakeControl (612 retweets)[22]
>   SHARE: Tomorrow is your chance to #VoteLeave and take back con-
> trol! (296 retweets)[23]

None of these tweets invoke the Invaded Nation scenario probably
because the official Vote Leave campaign was aware of the dangers of
deploying this scenario as it risked accusations of racism. Clearly, the
organisers of the Leave campaign realised the argumentative potential of
the Sovereign Nation scenario. The logic of 'take back control' is like this:

PRESENT SITUATION (PRE-REFERENDUM)
[**Major premise—Implied**] Britain once had control
[**Minor premise—Implied**] Britain has lost control to the EU
[**Conclusion**] Britain should therefore take back control

As seen previously with enthymemes, the argument does not need to be spelled out so it didn't indicate *who* control had been lost to—some would argue that it was really technology and the Tech companies of Silicon Valley that controlled the lives of most people. The idea of taking something 'back' in the major premise implies that Britain once had control because you can only take 'back' something that you once 'had'. The minor premise that it was membership of the EU that had caused loss of control also had to be worked out by inference.

As one Remain supporter tweeted:

> 'Take back control'. Such loaded, ominous words.[24]

'Army' was a keyword on Twitter during this period because a major concern for many voters was the proposition that there might be a European army and the Sovereign Nation scenario was deployed in moral reasoning on this topic. It was opposition to a European army that accounted for the very high number of retweets of the word 'army':

> Cameron says fears over an EU army is a lie: but his boss in Brussels has a different idea. #bbcqt #VoteLeave + quote from Jean-Claude Junker "In the very long we will need a European army. Because we have to be credible when it comes to forgeign policy". (559 retweets)[25]

This post was later deleted and the account name had been changed from 'Ben Brittain' to 'Benjamin Evin'—suggesting an attempt to cover over the trail of a propaganda message. The concept of a European Army came to symbolise the possibility of the end of the sovereignty of the nation state in the eyes of many Leave voters: the historic memory of heroic survival in the two World Wars, sustained by the popular media, was, alongside the national football team, the ultimate symbol of a sacred English national identity. With its 'barmy army' following the national cricket team and the regular chants at every professional football ground in the country that follow the pattern 'NAME OF COACH + APOSTRAPHE + TEAM'S COLOURS + ARMY' (for example 'Gary Hill's red and white army') has created a surrogate form of populist English identity. While very few people actually serve in the army, it is viewed as the embodiment of national heroism in the face of adversity, and evokes nostalgia for the British Empire. The army also provides a scenario for the British class system—with a high number of lower ranking recruits from areas of higher unemployment in parts of the north of England and officers drawn more from the Home Counties. However, it also serves as a means for inter-regional contact since recruits are drawn from all areas of Britain and hence leads to ideas of British identity in which accent is an acceptable and, even valued, expression of identity. This underlying symbolism of the army as a sacrosanct institution seemed to be threatened by the prospect of a European Army, and as always the experts of the Leave campaign had their finger closely on the pulse of the national mood when they voiced concerns about a European army:

> No EU Army! Liars it's already here training on Salisbury Plain Lord Guthrie now for #leaveEU over EU army #Brexit + link to Daily Mail article (175 retweets)[26]
> If you want a #euarmy vote remain if you want to keep a sovereign British Army as part of NATO #VoteLeave #newsnight (168 retweets)[27]
> There can be no plausible reason as to why a common market would want or need an EU army... (130 retweets)[28]

It seems that Jean-Claude Junker offered the Leave campaign a golden gift with the expression of his personal view of the need for a European army as it could easily be exploited in the moral reasoning of the Sovereign Nation frame.

The 'Invaded Nation' on Twitter

The following was extensively retweeted in the week before the Referendum and demonstrates activation of the Invaded Nation scenario by Leave supporters:

> Debts, war, terrorism and mass Islamic migration: EU is a danger for a safe and peaceful Europe. #Brexit #VoteLeave (622 retweets)[29]

Here 'war' is classified alongside other agents that are threatening to invade Europe and are strongly associated with the EU. The tweet lists apocolyptic threats in a confused muddle and is a scaremongering tactic designed to motivate a vote for leave. In the week following Farage's 'Breaking Point' poster this tweet reinforced a nightmare vision of a world in chaos—confirmed by breaking news media accounts of migrants crossing the Mediterranean and razor wire fences being erected across Victor Orban's Hungary on the migrant route to the north. The image of a highly threatening and unstable world was designed to create a 'fortress' mentality.

In this view the values of 'our' group were endangered by real external threats, as if the invisible forces of globalisation had suddenly taken on a human face—that of a refugee from a war zone or an economic migrant from a failed state. There had been plenty of material for such a Dantean image to feed on in the aftermath of the 2008 economic crisis. Combined with the political crisis in Syria and ongoing instability of a range of 'failed' states in the Middle East and Africa that appear to have stemmed from years of poor government combined with inadequate international solutions. The Leave campaign viewed the EU—and especially the open-door immigration policy adopted by Angela Menkel in Germany—as encouraging a migrant invasion and therefore aroused the moral foundations of Harm, Subversion and Degradation. This view was countered by Remainers who drew attention to the role of the EU in preventing further war in Europe:

> @Harryslaststand and fellow Second world war veterans urge Britain to stay in the EU #VoteRemain (37 retweets)[30]

However, Leave arguments seemed to address more current anxieties and intuitions triggered by the influx of immigrants who were risking their lives to cross the Mediterranean.

Even if they could not guarantee winning the war, both 'sides' seemed ready to frame issues in terms of war—although leave supporters more so. When we look in the British National Corpus at phrases commencing 'battle of' we find 'Britain' (185), followed by 'Hastings' (32) and 'Waterloo' (21). There are similar findings in Hansard, the most common phrases are: 'Battle of Britain' (1008) and 'Battle of Waterloo' (462). These battles were invoked in tweets before the referendum:

> I still don't think the #Brexit camp will pull it off but you never know. Battle of Hastings - remind me what happened there?[31]

There were 8 tweets that referred to the Battle of Waterloo in this week and imply the Invaded Nation scenario:

> Today is the Anniversary of the Battle of Waterloo, this week we face our 2nd Waterloo, the EU referendum #Brexit (344 retweets)[32]
> It wasn't very clever of French Economics Minister Emmanuel Macron to insult the UK on the anniversary of the Battle of Waterloo #VoteLeave (144 retweets)[33]

In the week before the referendum the French Prime Minister had expressed quite forthright views about the hardline that would be taken if the UK voted to Leave the EU arguing that it would leave Britain as a small isolated nation on the edge of Europe. What is curious is the reference to the Battle of Waterloo since there is no particular reason why a French minister should know the date of a French military defeat. The 'battle' term became one that Leave tweeters saw as largely favourable to their cause:

> 80% of Dutch support #Brexit. 88% want a #Nexit referendum. Great Britain we support your battle for freedom! No #EU (199 retweets).[34]
> Boris Johnson gives #Brexit battle cry as historic referendum nears http://shr.gs/6N0QKSl #EUref #VoteLeave (22 retweets)[35]
> This referendum is not just a choice over EU, it's a battle for the soul of the British nation - #InOrOut #Brexit (18 retweets)[36]

By analogy with popular view that Wellington misled Napoleon into underestimating the size of his army, so the Vote Leave campaign managers held back many of their financial resources to the very end of the campaign:

That was the Waterloo strategy...Basically spend a shitload of money right at the end. We tested over 450 types of Facebook ad to see which were most effective. We spent £1.5 million in the last week on Facebook ads, digitial ads and videos. We knew exactly which ones were most effective.[37]

Other more overt instances of the Invaded Nation scenario were references to 'Hitler' and iconic events such as 'D-Day':

#BREXIT #FascistEU was HITLER'S idea and it proves #Germany WON the Second World War #TotalitarianEU #Immigration + link to Express article (20 retweets)[38]
    One last drink before D-Day tomorrow. All the troops have worked really hard. Big push coming!#VoteLeave #Brexit (72 retweets)[39]

In *Heroic Failure* Finton O'Toole argues that part of the English psychodrama is to actually desire invasion so as to be able to die as a martyr in an orgy of masochism. I find this rather exaggerated, and although the popular press alludes to German success in the war, and evokes historic myths of national resistance it often does so in a way that is humorous rather than serious. It's Dad's Army rather than Colditz. The so-called Barmy Army that follows England's cricket team around the world is not averse to heroic allusions to 'victory' and 'no surrender',

Table 4.1 Comparison of 'Invaded Nation' keywords in referendum week tweets

Keyword	Leave multiple retweets	Remain multiple retweets
war	46	14
destroy	49	6
attack	52	1
battle	22	1
defend	13	5
invade	11	1
surrender	6	1
enemy	4	2
bomb	4	0
Hitler	3	0
Total	210	31

but O'Toole overlooks the self-irony that is an essential way of 'doing' English identity.

Comparing 'Leave' and 'Remain' Use of the 'Invaded Nation' Scenario

In this section I compare the use of the Invaded Nation scenario by the Leave and Remain sides on Twitter in the week before the referendum. Close analysis of keywords in multiple retweets (i.e. tweets that were shared more than 10 times in this week) shows that Leavers employed the scenario much more frequently than Remainers, as shown in Table 4.1.

The table shows that Leavers deployed keywords associated with the Invaded Nation scenario around 6 times more frequently than Remainers, and used all of the keywords for this scenario more frequently.

It was not that Remain avoided the War & Invasion frame, but that the frame had been systematically developed by Leave strategists and tweeters to which Remainers were responding rather than initiating frames of their own, and for this reason their tweets did not generate anything like the number of retweets. For example, if we consider *only* tweets that were retweeted more than 100 times in the week before the Referendum, there were at least 10 Leave tweets but only one Remain tweet. Consider the following:

> The EU is destroying Europe, the UK needs to take our chance & abandon the sinking ship. It's now or never #Brexit+ image of sinking Euro ship (591 retweets)[40]
> Paul Joseph Watson @PrisonPlanet 21 Jun 2016.
> White, middle class leftists attack black #VoteLeave supporters for handing out leaflets, label them "Nazis". (363 retweets)

Paul Watson is a successful 'Alt Right' online personality with over one million subscribers and here demonstrates his skill in attributing an act of aggression to Remainers. Since Watson claims that "Nazis" is used as a 'label' by the group he is opposing, and scare quotes are put around this word, we assume sympathy for those who are wrongly accused of being "Nazis"—the ambiguity created by 'label' and "Nazis" is rhetorically successful because it invites reflection as to how Vote Leave supporters can be Nazis if they are 'black'.

To explore further an important linguistic characteristic of the key verbs for the Invaded Nation scenario we need to understand the concept of transitivity. Analysing transitivity is crucial in identifying the relationships between participants and may be briefly summarised as specifying: WHO does WHAT to WHOM. So in the above tweet 'white middle class leftists' are agents who are claimed to have acted aggressively towards 'black VoteLeave Supporters', who are represented as victims. Consider how the evaluation would be different if phrased along the lines: "Vote Leave supporters provoke Vote Remain supporters". The addition of identity labels such as 'white', 'middle class' 'black' and "Nazis" arouses moral intuitions by bringing cultural identity into the Brexit debate because once an action is represented as an 'attack' it argues that defence is both a legitimate and morally justified response. In the tweet above Leavers are represented as being threatened rather than as aggressors.

In the Leave campaign's social media discourse a range of threatened entities are identified—these are abstract entities such as 'jobs', 'business' or 'our culture and country' or they are the more emotive 'people' victims such as 'British drivers' or 'UK women'. The War and Invasion frame implies that the OUT-GROUP—the European Union—is causing harm by 'destroying' threatened entities. Sometimes the Sovereign Nation scenario predominates:

> A vote for #Brexit is a vote to uphold parliamentary democracy. A vote for #Remain is a vote to destroy it (36 retweets)[41]

Here 'parliamentary democrary' is in the victim role and it is implied that Remain will destroy this sovereign entity so defending it is morally justified on the grounds of Care. Or the Invaded Nation scenario can be used:

> The EU destroyed our fishing industry, our farming capacity and British manufacturing, in turn benefitting everyone else. #VoteLeave #Brexit (11 retweets)[42]

Here the EU is construed as an aggressive agent and various areas of the British economy—fishing, agriculture etc. are in the victim role. The verb 'destroy' implies a higher level of physicality as they refer to some form of physical aggression and arouse the moral foundation of Harm. The agent that 'attacks' or 'destroys' emphasises the agency of highly threatening groups such as 'Islamists' or 'Eurocrats'. The use of human references in the agent and patient roles heightens the political emotions that are aroused and is therefore more likely to provoke a response in the form of a need to 'defend'. The above narrative referred to by the right wing blogger Paul Joseph Watson was adopted by another right-wing blogger:

> Black Brexit campaigner attacked in London by white #Remain campaigners. (161 retweets)[43]

Once an attack involves physical violence the word is of course no longer a metaphor but a literal description that evokes moral intuitions as to a just response; the keyword 'attack' was used in accounts of other event involving physical actions that were referred to as 'attacks' that legitimate 'defence':

> Migrants attack British fans returning from France and stone their cars. (+ link to Express article) (212 retweets)[44]

The Invaded Nation scenario invites acts of legitimate self-defence, making 'defend' a keyword:

> I stand with the #UK in it's Fight to defend #Democracy from #Islamists & Eurocrats #BREXIT #RegressiveLeft (112 retweets)[45]

The moral reasoning that is implied and the moral intuitions that are aroused is that your own group is in need of legitimate defence against aggressive others. This opens the door to identity politics; the following tweeter represents his 'race' as threatened:

THE DAILY EXPRESS
Defend the Father Land!
Keep our race clean!
#VoteLeave (11 retweets)[46]

The notion of a 'clean' race implies the moral foundation of Sanctity/Degradation.The emotionally provocative and manipulative potential of the Invaded Nation scenario provided an almost limitless reservoir from which the Leave campaign could draw and created networks of affiliation around a range of identities—white, British etc.—so that it was no longer just the nation that was being invaded, but identity itself. This raises the question of exactly what was represented as being under attack; Fig. 4.1 shows the transitivity relationships in the Invaded Nation scenario by showing the entities that were construed in multiple retweets as being 'under attack'. The top half of the diagram shows active forms of the verb so the agents, or subjects precede the 'victims' that they 'attack'. The lower half of the diagram shows passive verb forms so that victims precede the agents that they are defended from:

A pattern that characterised tweets from the Official Vote Leave campaign was to represent its leaders as victims of 'attacks' by Remain supporters: for example, following one of the three televised debates:

Andrea, Boris & Gisela rose above the IN campaign's personal attacks to provide a positive vision of why we should #VoteLeave (94 retweets)[47]
Grubby, personal attacks show that Remain know they're losing the arguments #VoteLeave (103 retweets)[48]
Horrible, personal attacks from Amber Rudd. Not a good look. #ITVEURef #VoteLeave (93 retweets)[49]

Evidently, there was a concerted strategy to gain voter sympathy and evoke moral intuitions by representing its *own* side as peace loving and Remainers as aggressive: this illustrates how Leave campaigners framed the referendum with the Invaded Nation scenario.

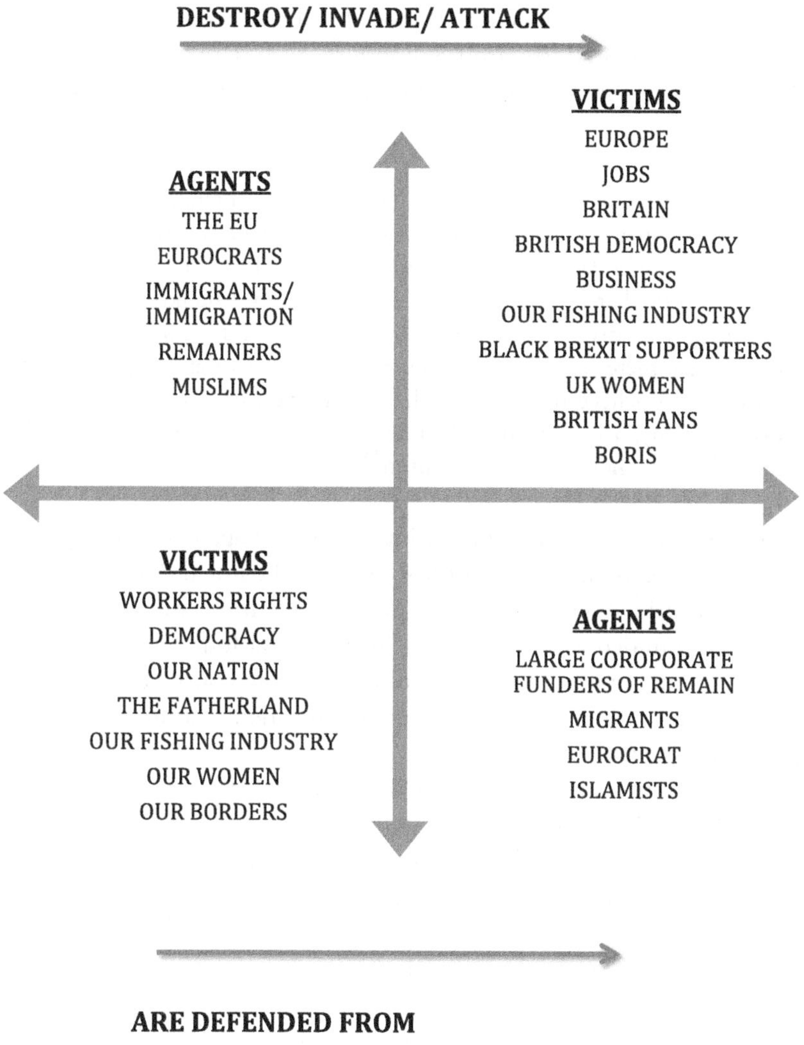

DESTROY/ INVADE/ ATTACK

VICTIMS
EUROPE
AGENTS
JOBS
THE EU
BRITAIN
EUROCRATS
BRITISH DEMOCRACY
IMMIGRANTS/
BUSINESS
IMMIGRATION
OUR FISHING INDUSTRY
REMAINERS
BLACK BREXIT SUPPORTERS
MUSLIMS
UK WOMEN
BRITISH FANS
BORIS

VICTIMS
WORKERS RIGHTS
DEMOCRACY
AGENTS
OUR NATION
LARGE COROPORATE
THE FATHERLAND
FUNDERS OF REMAIN
OUR FISHING INDUSTRY
MIGRANTS
OUR WOMEN
EUROCRAT
OUR BORDERS
ISLAMISTS

ARE DEFENDED FROM

Fig. 4.1 Transitivity analysis of leave's 'Invaded Nation' scenario

There is some evidence that the Invaded Nation scenario was deliberately exploited to arouse populist and nativist instincts; this was the view expressed by a South African political strategist Ryan Coatzee:

> The spent lots and lots of money online and in their literature were telling people stuff that is not true. It was designed to make you fear foreigners, I do…It was mendacious and xenophobic. In the English language, those are the words that best describe what they did. And frankly I personally don't care what people did; that's the truth. They did it into an environment where there was so much paranoia and distrust that people were all too ready to believe this stuff…What the Leave campaign offered them was an enemy, a bogeyman, What Britain needed to offer those people (left behind by globalisation) is a future.[50]

There is certainly evidence on Twitter of a propaganda campaign that systematically exploited fears but it should also be noted that the Invaded Nation scenario draws on other aspects of identity politics in nativist discourse grounded as I have shown in the moral foundations of Harm, Disloyalty, Subversion and Degradation. We may consider at this point the response by Remain to the dominant Invaded Nation scenario that Leave had initiated.

Remain arguments on social media relied much less heavily on the War and Invasion frame—they tended to avoid hyperbole, though at times showed considerable passion. They appealed partly to anxieties about the economic impacts of leaving; for example, the only high volume retweet in the referendum week was by the Labour MP (and former Cabinet Minister) John Prescott:

> John Prescott Retweeted Jim Pickard Thatcher's favourite economist on how destroying manufacturing is a price worth paying to leave. Crazy. #VoteRemain (218 retweets).[51]

For some remainers the Leave cause was tainted because of its association with the racism of the far right:

More and more recently, I feel like I am living in 1930's Germany. The racists are becoming emboldened. #VoteRemain (link to Independent article). (36 retweets)[52]

Please, if you're going to #VoteLeave at least do it because you've done your research and not because you're an ignorant racist. (31 retweets)[53]

God, this nasty bigoted racist xenophobic anti-people-like-us rhetoric is contemptible isn't it? I hope we can come back from it #VoteRemain. (23 retweets)[54]

A perspective of the Leave campaign as inherently racist increased after the Breaking Point poster:

@HumzaYousaf: UKIP's immigration poster was "xenophobic and frankly bordering on racist" #BBCDebate #VoteRemain #EUref (39 retweets)[55]

Mirza Waheed @MirzaWaheed 16 Jun 2016

Racist person poses in front of a racist poster for a racist campaign. #VoteRemain + Image of Nigel Farage stood in front of 'Breaking Point' advertisement board). (126 retweets)

This Invaded Nation rhetoric reminded tweeters of Donald Trump's campaign that had directly appealed on identity lines to white 'disenfranchised' working class voters:

Remarkably many Brits deride Trump as racist, backward-looking & isolationist but can't see #VoteLeave is direct UK equivalent. #r4today (51 retweets)[56]

While Leavers' use of the Invaded Nation scenario tended to demonise social groups—migrants, Muslims etc.—it very rarely named individuals. By contrast, many Remain tweets made highly personalised attacks on individuals, in particular Nigel Farage (as illustrated above), but also towards Boris Johnson:

Dear Boris,

Did your Nasty Norman ancestors arrive via an Aussie points-based system or did they invade & destroy? (12 retweets)[57]

One account in particular targeted Boris Johnson:

> Tom London @TomLondon6 20 Jun 2016.
> Johnson is prepared to do ANYTHING, including trash the country, if he thinks it might get him to No. 10
> Disgraceful
> Vote #Remain (32 retweets)
> Sickening how the media have indulged Boris Johnson as if he is a gifted child. He is not - he's a nasty piece of work. (152 retweets)[58]
> I think Johnson should be called by his surname like all other politicians. Calling him Boris is part of media's absurd indulgence of him. (201 retweets)[59]
> Boris Johnson is not royalty or a pop star. He should be called by his surname like other politicians. Not indulged by a sycophantic media (141 retweets)[60]

The sustained nature of 'Tom London's' social media attack on an individual politician goes against a focus on ideas alone, which was more typical of the official Remain campaign. On February 14th 2017 the Tom London account had 24,700 followers and had posted 35,100 tweets and by May 9th 2019 this had grown to 46,700 followers and had posted 61,800 tweets. Other postings suggest that its successful social media profile is aligned with the political left 'Momentum' movement that supports Jeremy Corbyn.

The difficulty faced by Remain was that its arguments were primarily economic—and most people's understanding of economics is not especially deep; there is a general mistrust of economics experts. Michael Gove made a very well received comment on a Sky News Question and Answer broadcast "people in this country have had enough of experts" and then followed this up with the comment: "I'm not asking the public to trust me. I'm asking them to trust themselves". This rejection of traditional sources of knowledge—"the experts"—is a typical populist strategy that had been successfully employed by politicians elsewhere following the failure of economists to find solutions to the aftermath of the 2008 financial crisis—let alone predict that crisis.

However, a number of Leave tweets explicity rejected the accusation of racism, framed in terms of the Sovereign Nation scenario:

Just because someone chooses to #VoteLeave, it doesn't automatically make them xenophobic or racist (162 retweets)[61]

It's not about race, it's about numbers! If a hotel is full the owner is not racist to say they are fully booked! #BBCDebate #VoteLeave (46 retweets)[62]

Everyone has their own reasons for wanting to #voteleave Don't assume we're all racists thanks (50 retweets)[63]

Voting to leave the EU isn't racism, it's getting the UK freedom from the social club of politicians who run Europe #VoteLeave (30 retweets)[64]

These Leave supporters were hurt by accusations of racism that were a slur on their character; they experienced them as ad hominem attacks, rather than as arguments based on evidence. They show varying degrees of of moral reasoning; for example in the last one the rejection of the ad hominem is accompanied by a statement of a reason *other than racism* for supporting Leave. Others used irony to raise identity related issues:

Replying to @DVATW

We are #VoteLeave on Thurs. Of immigrant parentage,we're both racist xenophobic Little Englanders…of course

(Selfie of interracial couple- ironic Tweet) (13 retweets)[65]

And others addressed the freedom of speech issue—viewing the claim that somone is 'racist' as a way of shutting them up and blocking any further examination of their views:

So not wanting my country to become islamified makes me a racist! When did that happen? #VoteLeave

(Image of woman with mouth taped up with this written beside 'The word 'Racism' is a simple term of slander used in psychological warfare to stop you speaking out about what is being done to your nation and people'). (117 retweets)[66]

The incorporation of the image shows how moral reasoning can be accomplished, and moral intuitions aroused, multimodally. Remain deployment of the Invaded Nation scenario therefore activated Leavers to respond by drawing on the Sovereign Nation scenario—illustrating the importance of distinguishing between these two scenarios in the discourse of Leave voters. Remain tweeters rejected the Invaded Nation scenario; however, by framing issues in terms of the 'Sovereign Nation' scenario initiated by the Leave campaign they strengthened the broader War and Invasion frame. In this regard their tweets potentially reinforced one of the two major scenarios of Leave rhetoric.

Summary

In this chapter I have illustrated two rather different strategies that were employed in the rhetoric of the Leave campaign; these I have described as 'scenarios' or characteristic arguments involving moral reasoning. One of these is by focusing on the in-group values shared by those who believe in the nation state—its historical and geographical reality, established institutions and shared values all of which demand protection. I have described this as the 'Sovereign Nation' scenario and suggest that it was especially important to the middle class voter who might be anxious about perceiving to respond to accusations of racism regarding their views on immigration. It appealed to the Care, Loyalty, Authority and Sanctity moral foundations by arguing that Britain's authority was being subverted by the EU and therefore the sanctity of the nation was under threat. The second scenario works rather differently as it focuses on the dangers presented by an out-group: typified by any entity external to the nation, whether it was the EU Commission, migrants who are seeking asylum in the UK, or jihadi terrorists. Its moral reasoning argued that the nation demands defence but it was also heavily reliant on arousing moral intuitions that are based on the Harm, Betrayal, Subversion and Degradation moral foundations. The moral reasoning of the 'Invaded Nation' scenario grouped together all perceived enemies of the English nation into a category of threatening entities that were attacking and desecrating established institutions, and shared values—whether it was democracy itself or the fishing industry, and that the nation was being degraded. This moral reasoning was therefore a post hoc justification of moral intuitions. The 'Invaded Nation' scenario was one that was developed by organisations such as Leave.EU that particularly targeted their messages toward working class voters in the towns and cities—especially where there were heightened concerns regarding immigration. By finding a set of symbols that expressed the shared intentions of these people they united them in defence of the idea of a Sacred Nation.

However, Remain rhetoric failed to distinguish between these two scenarios and in doing so often ended up using the Invaded Nation scenario, for example when its moral reasoning attacked the Leave campaign as uniformly racist such claims were really based in moral intuitions for which moral reasoning only offered a form of a post hoc justification. Since the Invaded Nation scenario appealed to disaffected working class voters—'the left behind'—such attacks failed to appeal to middle class voters. When there were accusations of racism Leavers could reason morally using the more acceptable Sovereign nation scenario. Ultimately, by engaging in a rhetorical slanging match involving metaphors from the frame of War and Invasion Remainers allowed the debate to be conducted on the cognitive psychological, and linguistic ground rules that had been established by the Leave campaign.

Notes

1. Shipman, T. (2016).
2. Clarke, H., Goodwin, M., & Whiteley, P., (2017).
3. Ibid. p. 37.
4. Davies, W. 'How feelings took over the world; Populist turbulence, viral panics, experts under attack: instinct and emotion have overtaken facts and reason in the digital age—can feelings now propel us into a better future?', *The Guardian*, September 8, 2018
5. Haidt (2012), p. 235.

6. Chilton, P. (2004), p. 204.
7. In a similar way the slogan for the American Republican Donald Trump's successful campaign for Presidency—'Make America Great Again'—presupposed that it was no longer great—though it had been previously.
8. Banks, A. (Oakeshott, I. ed.) (2017), p. 83.
9. Ibid. p. 102.
10. The use of social media profiles by political consulsting agencies such as Cambridge Analytica was exposed in March 2018. https://en.wikipedia.org/wiki/Cambridge_Analytica.
11. Nigel Farage Speech https://www.independent.co.uk/news/uk/politics/eu-referendum-nigel-farage-4am-victory-speech-the-text-in-full-a7099156.html.
12. Shipman (2016), pp. 428–29.
13. Rees-Mogg Speech, 27 March 2018.
14. Ibid.
15. Ibid.
16. Ibid.
17. Rees-Mogg Speech, 10 September 2018.
18. Quoted in Shipman (2016).
19. Vote Leave @vote_leave, 22 Jun 2016.
20. Boris Johnson, *The Sun,* 23 June 2018.
21. Ranil Jayawardena MP @TellRanil, 22 Jun 2016.
22. Vote Leave @vote_leave, 22 Jun 2016.
23. Vote Leave @vote_leave, 22 Jun 2016.
24. Alan TurkINgton @thisisalanturk, 22 Jun 2016.
25. Ben Brittain @Of_Mice_And_Ben, 19 Jun 2016 (Subsequently deleted).
26. Leave the EU @Trev_Forrester, 17 Jun 2016.
27. Brexit Now @StrongerOut, 20 Jun 2016.
28. Stop the EU @Stop_The_EU, 21 Jun 2016.
29. Voice of Europe @V_of_Europe, 20 Jun 2016.
30. Mike @mikeo111, 20 Jun 2016.
31. Ruth Robinson @RuthRobinsonLon, 19 Jun 2016.
32. David Jones @DavidJo52951945, 18 Jun 2016.
33. Simon Richards @simplysimontfa, 18 Jun 2016.
34. Mis Standen @Dwalingen, 18 Jun 2016.
35. Charlton Edwards @Charlton_UKIP, 20 Jun 2016.
36. JW™ @WillemXIII, 20 Jun 2016.

37. Shipman (2016), p. 413.
38. Brexit Now @BrexitNoww, 18 Jun 2016.
39. David Roach @davidroachcouk, 22 Jun 2016.
40. David Jones @DavidJo52951945, 17 Jun 2016.
41. Christopher J. Green @DefiantLionUK, 20 Jun 2016.
42. Luke Graves @lukegraves13, 20 Jun 2016.
43. James Delingpole @JamesDelingpole, 21 Jun 2016.
44. Supreme Dark Lord @voxday, 21 Jun 2016.
45. Aisha Akbar @AishaAkbar17, 22 Jun 2016.
46. B.B.C @mediabias_inUK, 21 Jun 2016.
47. Vote Leave @vote_leave, 9 Jun 2016.
48. Vote Leave @vote_leave, 9 Jun 2016.
49. Vote Leave @vote_leave, 9 Jun 2016.
50. Shipman (2016), p. 298.
51. James W. John Prescott @johnprescott, 19 Jun 2016.
52. Chelley Ryan #RJCOB @chelleryn99, 18 Jun 2016.
53. Euan Parfitt @euan_parfitt, 22 Jun 2016.
54. Edana Minghella @edanaming, 22 Jun 2016.
55. The SNPVerified account @theSNP, 21 Jun 2016.
56. David K. Smith @professor_dave, 21 Jun 2016.
57. Matthew Ward @HistoryNeedsYou, 21 Jun 2016.
58. Tom London @TomLondon6, 1 Jul 2016.
59. Tom London @TomLondon6, 13 Jul 2016.
60. Tom London @TomLondon6, 4 Dec 2016.
61. Lucy @LucyAVFC_, 22 Jun 2016.
62. Tay @talorvic, 21 Jun 2016.
63. Alex @paealla, 17 Jun 2016.
64. Sam Rawlings @sam_rawlings7, 17 Jun 2016.
65. Bernie Briffa @goonerbeau, 20 Jun 2016.
66. Based Tacita @GaiaTacita, 20 Jun 2016.

References

Banks, A. (2017). *The Bad Boys of Brexit* (Oakeshott, I. ed.). London: Biteback.
Chilton, P. (2004). *Analysing Political Discourse*. London and New York: Routledge.

Clarke, H.D., Goodwin, M., and Whiteley, P. (2017). *Brexit: Why Britian Voted to Leave the European Union*. Cambridge: Cambridge University Press.

Haidt, J. (2012). *The Righteous Mind: Why Good People are Divided by Politics and Religion*. London: Penguin.

Shipman, T. (2016). *All Out War*. London: Collins.

5

Conceptual Metaphors: 'Eurocrats Living in the Brussels Bubble'

Introduction

The idea of 'framing' situations as I have described in earlier chapters has its origin in conceptual metaphor theory (Lakoff and Johnson 1980). This theory was first illustrated with a conceptual metaphor ARGUMENT IS WAR and the authors proposed that the reason why we use expressions such as 'your claims are *indefensible*' and "he *shot down* all my arguments" is because argument (in general) is 'partially structured, understood, performed and talking about in terms of WAR'.[1] This is because war fundamentally involves imagistic ways of thinking which helps us to better understand argument; the claim is that this is not a poetic or fanciful way of talking about argument but one that is unconsciously adopted and widespread in everyday language about argument. We have seen in the previous chapter how arguments about Brexit were commonly talked about in terms of war and so we could modify the conceptual metaphor that was produced for language in general to summarise the moral intuitions behind Brexit by the conceptual metaphor: BREXIT IS WAR.[2] Conceptual metaphors propose that everything we know about war—the 'source domain'—can

© The Author(s) 2019
J. Charteris-Black, *Metaphors of Brexit*,
https://doi.org/10.1007/978-3-030-28768-9_5

be transferred to the more abstract 'target' domain of Brexit-related argument. For example, the knowledge from war that there are two competing sides each united under a flag and involved in a conflict with each other, pursuing a strategy to achieve the goal of victory could be transferred to the target domain of Brexit. The source domain has target domain roles for generals (e.g. Nigel Farage), troops (UKIP or Remain supporters), cannon fodder (the general public) and victims (perhaps immigrants).

Another example of a conceptual metaphor in political discourse is the view of nations as couples in a relationship and this could be represented as the NATION IS A PERSON.[3] Just as people can either be in conflict or at peace, so nations in alliance can be conceptually understood in terms of POLITICAL UNION IS MARRIAGE.[4] Diverse and often conflicting representations depend on the argument being made. Conceptual metaphors usually combine two nouns and these conceptual metaphors imply that what we know about interpersonal relationships can be mapped onto to what we know about relationships between political entities but this dependence on nouns tends to overlook the more dynamic framing that can come from verbs.

As Musolff points out, the choice of a form such as ARGUMENT IS WAR is quite arbitrary since at a more abstract level these expressions could equally be construed as ADVERSARIAL ACTIVITY IS FIGHTING.[5] There are no constraints on the wording of conceptual metaphors; for example, if we commonly discuss England being 'married to' Scotland, this could be based as much on the conceptual metaphor ENGLAND AND SCOTLAND ARE A MARRIED COUPLE as it is on the more general POLITICAL UNION IS MARRIAGE. The first is more specific and might be called a metaphor domain, whereas the latter is less so; the second could be worded even more generally as UNION IS MARRIAGE to describe situations outside of the domain of politics, so the question arises of how far conceptual metaphors are restricted to particular domains. Some researchers follow Lakoff in using 'image schema' to refer to the most abstract idea but there are no fixed rules as to whether the more particular domain form or the more general, image-schematic form is preferable.

A further claim of conceptual metaphor theory is that *everything* we know about the source domain, in the cases above, war and marriage, is mapped onto the target domains. We know that war entails actual physical conflict, and yet, fortunately, very few (if any) people have lost their lives over Brexit (apart, perhaps, from Jo Cox) so this aspect of the source domain does not really transfer to Brexit. Similarly, in the case of marriage we know that the physical and emotional closeness, the need to work on the relationship to prevent it from ending etc., can be applied to the relationship between two countries. But in the case of the union between England and Scotland: do we really think about them as having a wedding or children—both of which are part of what we know about marriage? Or is the metaphor just a way of reasoning about the political idea of their interdependence, without specifying what contributes to this?

While conceptual metaphors have their place in identifying patterns of metaphor, they do not reveal the reasoning devices and how these interact to make arguments. So a problem with this approach is that it treats metaphors as static rather than dynamic. Conceptual metaphors are sometimes too fixed to capture the *full verbal action* of framing: the moral reasoning processes through which opposing positions are contested. Conceptual metaphors are insufficient in themselves to describe the moral intuitions and moral reasoning through which Brexit was debated. Identifying conceptual metaphors does not tell us how the frame is applied in making particular arguments. For this reason, I suggest that while conceptual metaphors provide a starting point they do not provide a rich explanatory account of contemporary political arguments. So if Brexit was framed *as if it were a war* or *an interpersonal relationship* this then needs to be supplemented by discussion of 'allegory', 'scenario', 'frame' so that there is an explanation of 'moral intuition' and 'moral reasoning'. Critical Metaphor Analysis accepts that conceptual metaphors can be a starting point but the explanation stage requires other concepts such as allegories and scenarios to understand moral reasoning and moral intuition, but it is still helpful to have some conceptual metaphors as a way of framing our understanding.

In this chapter I would like to illustrate some of the conceptual metaphors that can be inferred from patterns of linguistic metaphor that occurred in the press, in speeches and online debates relating to Brexit in the period 2016–2018. I will concentrate on two types of conceptual metaphor: containment metaphors, and games' metaphors. This will then provide a starting point for understanding both the frames already introduced and those that follow in the remaining chapters.

Containment Metaphors

'Containment' metaphors are metaphoric uses of words that imply some sort of a bounded space, for example:

> Tomorrow let's take back control of our money, economy, *borders*, security and taxes #VoteLeave #TakeControl (612 retweets)[6]

Such metaphors are of interest in critical linguistics because they because they contrast entities that are within the container with those that are outside the container and so are helpful in contrasting 'Us' groups such as the family or the nation with 'Them' groups who are framed as **not being** part of the family or nation and hence framing political actors as 'insiders' or 'outsiders'. A further reflection is that words, phrases and sentences are themselves often thought of as containers of meaning, they can be transmitted along conduits and unpackaged at the other end by their receiver.[7] In this regard boundary making is fundamental to language, just as it may be in terms of identity and morality. We speak of actions also as coming 'within' the law and reject those that are outside the law. The container metaphor is not therefore cognitively limiting, although it may be over-simplifying, because it proposes that boundaries, lines and containers are an essential part of how humans create meaning. In the case of political meanings this could be summarised using the following conceptual metaphors:

BOUNDARIES ARE CONTAINERS
SUPPORTERS ARE THOSE IN THE CONTAINER
OPPONENTS ARE THOSE OUTSIDE THE CONTAINER

In context the evaluation of container metaphors is not ambiguous and since we know that all containers, like words, share the same properties of distinguishing unambiguously between an inside and an outside they are potentially an influential means for framing situations according to two categories 'in' or 'out': it is for this reason that they have a tendency to over-simplify. It shows linguistically how Haidt's moral foundation of Loyalty/Betrayal is realised through metaphor. Creation of categories—another type of container—is fundamental in linguistics—much of which concerns the appropriate arrangement of categories in relation to each other. Since the referendum itself was about remaining 'in' or going 'out of' the EU, it is not perhaps surprising that container metaphors were used to frame the UK as a container that needed protecting from outside.

However, container metaphors differ between viewing a situation from the perspective of within a three-dimensional container, and from an outside perspective observing the container from an external viewpoint. Consider the following:

Eurocrats living in the Brussels *bubble*...[8]

Whereas the 'borders' metaphor (above) evaluates a situation from the perspective of someone inside a container that is valued, in the 'bubble' metaphor the author is viewing the bubble from the perspective of someone *outside* the container and so is critical of 'Brussels' for being detached from the world outside their container. The expression 'Westminster bubble' became so widely used in this period that in September 2016 it was added to the Oxford English Dictionary; the definition given was 'n. the politicians, civil servants, and journalists working in and around the Westminster parliament, characterized as an insular community, out of touch with the experiences and concerns of the wider British public.' This shows a different concept along the lines: CONTAINERS ARE BOUNDED SPACES. Consider two groups of typical container metaphors:

Group 1: 'border', 'red lines', 'home', 'house'.
Group 2: 'prison', 'bubble' and 'echo chamber'.

Group 1 metaphors motivated by BOUNDARIES ARE CONTAINERS view a situation from a perspective of within the container and imply that the container is protective and therefore good;

these metaphors evaluate positively the 'Us' that is in the container and negatively the 'Them' entities that threaten the integrity of the container.

Consider, for example, when someone sets out their 'red lines'—an expression widely used referring to negotiating positions in the withdrawal period. What the speaker is doing is setting out a clearly defined boundary around a certain position beyond which they will not go and in doing so defining a political position. So everything this side of the red line is positioned as acceptable to 'us', but the other side of the red line is unacceptable. It is also found in expressions such as 'beyond the pale', which originated in the name given to the area of Ireland that was controlled by the English that was known as 'The Pale'. It is also found in the notions of 'cis' and 'trans' gender, in which 'cis-gender' refers to this side of the gender boundary in which personal identity coincides with sexual identity while 'trans-gender' refers to those whose gender identity and sexual attributes do not coincide. In the case of the BOUNDARIES ARE CONTAINERS conceptual metaphor the container need not necessarily have depth, and can be two-dimensional, but it is nevertheless a clearly demarcated boundary and is a concept that is relied on when evoking moral intuitions in political argument.

By contrast, with group 2 metaphors ('bubble', 'echo chamber' etc.) the container is viewed from an external perspective and they make a strongly negative evaluation of the inward-looking nature of those inside the container. Consider the following uses that are taken from the UK press during the week leading up to the Referendum:

He then told Dale he "lived in a media *bubble*[9]
That's why the social media *echo chamber* is so dangerous.[10]
You're living in a narcissistic *echo-chamber*.[11]

In each case the journalist is commenting negatively on the topic, when people are said to be 'In a bubble' it means their understanding of reality is obscured by their limited experience; and similarly the 'echo chamber' effect of social media refers negatively to the confirmation bias that characterises much social media interaction by which people only share similar opinions with others who already think the same way, thereby reinforcing and intensifying these opinions rather than exposing them to fresh thinking about a topic. So this type of containment is a form of imprisonment of thought, here the actual container itself, by implying that it blocks or obstructs, suggests a conceptual metaphor CONTAINERS ARE BOUNDED SPACES. This corresponds with a different moral foundation, the Oppression component of Liberty/Oppression. Consider the following: 'We keep hearing wise-heads falling back on the now-clichéd expression "the Westminster bubble". On the radio over the weekend I heard a metropolitan commentator concede that "of course we live here in a London bubble". And I—and, for all I know, you—nestle snugly and smugly within the "metropolitan elite" bubble, don't we?' (*The Times*, 22 June 2016). Here there is the idea that people are intellectually restricted by being confined within a 'bubble'.

Evaluation is quite complex as group 1 BOUNDARIES ARE CONTAINERS metaphors express an 'Us' perspective, it is desirable to be safe inside a place where we might want to be, such as a cocoon or a ship, and are therefore positive, but when those who are metaphorically 'in' the container don't want to be there, there is a switch to another conceptual metaphor: CONTAINERS ARE BOUNDED SPACES. This is the case with the 'prison' metaphor: but it is undesirable to be in a place where we would rather not be such as a 'prison' or 'bubble'. For those supporting Leave, the EU was framed as a type of container from which the UK needed to break out in order to gain its freedom:

> #Brexit will reinvigorate our economy, our democracy & our *liberty* (+ link) (115 retweets).[12]

This was closely related in these framings to ideas of democracy and sovereignty:

> #UKIP Cllr Luke Spillman - #VoteLeave for *Freedom*, democracy, *liberty* and *sovereignty*[13]

The EU was viewed by Brexit supporters as equivalent to living in a prison:

> I'd rather be poorer with the option of prospering rather than being a *prisoner* in the undemocratic #eu.#Brexit best for Britain.#Peston[14]

In the CONTAINERS ARE BOUNDED SPACES conceptual metaphor being in the EU was equivalent to voluntarily putting oneself in a cell and handing over the keys to the European parliament:

> Dave saying *leaving the EU is irreversible is like saying to a prisoner you'll never get back into jail.* #VoteLeave #Remain in dreary land.[15]

Clearly these framings of Britain as struggling to gain its freedom from imprisonment within the EU depended on the idea of a rigid, unyielding container; rather than being part of the EU, the UK was trapped within a container from which it sought to liberate itself by breaking out into a free world. The nature of the container itself here was what is salient because the implication of the metaphor is that it is a hard and oppressive container as the 'Iron Curtain' had been for those living under the influence of the Soviet Union. Leavers, though viewing the national borders as a form of container, aspired also to be in a borderless world of free trade.

Other uses of the CONTAINERS ARE BOUNDED SPACES conceptual metaphor profile the apertures in the container:

> We do not want to *haul up the drawbridge* and we certainly don't want to deter the international students
>
> They fear that leaving the EU will mean that the UK *will slam the door on the world.*

In framing situations influencers like to consider the nature of the container: what it is made of, what shape it is, what is its function, whether or not it has an opening. Here the 'castle' and 'house' containers are protective, but also have a means of legitimate entry. In the following chapter I explain how containment conceptual metaphors were taken up by Boris Johnson in creating an allegory of unjust entrapment. However, an important version of this metaphor, because of its cultural salience, involved maritime frames.

A very influential type of container metaphor used by supporters of Leave in the UK referendum was one that explored 'Them' and 'Us' relationships by framing the UK as a ship and the rest of the world as a potentially dangerous sea. It activates the moral foundation of Care/

Harm. This metaphor also introduces other source domains such as water, weather conditions and a control frame. The 'ship of state' metaphor has a long history that can be traced back to Plato who likened the governance of a city-state to the command of a naval vessel. It has been used at least 295 times in the British parliament; for example:

This Parliament has come together to *pilot the ship of State through the most perilous and difficult seas amid* which we live, and *to bring that ship and its precious cargo with all the fruits of victory into a peaceful harbour*....[16]

Those in charge of the 'ship of state' have a moral responsibility to chart a safe course through troubled waters, and for Plato's Socrates the ship's navigator, a stargazer, is the only true philosopher. Since it has a deep cultural and historical basis these container metaphors suggest the concept a NATION IS A SHIP. With this cultural pedigree it is little surprise that, as one tweeter wrote:

#Brexit are obsessed with *boats*.[17]

There were over 189 tweets in the Referendum week that referred to 'boats' of which 9 were retweeted more than 10 times. There were of course different types of boats: the safe boat of Britain once it had detached itself from the EU and the unsafe, leaky EU boat that was prone to disaster. There were also aspects of the political situation that encouraged actual uses of real boats that then contributed to a frame of reference for metaphors for THE NATION IS A SHIP. Sturdy boats of fishermen are normally valued in British culture, small boats could be used for people smuggling:

#Calais jungle dwellers use tiny boats to cross English Channel to illegally enter Britain[18]

Cameron and Osborne big claim on immigration yet cannot send packing 6 Afghans found in a boat in the English Channel.[19]

With boat loads of economic migrants arriving there'll be houses built on it soon enough if we stay in.[20]

So a contrast was set up over the 'good' boats of fishermen and the 'bad' boats of people smugglers and it was very clear into which of those categories the EU boat was metaphorically associated:

> @StrongerInPress @vote_leave EU will integrate anyway leaving us as a 2nd class member on slow *boat* to nowhere. Take this chance #VoteLeave[21]

By contrast, for Leavers, the UK was a 'lifeboat':

> #Brexit is the *lifeboat*. #VoteLeave (53 retweets[22])
>   Master Investor @masterinvestor 22 Jun 2016 "UK better off on *'lifeboat'* than *EU Titanic*" - Jim Mellon speaks to @cnbc about voting (32 retweets)

As we saw in chapter one the introduction of the large ship/titanic frame made available allegories of immanent disaster that could be used to arouse fear of mass immigration across Europe from the crisis in Syria, and the Horn of Africa and elsewhere. It is therefore not surprising that the container frame interacted with frames of water and disaster, consider:

> The #EU is a *sinking ship* what we have to abandon
>   Reclaim your sovereignty before it's too late! (49 retweets)[23]

The EU was commonly referred to generically by the Leave campaigns as a 'sinking ship', as in this tweet from the EU Leave campaign:

> Former adviser to PM says EU referendum is a LIFELINE from the *sinking EU ship*[24]

The sinking ship concept is motivated by fear and, that most primal of all instincts, the desire for survival and triggers the moral foundation of Harm. In the Twitter referendum debate there is further allusion to this allegory; any reference to the Titanic was relatively uncommon a year before the referendum but reached a peak with over 100 tweets containing this keyword in the Referendum week, although with the continuing uncertainty after the referendum, the allegorical allusion was still active 6 months later. While presenting an award to George Osborne at the Spectator magazine's Parliamentarian of the Year ceremony Boris Johnson alluded humorously to the Titanic allegory: "In the words of our great prime minister... I understood that Brexit means Brexit and we are going to make a Titanic success of it."[25] The sense of immanent disaster was further stimulated by the continuing rise of right wing populism in Europe, which increased anti-EU voices across Europe.

Closely related to 'sinking' metaphors for immanent disaster are metaphors such as 'tsunami', 'waves', 'floods' or 'influxes'; in all of these large quantities of an alien element threatens to break the boundaries of the nation-ship, as in the following:

> Curious how showing an actual image of the mass illegal economic migrant *tsunami* sweeping Europe is now characterised as "hate". #Brexit (103 retweets)[26]

The imagery of water has long played a significant role in British political discourse especially in relation to the issue of immigration. As I have pointed out elsewhere[27] immigration has long been likened to large movements of water—floods, tidal waves or tsunamis of immigrants—and fear of being overwhelmed by a vast quantity of 'otherness' that will 'swamp' native English identity has always been a strategy of the political right. From Enoch Powell, to Margaret Thatcher and Nigel Farage, the discourse of the political right has emphasised the scale of immigration by thinking of it in terms of an unstoppable influx of water. Enoch Powell's notorious prophecy that 'Like the Roman, I seem to see the River Tiber foaming with much blood' aroused the worst fears that the out-group—New Commonwealth citizens would displace the in-group (Native white English people) by outnumbering them, taking over their inherited economic and social resources and diluting or contaminating their identity. A sense of impending disaster surrounding the immigration issue was encapsulated by what are also FORCE metaphors that referred to migration as a tsunami:

BREXIT & ESCAPE DEADLY *TSUNAMI* OF 3 MILLION TURKISH MIGRANTS WAITING 2 ENTER #EU! (21 retweets)[28]

The concept of a tsunami only became introduced into political language after the 2007 tsunami in Sri Lanka, previously the preferred right-wing metaphor for the immigration was 'tidal wave':

> Britain is facing a *nightly tidal wave of asylum* seekers from Cherbourg, France's second biggest port.[29,30]

However, the more exotic and foreign sounding 'tsunami' seems to have gradually replaced it. For example, in *Daily Mail* headlines over a two year period (February 2015–2017) there were 7 uses of 'tsunami' but only one of 'tidal wave'. The use of a metaphor like 'tsunami' is related in cognition to what we may call the FORCE metaphor. The most significant one used in the Brexit campaign was a poster showing the front of an endless column of refugee-migrants (non-ethnically white) with the words 'Breaking Point'. The press published images of Nigel Farage standing in front of the poster and endorsing it. When pressure builds up so much that it risks breaking the boundaries of a container, the container no longer has a boundary and its rupture symbolises a disaster. This is also the case as in other metaphors that imply the complete rupturing of a container such as 'meltdown'. Words work differently because their meanings are allowed to shift over time, as long as such shifts are acknowledged by a sufficient number of speakers. Conceptually, these metaphors imply a massive amount of physical force that goes beyond what the container is able to sustain: they evoke moral intuitions by threatening survival.

Although Boris Johnson avoided the 'flood' term in relation to immigration, it nonetheless found its way into his first 'Out' article:

> That is the thing about EU law: it is supreme, irreversible, and in danger of *flooding out* national discretion. Human rights law fetters the ability of the British army to fight. (Shipman 2016: 611)

Earlier in the speech he argued that: 'Sovereignty is the ability to make our own rules when we desperately need them; and conversely, to stop the *flood of* new rules that we don't want'. For a skilled rhetorician like Johnson (as we will see in the next chapter), there is clearly a reason why he combines the water metaphor with a 'prison' metaphor ('fetters') in this critical article and I suggest it is because he is seeking to combine CONTAINERS ARE BOUNDED SPACES with the culturally salient THE NATION IS A SHIP conceptual metaphor. The threats are infringements on British sovereignty, but the water metaphor evokes fears of an influx of European workers and illegal immigrants arriving on lorries from Calais. Against this background the British boat was clearly being rocked, and even threatened by sinking with all those on board drowning:

> We aren't at the *helm*, we're being *dragged along in a lifeboat* and need *to cut the rope* and #Brexit[31]

The activation of metaphor frames by alluding to actual current political events characterises many boat-related metaphors as the political situation became the ground for such metaphors. Many tweets referred to a publicity campaign by Leave involving the use of fishermen's boats. Nigel Farage is both personally interested in sea fishing but has been constrained by EU law from landing sea bass and views the fishing industry as likely to benefit from Brexit; according to his spokesman Gawain Towler: "It matters to him, it is deeply symbolic, we are an island nation...A nation should control its own waters". The stunt was intended to evoke nostalgic memories of Dunkirk. He was approached by groups of Scottish and Essex fishermen to arrange a flotilla of 35 vessels to head up the Thames on June 15, with some of them continuing on to Westminster. Hearing of this, Bob Geldof, who founded Live Aid, sought to ambush the event with a display of pro-Remain banners hanging from Tower Bridge and a rival flotilla of dinghies. Another patriotic expression was 'our waters' used to imply a moral intuition that it is only right to protect the national interests of an island nation:

> #Brexit Britain: Foreign boats catch fish in *our waters* & ship it back to us #EU #referendum #voteleave[32]

Here the waters themselves have become included in the container of Britain, so that like a bath in which a boy is floating a boat, the bathwater itself is part of the bath container.

Populist press accounts represented Geldof and his crew as an arrogant crowd of 'toffs' on a pleasure cruiser, and Farage and his fishermen as humble defenders of an island nation that—drawing on the Invaded Nation frame- sought to 'take our waters back'. The class divide element was taken up by some tweeters:

> If Bob Geldolf drives by in his private boat giving the two fingers to working fishermen & that's seen as an advocate to remain? #VoteLeave[33]
>
> This is the rich elitist boat of people sticking twos up at the hardworking fishermen of this country. #VoteLeave[34]

One conspiratorially minded tweeter claimed that Geldof's boat was funded by Goldman Sachs:

> Breaking: Bob Geldof's boat funded by Goldman Sachs with BBC director in tow. (852 retweets)[35]

Farage's background as a banker seemed soon forgotten in his fresh identity as a man of the people. The EU had become a sinking ship that it was necessary to abandon by taking refuge on the lifeboat of Britain defended by its flotilla of fishermen:

> A #Brexit flotilla is sailing on the #Humber, lead by @UKIP's @MikeHookemMEP & east coast fishermen (59 retweets)[36]

The symbolism of the 'flotilla' is that it integrated the moral foundation of Sanctity originating in the heroic rescue from Dunkirk, with economic concerns over EU fishing quotas that had lead to many fishermen supporting the Leave campaign. Blurring categories together is characteristic of populist metaphor frames: it appealed to boat ownership—which permeates the culture from narrow boats on canals, to launches on bigger rivers and yachts on the sea. The deep nostalgia for the sea has been testified by many commentators on English cultural identity who note the appeal that the seaside has for families on holiday, caravan and mobile home parks by the sea and the ultimate dream of many for retirement by the sea—preferably with a sea view (if affordable).

Unlike the titanic, the flotilla is comprised of small boats, not large showy ones, ones that people who are only modestly well-off might still be able to afford. Somehow the image of the wealthy pop star with his loudspeaker implied privilege and a sense of elitism, while the trawler-mens' boats symbolised the moral intuitions of a group of working men marginalised by globalisation. In the allegory of English national iden-tity, there are corrupt politicians who are seeking to enrich themselves, through endearing themselves to foreign sources of authority, at the expense of brave seamen who are defending the homeland, and hard-working fishermen who are prevented from fishing in 'our waters' and know what a hard days' work is like:

> The fishermen should take Geldof out on one of their boats, in high seas. Then he would know what a proper job is! #Brexit[37]

Not all images of the flotilla were in favour of Leave; there was also evi-dence of counter-messages that create metaphor:

> Thought the #FarageFlotilla was a lovely metaphor for the UK after a #Brexit vote. A bunch of small boats cast adrift.[38]

Here the EU is a harbor from which the UK has become detached put-ting itself at the mercy of the oceans. As in a medieval morality tale, the battle on the Thames created an allegory out of the Brussels elite and out of work fishermen: it is a political allegory that rejects much of modernity and most of globalisation bringing out a yearning for better times when honest men and women did a hard day's work—and were not tempted by the Brussels 'gravy train'.

The 'Game' Conceptual Metaphor

A further conceptual metaphor that dominated the Referendum and the Withdrawal period was POLITICS IS A GAME. Leading 'players' on the Leave side frequently used the source domain of playing cards when talking about making 'an opening bid', 'playing their hand' as they negotiated a 'deal'. Then they sought to 'tackle' the opposition, while ensuring that the game was played on a 'level playing field', and they even referred to 'Brexit' as a 'prize' to be won. The Referendum was characterised as a competitive game—cards, cricket, rugby or chess—between two sides, each of which had their 'captains', with their 'strategies', while they sought to attain victory. They claimed to be following the rules laid down by the Electoral Commission as regards declaring expenditure and keeping within the permitted spending limits. This therefore corresponds closely with the Fairness/Cheating moral foundation.

However, as is not uncommon in high stakes games, the Leave side did not play entirely be the rules as it seems that certain elements relied on the services of Cambridge Analytica to purchase large datasets from Facebook to enable target marketing strategies. These entailed directing those messages that would be likely to most effective to particular social media users that came within specific demographics. So, for example, we have seen in Chapter 4 how the War and Invasion frame was likely to appeal to older voters in working class areas in parts of the North and Midlands, some of whom felt that there country had been 'invaded'. However, this frame was unlikely to appeal to younger voters in the south of England, where concepts like 'playing', 'risk-taking' and 'gambling' were likely to be more attractive. In a tweet on 28 August 2019 the Labour MP Jess Phillips commented: 'Before entering parliament I had truly never met the kind of people who game a system just for the sake of winning a game'.

Games metaphors retain the competitive race frame of war[39] in which there are winners and losers, stakes, rules and clearly defined outcomes but they do so in a way that is likely to put emphasis on sophisticated knowledge of the rules of the game, and the high level strategies involved in outsmarting an opponent, if POLITICS IS A GAME then Brexit was a very high stakes one and gave full opportunity for the players to display their most competitive instincts. I will first consider metaphors to do with playing the game, then those about playing by the rules before considering metaphors for the game's outcome, or result. At all times choices as regards metaphor were influenced by creating appropriate moral scenarios in which moral reasoning required knowing the rules of the game, while the desire to win was assumed as a taken for granted moral instinct. Evidently, at times, the two were in conflict with each other, as we know in competitive games the desire for victory can overwhelm considerations of *how* it is achieved. This should not surprise us as some research has shown that even moral philosophers cheat if they think they can get away with it[40]!

The POLITICS IS A GAME conceptual metaphor was especially evident in the language of Boris Johnson, whose career has sometimes resembled a game, deciding for example whether to support Leave or Remain, and then what position to take in relation to the deal negotiated by Theresa May. One has always sensed that he is playing something of a long-term strategy, with each move being calculated according to his ultimate objective of becoming Prime Minister. He has always been keen to draw on all types of competitive frame and in the following he blends together POLITICS IS A GAME with BREXIT IS WAR:

> So I gather *they think it's game over.* The Bremainers think they *have bombed us into submission.*[41]

Political observers were keen to frame Boris Johnson as a game player as in the following comment on Boris Johnson's criticism of Barack Obama for removing a bust of Winston Churchill from the Oval Office:

> He added, in a brilliant touch, that if you have too many busts in the Oval Office, it starts looking a little cluttered. *Game, set and match* to the President. But why did Boris ever *get himself into a contest* he was so *likely to lose?*[42]

This was probably because Johnson himself had a tendency to use metaphors from the world of competitive sports: he is known to be highly competitive, as when in October 2015, during an overseas trip, he sent a 10 year old Japanese boy flying when playing touch rugby. It is ironic that when talking about others he exhorts them to play fairly, without too much competitiveness:

...but I hope we can all agree to concentrate on the arguments; *to play the ball and not the man*. At the end of it all, we want to get a result, and then get on and unite around David Cameron[43]

The phrase 'play the ball and not the man' could have come straight from Matthew Arnold who saw the public schools as the correct moral grounding on how life should be lived. A good example of Johnson's public school mentality living in a world where success is measured in terms of cups and prizes is his use of the metaphor 'prize' in press articles to refer to Brexit:

If we get it right, we can have a better and more honest relationship - and that means leaving the EU, but emphatically not leaving Europe. *That is the prize.*[44]

He also used the 'prize' metaphor in his speeches:

That was the vision of Brexit we fought for; that was the vision the Prime Minister rightly described last year. That is *the prize that is still attainable.*[45]

Who, I wonder, does Boris Johnson imagine walking up on the podium to receive the prize while the audience applauds rapturously? But the central importance of the GAME metaphor in his thinking shows when in his resignation letter, he described Theresa May's unpopular deal as follows:

What is even more disturbing is that this is *our opening bid.*[46]

During the Brexit negotiations he frequently used card-playing metaphors:

The EU, by discourteously *overplaying its hand*, has offered us real freedom and the Prime Minister looks willing to grasp the initiative.[47]
    This means the country could spend £39 billion without knowing what the future agreement is going to be, so our *strongest negotiating card has been played* for nothing in return.[48]

Given the importance of POLITICS IS A GAME in his framing of Brexit, it is not surprising that political commentators used game playing metaphors when describing Boris Johnson's approach:

> It is telling that, *knowing the game*, Johnson decides to play it anyway, putting down a firm marker on why Britain's *"end state" deal* with Brussels must allow the UK to diverge from EU laws once we have left...[49]

An important component of conceptual metaphors is that they become wired into the brain and serve as filters for interpreting situations, so once the game playing frame was established it prevented moral questions from being explored in depth—such as what kind of debts had been incurred by Britain as a member of the EU for 43 years, a period during which it had enjoyed the full game-playing opportunities offered on the Brussels chess board. Boris Johnson was aware of the long-term strategies employed by EU negotiators:

> In presuming to change the constitutional arrangements of the United Kingdom, the EU is treating us with naked contempt. *Like some chess player triumphantly forking our king and our queen*, the EU Commission is offering the UK government what appears to be a binary choice.[50]

In fact, the game-playing frame is usually about binary choices once teams have been allocated, and the difficulty faced by the UK was that it had put itself in a position where there were 27 players on one side, and only one on the other!

Game metaphors were not the exclusive preserve of Johnson, and as we see in the next chapter he used many other frames too, but they are indicative of a political style of moral reasoning. This was especially the case with another leader of the hard Brexiteers, Jacob Rees-Mogg who—as we saw in the last chapter—projected an erudite persona that was well grounded in a moral code; he frequently employs thePOLITICS IS A GAME conceptual metaphor when arguing for fairness, as in the following:

> The UK has also agreed to *a level playing field* but this is code for adopting EU inefficiencies...... *A level playing field must not become a sticky wicket.*[51]

Here he elaborates the conventional 'level paying field' metaphor as a way introducing the more abstract concept of the force of gravity: we know that when a playing field is not level it will give an unfair advantage to the team playing downhill because they have the assistance of gravity and therefore need to expend less effort. He draws on the 'cheating' component of the moral foundation of Fairness and Cheating for moral reasoning with the idea of a playing field that can be deliberately tilted:

> The Government has clearly tried *to tilt the playing field* in its direction, spending taxpayers' money on an inaccurate leaflet, and flooding its websites with lies about the economy.[52]

It was an important part of the Leave campaign to argue for the moral legitimacy of their cause and so the idea that the Remain campaign was being unfairly advantaged was a means of undermining its moral legitimacy. Moral reasoning was also developed by linking the POLITICS IS A GAME metaphor with other notions related to responsibility, for example ideas of excessive risk:

> In response Europe has chosen to *play a risky game* of banking all our concessions and offering no goodwill in return. This is the surest guarantee that we will *leave without a deal.*[53]

All other 'players' were represented as taking irresponsible risks while only Leave was exerting appropriate moral caution:

> While some Lords are intent on *playing the compulsive gambler* continually *spinning* the *legislative dice until they hit the double* Remain, it is time they call it a day.[54]

For many, the idea that Brexit was some sort of game to be played was anathema because they felt that the outcomes affected their lives, their identities and their economic wellbeing; however, they did not always come up with a sufficiently well grounded account that was based on how language and the brain works.

Summary

In this brief account of conceptual metaphor theory and its application to the metaphors of Brexit, I have compared two different conceptual metaphors: containment metaphors and game related metaphors. I have summarised these in terms of:

BOUNDARIES ARE CONTAINERS and its most common implications:

SUPPORTERS ARE THOSE IN THE CONTAINER
OPPONENTS ARE THOSE OUTSIDE THE CONTAINER

Which corresponds with the moral foundation of Loyalty/Betrayal and
CONTAINERS ARE BOUNDED SPACES
That corresponds with the moral foundations of Liberty/Oppression. Both conceptual metaphors correspond with the Care/Harm moral foundation.

I have illustrated containment metaphors convey positive evaluations of entities construed as within the container, so THE NATION IS A SHIP has very positive evaluations of those who are on HMS Britain. Conversely, when negatively construed, the conceptual metaphor CONTAINERS ARE BOUNDED SPACES represents containers such as the EU, or echo chambers and media bubbles as oppressive entities that constrain the freedom of the supporters trapped within the container. Ultimately it was the CONTAINER of Brexit itself that proved to be a BOUNDED SPACE. Having clambered down into the dark hole of Brexit, the British Body Politic found itself in a deep and dark hole from which whatever efforts it made to clamber out of served only to push it further back into the hole. Like some gaudy Egyptian sarcophagus, Brexit became a funerary coffin that consumed the body politic.

The POLITICS IS A GAME conceptual metaphor activated a frame with roles for: competition, skill, guile, cunning and strategy; it was employed especially by leaders of the Leave campaign and corresponded with the moral foundation of Fairness/Cheating. Depending on the moral reasoning involved, they also advocated taking or avoiding risks, a focus on the ultimate 'goal' or 'prize' and claimed to be 'playing by the rules'. However, others viewed the concept of viewing politics as a game as fundamentally opposed to their moral intuitions about how society should be governed. Certainly others will come up with alternative conceptual metaphors, and frames that may further contribute to understanding the metaphors of Brexit and their influence on the body politic.

Notes

1. Lakoff & Johnson (1980), pp. 4–6.
2. Conceptual metaphors are always written in capital letters to distinguish them from ordinary linguistic metaphors.
3. This is discussed in more detail in Chapter 7.
4. This is discussed in more detail in Chapter 8.
5. Musolff (2016).
6. Vote Leave @vote_leave, 22 June 2016.
7. This is known in cognitive linguistics as the 'Conduit' metaphor and originates with the work of Reddy (1979).
8. *Express Online*, 20 June 2016.
9. *Express Online*, 21 June 2016.
10. *The Guardian*, 17 June 2016.
11. *Telegraph.co.uk*, 24 June 2016.
12. Reaction @reactionlife, 20 Jun 2016.
13. thebrexiteer@twsud, 22 Jun 2016.
14. English patriot ﺝ ﺍﻝ‫ﺱ‬ @englishmanshome,19 Jun 2016.
15. Nicholasjf@nicholasjf1, 19 Jun 2016.
16. Wisnton Churchill, 31 March 1919.
17. nickyclark @MrsNickyClark, 16 Jun 2016.
18. Europa News @europafreunde, 19 Jun 2016.
19. UK Justice Forum @Justice_forum, 19 Jun 2016.
20. smithy @bunteryid, 18 Jun 2016.
21. Rob Ryan @robryan_uk, 22 Jun 2016.
22. Ann Sheridan @bernerlap, 17 Jun 2016.
23. lisa henegauwen @LisaHenegauwen, 22 Jun 2016.
24. LEAVE.EU @LeaveEUOfficial, 19 Jun 2016.
25. Boris Johnson, 3 November 2016.

26. David Vance @DVATW, 19 Jun 2016.
27. Charteris-Black, J. (2006).
28. Eta Centauri (η Cen) @ECentauri, 19 Jun 2016.
29. *News.Telegraph*, 25 August 2002.
30. The metaphor of the 'tidal wave' pre-dated the devastating tsunami of December 2004.
31. NO2USE @NO2USE, 20 Jun 2016.
32. SRAEL BOMBS BABIES @Col_Connaughton, 16 Jun 2016.
33. Chris Bruce @Bruceyy9, 22 Jun 2016.
34. Simon Cullen @simoncullen01, 16 Jun 2016.
35. #BBCequalsFakeNews @ExposingBBC, 16 Jun 2016.
36. James Piekos @Piekos, 20 Jun 2016.
37. Tim H @Timzere65, 16 Jun 2016.
38. Grumpy dad @hood1960, 16 Jun 2016.
39. See Charteris-Black (2017) for a detailed discussion of this frame.
40. See Haidt (2012), p. 104.
41. Boris Johnson, *telegraph.co.uk*, 24 April 2016.
42. Andrew Gimson, *Mail on Sunday* (London), 24 April 2016.
43. Boris Johnson, *The Daily Telegraph*, 22 February 2016.
44. Boris Johnson, *MailOnline*, 21 May 2017.
45. Boris Johnson, Speech 18 July 2018.
46. Boris Johnson Resignation Letter July 10, 2018.
47. Jacob Rees-Mogg, *MailOnline*, 22 September 2018.
48. Jacob Rees-Mogg *telegraph.co.uk*, 29 November 2018.
49. Tim Shipman, *The Sunday Times*, 17 December 2017.
50. Boris Johnson, 14 October 2018.
51. Jacob Rees-Mogg *Sunday Express*, 25 November 25, 2018.
52. Jacob Rees-Mogg *MailOnline*, 29 May 2016.
53. Jacob Rees-Mogg, *The Express*, 25 April 2018.
54. Jacob Rees-Mogg, *MailOnline*, 17 June 2018.

References

Charteris-Black, J. (2006). Britain as a Container: Immigration Metaphors in the 2005 Election Campaign. *Discourse & Society* 17, 6: 563–582.

Charteris-Black, J. (2017). Competition Metaphors & Ideology: Life as a Race. In R. Wodak and B. Forchtner (Eds.), *The Routledge Handbook of Language and Politics* (pp. 202–217). London and New York: Routledge.

Haidt, J. (2012). *The Righteous Mind: Why Good People are Divided by Politics and Religion*. London: Penguin.

Lakoff, G. and Johnson, M. (1980). *Metaphors We Live By*. Chicago, IL: University of Chicago Press.

Musolff, A. (2016). *Political Metaphor Analysis: Discourse and Scenarios*. London: Bloomsbury Academic.

Reddy, M.J. (1979). The Conduit Metaphor: A Case of Frame Conflict in Our Language About Language. In A. Ortony (Ed.), *Metaphor and Thought* (pp. 284–310). Cambridge: Cambridge University Press.

Shipman, T. (2016). *All Out War*. London: Collins.

6

The Metaphors of Boris Johnson

Introduction

Alexander Boris de Pfeffel Johnson is among the most controversial of contemporary politicians. As a former mayor for London, Minister, MP, minor television celebrity and successful journalist he has a wide following and a significant influence on public opinion. He has a reputation for philandering and infidility in marriage, rather than for a coherent set of political beliefs. His appeal arises from a style based on surreal humour, eccentric appearance and considerable linguistic skill. He arouses interest by challenging established attitudes and ridiculing opponents. He can be readily named: we all have an image of the disheveled, blond, larger-than-life schoolboy blasting at an opponent or getting stuck on a zip wire. As a carefully manicured brand, 'Boris' is often provocative, sometimes funny, but always colourful, standing out from the surrounding grey. In evaluating him it is essential, then, to remember in times dominated by difficult social issues and political crises, he has the ability to entertain readers through studied provocation, challenge to conventions of dress, appearance, and behaviour, and by stylish use of metaphor. Appraisals of Boris depend on whether one

© The Author(s) 2019
J. Charteris-Black, *Metaphors of Brexit*,
https://doi.org/10.1007/978-3-030-28768-9_6

is evaluating the journalist, the politician or the man; since the focus of this chapter is on metaphor, at which he is skilled, it is likely that the judgement will be more favourable than had it been based purely on his personal reputation.

He has developed a journalistic narrative that appeals to the Middle England of readers *The Daily Telegraph* with a mixture of pride in village greens, women's institutes, red letter boxes and the other patriotic symbols explored in Chapter 3. He has taken a consistently anti-European Union position reporting on the dastardly plots of Johnny Foreigner and the endless red tape and absurdities of the European Commission—whether banning prawn cocktail crisps or straightening bananas. As a journalist, he stimulates and feeds the desires of his middle class readers; but his euro-scepticism was readily adapted to offer other versions of the 'national' story to the less middle class readers of *The Express* and *The Sun*. While many readers share his moral intuitions about the EU, as a politician he has been inconsistent to the extent that few colleagues trust him. He is the only living politician who is regularly referred to by his nominal first name, the pseudonym 'Boris', though his family addresses him as 'Alex'. It is not always clear whether this is because he is thought of affectionately, or, like a recalcitrant teenager, just not taken too seriously. Since 'Boris' is less ambiguous than 'Johnson', I will use 'Boris' in this chapter.

Boris goads opponents with a mixture of colourful ad hominem attacks and public school humour framed in imaginative metaphor. On Tony Blair he commented: "It is just flipping unbelievable. He is a mixture of Harry Houdini and a greased piglet. He is barely human in his elusiveness. Nailing Blair is like trying to pin jelly to a wall".[1] During a London Assembly meeting following the publication of the 2014 budget for London he referred to his political opponents as "great supine protoplasmic invertebrate jellies".[2] His metaphors shift their target down the hierarchy of the Great Chain of Being[3] from human via animal to jelly. In an article for *The Express* he described Jeremy Corbyn as having 'an innocent and vole-trousered air'[4] and in for the *MailOnline* he asked: "How on earth is Corbyn the hokey-cokey artist going to take back control of immigration?" then continued: "The answer is that he would fail - not just because he would have Nicola Sturgeon and Tim Farron perched like monkeys on his back, one demanding another EU referendum and the other trying to destroy our fantastic United Kingdom" before delivering his final ad hominem: "He would go into the negotiating chamber with all the authority of a smacked blancmange".[5] The progression from 'artist' to 'monkeys' to 'blancmange' descends the universal hierarchy of the Great Chain so the targets of his epithets become increasingly less animate until they end up as just things or mass produced objects. Referring to Jeremy Corbyn in a speech following his defeat in a vote that prevented the UK leaving the EU without a deal he observed: "There's only one chlorinated chicken that I can see … and he's on that bench." In an article for *The Daily Telegraph* he described the former Liberal Democrat leader Nick Clegg as a 'cutprice edition of David Cameron hastily knocked off by a Shanghai sweatship to satisfy unexpected market demand'.[6] His metaphoric ad hominems amuse and invite the reader to join in the mockery: many other populist politicians insult but rarely to such suppressed laughter—evoking the thought: "Did he really just say that?"

Is this the harmless invective of a gifted satirist or does it reflect a ruthless and vindictive politician? Perhaps Boris views journalism and politics as a highly competitive game—adversarial and combatitive in nature—like a boxing match, with the rhetorical knockout blow being the only measure of debating success? The answer is probably both, as one of his critics has noted: 'Like Lord Palmerstone, Boris does not have friends, merely interests'.[7] Yet, as a journalist he is creative and imaginative; his metaphors engage audiences, and combine moral reasoning with emotionally persuasive arguments. For example, at the Conservative conference in Manchester in October 2009 he warned his audience in a flurry of metaphors: "I know how unpopular these bankers are and I know how … I now seem to be sticking up for these pariahs. But never forget all you banker-bashers that the leper colony of the City of London produces 9 per cent of UK GDP and 13 per cent of value added", here moral intuitions were challenged by reasoning.

His metaphors (in italics) offer psychological release from the constraints of literal language. Many are concerned with force: physical constraint, and release from such constraints in line with the

CONTAINERS ARE BOUNDED SPACES conceptual metaphor described in Chapter 5. Consider the following:

> If we vote Remain, *we stay locked in the back of the car, driven by someone with an imperfect command of English, and going in a direction we don't want to go.*[8]
>
> And that is why it is such a mistake for us to leave on the Chequers terms, *locked in the tractor beam of Brussels.*[9]

As an extended metaphor, these images of constraint and entrapment contrast with images of release from confinement:

> And that *open* Brexit will *unleash this country* to go *back to its roots* as a great global trader not just in goods …[10]

Just as he views Brexit as an opportunity for a powerful and energetic Britain to be released from the restraining force of the European Union, so, as a journalist, Boris finds in metaphor a release from the constraints of the literal language of less charismatic politicians. Such ordinary mortals may pay greater attention to detail but lack the bigger mapping possibilities offered by his metaphors. The vigorous intensity and the intuitive moral judgements provided by his metaphors makes them highly quotable.

In October 2016 Boris drafted two versions of an article—with one advocating remaining in the EU and the other leaving; this duplicity has given rise to a view that as a politician he lacks principles and selects policies likely to lead to his own self-advancement. On moving back to London in 1994 he is reported as saying that he was a 'bit worried (as) I haven't got any political opinions'.[11] Of course, many individuals struggled over how they would vote in Brexit: there seemed to be arguments both ways and Boris was using parody to straddle these. However, moral intuitions evoke a higher level of emotional engagement and moral questioning had been at the root of Boris's critique of the EU as a journalist. Many people experienced a stronger emotional attachment to 'Westminster' than they did to 'Brussels'. Whatever he really believed, Boris understood and exploited these emotionally based moral intuitions for his own career advancement—first in journalism and then in politics. His decision to become, at least at one time, the major mainstream politician advocating Leaving the EU was consistent with a persona developed by appeals to emotion rather than to principle. The will to power relies on emotional intuition more than reasoned argument and was more credible in his journalism than in his wavering political stance. Whatever he really thought about EU membership, given the anti-European persona developed through his journalism, he was hoisted on his own petard as he would appear hypocritical if he failed to support Leave.

On Twitter many rejected Boris's populist arguments on the grounds that he was inherently untrustworthy as a politician:

> The blond guy on the pic is leading UK towards #Brexit to defend the working class against Brussels' elite, right? (11 retweets) (Picture of Boris dressed for Bullingdon club dinner)[12]
>
> Every time Boris Boris says "Take back control", I just hear it as "Give control to me." No thank you, Boris. I don't trust you. (55 retweets)[13]
>
> When Leave claims we will take back control, who's "WE"? Boris Boris & his water cannon say it's not you. (13 retweets)[14]

Politically, there was considerable mistrust of Boris by many from the metropolitan left who saw his political manoeuvering over Brexit as self-seeking and lacking a plan, the following link to the incumbent mayor of London speaking on a BBC TV debate was retweeted 405 times:

> "A slogan is not a detailed plan, Boris. What is your plan?"—Sadiq Khan (405 retweets)[15]

His most recent biographer, Purnell, recognises these deficiencies:

> …blessed with immense charisma, wit, sex appeal and celebrity gold dust; he is also recognised and loved by millions—although perhaps less so by many who have had to work closely with him (let alone depend on him). Resourceful, cunning and strategic, he can pull off serious political coups

when the greater good happens to coincide with his personal advantage but these aspirations are rarely backed up by concrete achievements, or even detailed plans.[16]

As a media-savvy performer, he rejects bland, neutral positions and demands a response from his audience. His supporters enjoy the bullish aspirational language while others view this as a populist guise for an elitist and class-based politician. For example, he often talks about 'fat cats' as if he were not himself a journalist who earns more than £250,000 a year in that capacity alone. He relies on metaphor as a way of framing political scenarios in general terms as in the following:

> The Bremainers think *they have bombed us into submission*. They think that we have just seen the turning point in the referendum campaign, and that the British people are so intimidated by these testimonials - American presidents, business leaders, *fat cats* of every description - that they now believe the British people will *file meekly* to the polls in two months time and consent to stay in the EU; and thereby to the *slow and insidious erosion of democracy* in this country.[17]

In a classic piece of 'them' and 'us' polarising rhetoric the metaphors include many of the frames identified in earlier chapters: patriotism ('the British people'), war and invasion ('bombed'), as well as distrust and betrayal ('insidious erosion'). There is also in 'fat cats' and 'file meekly' a frame I will explore in Chapter 9—the Human as Animal frame. All these metaphors are based on moral intuitions rather than reasoned argument.

Boris's journalism shows a 'ludic' style that intends to give pleasure and engages audiences by playing with language. He is renowned for his innovative use of language: he reinvents old words for example 'wiff waff' (an early nickname for 'ping pong') and 'mugwamp' for Jermy Corbyn. He even invents completely new words, for example in an article on children's accidents in playgrounds he coined 'scabophobic'[18]: in each case it is the sound and rhyme of the words that is crucial: the article had four other instances of 'scab', 'wiff' 'waff' sounds like 'toff' and 'mugwump' sounds like 'chump'. His lexicon is innovative and characterised by vigorous consonant sounds:

> Why, then, are we proposing to turn the UK, in important respects, into the perpetual punk of Brussels? Chuck Chequers.[19]

He repeats 'punk' several times in this article with the less familiar sense of 'a young person who behaves in a rude, aggressive, or violent way' (Collins) and combines two alliterations. An article from *The Express* is entitled 'Boris gives them sunshine, but the PM stays away'. The article, authored by Boris, celebrates his jokes then continues: "The conference in Manchester was finally roused from post-election misery by the party's chief sunshine dispenser".[20] Boris is keen to sustain the myth of the joy that he brings as a dionysian life force.

For metaphor junkies, Boris is your fix: in his journalism, he invents novel metaphors that communicate a personal psychological stance and has established an impressive reputation for forceful opinions and colourful language. But as a politician he is barely trusted by party members: he may have been more successful in a political culture that accepts a higher level of emotional engagement. His populist style, like that of other ludic politicians of the right and far right such as Nigel Farage and Beppo Grille in Italy, has given voice to popular feelings of frustration with the European Union, but has probably pushed him too far to the right to be politically credible to the general public. His desire to use language to please has offended many who are more concerned about its implications for his policies.

In this chapter I first consider his journalistic frames and then his political frames. To assist with this I have used two datasets: 82,000 words comprising all his press articles during the period 2016–2018 and 40,000 words of his speeches that I collected from the period October 2011 to October 2018. These two datasets were examined manually but with the assistance of software to identify keywords. I will interpret Boris's metaphors in terms of simulated embodiment: his journalistic metaphors are framed by concepts of physical constraint and release from constraint and what I describe as the allegory of unjust entrapment. His political metaphors are framed by typical Leave frames such as 'Patriotism and the Nation' and 'War and Invasion' as well as the nation-as-body and the nation-as-family frames that I explore in the next chapter. As a journalist, moral reasoning is often replaced by moral intuition as when he called the EU 'playground bullies', or made analogies between the European Union, Hitler and Napoleon. The moral reasoning behind viewing Britain as a defeated colony— part of someone's else's empire—hardly stands up to analysis but it is attention grabbing and its moral indignation is emotionally appealing and intuitive, at least for some of his followers. As a journalist, he is an inveterate metaphor addict, and while even fellow politicians find him untrustworthy and duplicitous, some of those who read his articles are addicted to their mixture of humour, moral reasoning and linguistic originality, as well as to moral intuitions that correspond with their own values.

Boris's Journalistic Frames: Constraint and Embodied Simulation

Boris's metaphors frequently break the normal conventions of language and delight in imaginative fantasy. For example, when questioned by the political editor of *The Mail on Sunday* about one of his marital infidelities he replied: "It is complete ballderdash. It is an inverted pyramid of piffle".[21] He has an appetite for food-related metaphors (as well as punning) that express schoolboy humour, sometimes at his own expense: "I think I was once given cocaine but I sneezed so it didn't go up my nose. In fact, it may have been icing sugar". As Boris himself put it: "I think it's important to remember that most people find politics incredibly dull, so I don't see any particular vice in trying to sugar the pill with a few jokes".[22] So linguistic entertainment by metaphor is a necessary prerequisite for engaging reader interest.

He employs visceral body metaphors when discussing political issues; for example on stag hunting he commented: "I remember the guts streaming, and the stag turds spilling out on to the grass from within the ventral cavity ... this hunting is best for the deer".[23] And he once claimed that: "Voting Tory will cause your wife to have bigger breasts and increase your chances of owning a BMW M3".[24]

His fans find his political views acceptable because their moral reasoning is framed humorously. Consider further the ad hominem towards Jeremy Corbyn mentioned above:

> ....this is the man who would be sent to go eyeball to eyeball with Jean-Claude Juncker and Angela Merkel. It would be a disaster. He would go into the negotiating chamber with all the authority of *a smacked blancmange*. How would our partners respond to the Corbyn approach? At first they would be puzzled. Then they would *probe the defences of the blancmange*.[25]

The metaphor is creative as it stretches the imagination to find resemblances between a politician and a type of sweet, soft pudding—white in colour and made from milk or cream and sugar—that needs to be 'smacked' in order to release it from the mould. Presumably the idea is that while, appearing to be pleasing the pudding-Corbyn lacks strength, tending to wobble and therefore would not offer resistance—and would be very easily consumed by hungry and rapacious European politicians. A similar effect was sought in the 'chlorinated chicken' epithet quoted in the introduction to this chapter. These are tenuous metaphors but serve his purposes in gaining media attention and evoking a few laughs while conveying the moral judgment that Jeremy Corbyn would not be competent in negotiating Brexit. The metaphor choices take into account his purposes when considering the psychological and cognitive frames of his intended audience—for example Boris knows that *Telegraph* readers will understand what a blancmange is and know that there is concern over American chlorinated chicken being sold in the UK after Brexit. The metaphors also fit current norms of political interaction in which light-hearted personal insults are acceptable if they are humourously or creatively articulated. They come over as banter, rather than as diatribe—and that is an important element in the communicative style that Boris seeks to convey, though categorising as 'just' banter can of course conceal harmful misconstruals too.

His interpretation of Brexit options is often expressed by food metaphors. Consider his distinction between those metaphors that have become almost entrenched in the Brexit debates, the distinction between a 'hard' and 'soft' Brexit:

"What type of Brexit will it be?" it is perhaps time to stop talking about the Brussels talks as though they were a kind of glorified cheeseboard. Some people still seem to think that we must make a choice: to go for a slice of camembert or parmesan, a hard Brexit or a soft Brexit, or perhaps a chunk of each. I am not convinced by this metaphor.[26]

The food frame is introduced for fun and then rejected. So the cheese metaphor engages his audience partly because it captures an association often made between Boris and food; for example, the i-Independent asked: "A Brexit bake-off may enable Mrs May to woo the Europeans, perhaps with some Danish pastries. Some Barnier barm cake. Macron macarons (mais bien sur!). A nice meringue for Merkel. And, erm, some humble pie for Boris?".[27] Apart from gaining attention, the extended 'cheese' metaphor is a rhetorical technique for counter-argument by rejecting his opponents' purported arguments for a simple choice between 'hard' or 'soft' Brexit. Later in the article he develops an argument that people 'fear that leaving the EU will mean that the UK will slam the door on the world', he then extends this metaphor: "You can take back control of borders without slamming the drawbridge on talent" to conclude the article with the aspiration that: "I believe people want an open Brexit, and a vision for Britain as a great global trading nation - and that is what we are going to deliver". He contrasts fears about separation and isolation ('door slamming') with the metaphor that Britain will be more 'open' outside the EU—clearly he is drawing here on the conceptual metaphor BOUNDARIES ARE CONTAINERS. He frames an issue through metaphor, and creates scenarios in which moral reasons are elaborated. Consider this article published soon after Theresa May's Chequer proposals (metaphors in italics):

So *it's ding ding! Seconds out! And we begin the final round of that international slug fest*, the Brexit negotiations. *Out of their corners* come Dominic Raab and Michel Barnier, *shrugging their shoulders and beating their chests* - and I just hope you aren't one of those trusting souls who still thinks it could really go either way. The fix is in. The whole thing is about as pre-ordained as a bout between *Giant Haystacks and Big Daddy*; and in this case, I am afraid, the inevitable outcome is a *victory* for the EU, with the UK *lying flat on the canvas* with 12 stars *circling* symbolically over *our semi-conscious head.* ... There may be some *confected groaning and twanging of leotards* when it comes to the discussion on free movement. But the reality is that in this negotiation the EU has so far *taken every important trick.*[28]

Boris comes over as a large man, he is a former rugby player, and affecianado of the Eton Wall game: a man who likes to throw his weight around. While taking part in an informal game of street rugby on a trip to Japan in October 2015 he flattened a 10-year-old schoolboy and in 2006 he headbutted the German international Maurizio Gaudino during a charity football match. It is therefore quite easy to visualise the author as a wrestler 'groaning and twanging his leotard' which invites the type of embodied re-enactment that readers go through when imagining what it is like to pick someone up and hurl them across a ring (even only in the highly artificially simulated world of wrestling). The metaphorical theme that POLITICAL CONTESTS ARE WRESTLING BOUTS is what Ray Gibbs describes as an allegory because it has a rich symbolic character that invites embodied simulation on the part of the reader. This he describes as: 'simulations of speakers' linguistic messages that involve moment-by-moment 'what must it be like' processes that make use of ongoing tactile-kinesthetic experiences'.[29] He also argues that such allegories take on a symbolic meaning that make them more than just extended metaphors. Here the allegorical meaning is that you can't trust the authenticity of the EU any more that you can believe that a WWF bout is an authentic wrestling match.

In this article Boris goes on to argue that: "In adopting the Chequers proposals, we have gone into battle with the white flag fluttering over our leading tank". Now this powerful symbolic imagery draws on deep ancestral memories of wartime. And in the very worst case scenarios of war: "to break free of the gravitational pull of the EU, and forced to sue for humiliating terms": so he has shifted from the ludic playfulness of 'ding ding' and 'slug fest' that invites embodied simulation to a much more symbolic and mythic allegory of conquest and defeat that evoke moral intuitions related to Sanctity and Degradation. 'Humiliation' became a Boris keyword after Chequers:

> ...to send that tax to Brussels - when Britain has no say whatsoever in setting that tariff. That isn't *taking back control*. It is *losing control*. It is an absolute *humiliation*, and it is quite incredible that the world's fifth biggest economy is willing to sign up for it.[30]

In September 2019 he claimed that the bill to stop the UK from leaving without a deal was a 'Surrender Bill'. While on a trip to India in January 2017 Boris controversially referred to the EU inflicting 'punishment beatings':

> If Mr. Hollande wants to *administer punishment beatings* to anybody who seeks *to escape [the EU]*, in *the manner of some World War II movie*, I don't think that is the way forward, and it's not in the interests of our friends and partners...[31]

I suggest the key to understanding Boris's metaphors is that they initially invite some form of neurological based empathetic response through a process of simulation. This is then developed through the allegories and scenarios that evoke moral intuitions. I suggest that his metaphors trigger embodied simulation on the part of his audience and this achieves rhetorical weight and force. Think for example of the metaphor 'gammon' to describe an angry white pro-Leave supporter who would be outraged by the idea of 'punishment beatings'. The metaphor (though not one likely to be used by Boris) describes the apopelectic reader's embodied simulation, as he turns red as a result of an increase in blood to the face. Consider the following metaphor describing the mental processes of a wavering voter in the polling both:

> You were about to *strike your own small but vital blow* for freedom and democracy - when you suddenly *bottled it. You swerved; you shied; you jibbed; you baulked. You screwed up your eyes* in the polling booth and you found yourself momentarily oppressed by the *sheer weight* of the Remain propaganda - all that relentless misery about this country and its inability *to stand on its own two feet*.[32]

In this extended metaphor we have the same embodied account of a rugby player or a boxer who is shimmying around, trying to stay upright while swaying—the mental turmoil over which way to vote is communicated by metaphors of physical motion. He then continues:

> For reasons you secretly know were nonsensical, you decided to go for what the gloom-mongers had told you was the safer option. *Nose held, eyes screwed tight,* you voted for Remain.[33]

Notice the feelings of physical constraint of the eyes and the nose that are associated with a vote for Remain. The sense of smell is closely related to emotional responsiveness. He then describes:

> A sense of morning-after shame and abject remorse: because the burble from the TV is informing you that Remain have won. Yes, by the narrowest margin you - and *fellow last-minute swervers - have helped to keep us locked in the back of the minicab, with a driver who barely speaks English, going in a direction we don't want to go.*[34]

Here the physical constraint image develops into a scenario in which someone is locked in a minicab and unable communicate with the driver implying that they have lost any physical or psychological control. Boris used the same image in another article only weeks previously:

> If we vote Remain, we *stay locked in the back of the car, driven by someone with an imperfect command of English, and going in a direction we don't want to go.*[35]

'Control' became an obsession for Boris and was expressed through the CONTAINERS ARE BOUNDED SPACES conceptual metaphor that I described in the last chapter. Over two years later the same image of being 'locked in' occurs when he humorously describes his old Japanese car in another extended metaphor:

And yes, it is true that my superb Japanese charabanc is now starting to show its antiquity. The exhaust is knackered, so that the car announces its approach *like a clanking convict;* and *at some speeds there is a tapping as though someone has been locked in a forgotten compartment of its capacious interior.*[36]

There is still the same imagery of physical entrapment within a confined space—that is now forgotten. Consider the following images of physical entrapment:

…with the result that we appear to be heading for a semi-Brexit, with large parts of the economy still *locked in the EU system,* but with no UK *control over that system.*[37]

Then, of course, there is a third way in which people can respond to the disaster of being *locked in a suboptimal currency zone,* when their own region is unable *to compete.*[38]

They cannot understand why we would want—after Brexit—*to stay locked in the orbit* of the EU.[39]

Then *we have locked ourselves in captivity,* by treaty—and *handed the EU the key.* If this is certainty, it is the certainty *of the jail.*[40]

This constant reiteration of a metaphor scenario drawing on the same conceptual metaphor is the basis for an allegory that communicates his moral intuitions about Brexit. The allegory is that national energies have been eviscerated by EU membership and left Britain entrapped and ensnared in the EU container. This is an allegory in which force is applied from the outside to keep Britain confined in a cage, jail or car boot. I will describe this version of the CONTAINERS ARE BOUNDED SPACES conceptual metaphor as 'the allegory of unjust entrapment' it derives from the moral intuitions of Harm, Cheating and, above all, Oppression. We know that our bodies resent being physically trapped—whether in wrestling or when arrested and that the natural response is to struggle for freedom from such entrapment. Consider the end of Boris's resignation letter:

As I said then, the Government now *has a song to sing.* The trouble is that I *have practised the words* over the weekend and find that they *stick in the throat*. We must have collective responsibility. Since I cannot in all conscience champion these proposals, I have sadly concluded that I must go…[41]

On the surface this might look like a singing metaphor, but I think an embodiment explanation works better: the words he wants to get out are trapped in his throat. On examining the force that is making them 'stick' he finds that it is current government policies—so in the moral intuitions that form the basis for the allegory of unjust entrapment the role of the government is identical with that of the EU, so the only just action is to leave the government. His metaphors provoke an embodied form of response because metaphor is a therapeutic reaction to the emotional and ethical disequilibrium caused by the whole issue of EU membership: it is restorative and therapeutic—even though it often works by transferring the pain to his readers.

The Allegory of Unjust Entrapment

Sometimes the allegory of unjust entrapment is creatively elaborated in a humourous, populist, style that is in keeping with the ludic nature of his political persona. Consider these extracts from an article for the Sun where I have numbered and italicised metaphors:

It was two years ago today that the people of this country stunned the world. They defied the experts. They *stuck up two fingers to the gloom merchants*. They disobeyed the warnings of every major political party. (1)

We voted to leave the *bosomy lavender-scented embrace* of the EU after 45 years of membership. In a heroic act of national self-belief we decided to *take back control* of our laws, borders, and all the cash we send to Brussels. (2)

They don't want some *bog roll Brexit - soft, yielding and seemingly infinitely long*. (3)

… We will have the freedom *to bust out of the corsets of EU regulation and rules* - to do things our way, to make the most of British leadership in the growth sectors of tomorrow… (4)

Brexit is the chance *to turbo-charge those capabilities and lengthen our lead*. (5)[42]

In 1 the 'people' have broken the normal constraints on behaviour through the embodied gesture of 'sticking up two fingers': which of us has not at some point responded to an unjust action in a morally intuitive way at some time in our lives? In (2) and (4) the EU is imagined as a bossomy encompassing female—a powerful, oppressive, controlling and unattractive aunt, but these personifications still evoke embodied simulations through their multimodal nature with the combination of smell and touch in (2) and pressure and texture in (3) and (4). Finally in (5) there is an image of release from constraint as Britain becomes a competitive racer. Women are often symbols of ensnarement in Boris's discourse but nearly always, as in the Sun article, humourously; consider another female metaphor that he used as the predominant scenario in a press article:

> We have become *so used to Nanny in Brussels that we have become infantilised, incapable of imagining an independent future.*[43]
> This is a moment to be brave, *to reach out - not to hug the skirts of Nurse in Brussels*, and refer all decisions to someone else.[44]

The nanny image was also alluded to in a different article 10 days later:

> Let's believe in ourselves again, rather than *clutching the skirts of Brussels.*[45]

He frames the EU as a controlling adult, not one of the family but with legitimate authority over the children; but 'Nanny' and 'Nurse' (notice the capital letter initials) are emotionally distant figures who constrain the child. This is an abuse of the Authority/Subversion moral foundation because it is a form of Oppression. The same distancing occurs with the depersonalising metonym 'Brussels' to refer to the European institutions. It contributes to his allegory of unjust entrapment because children cannot choose whether or not they will have a nanny, or nurse, but they usually have to accept their authority over them. The nature of the constraining force implied by the allegory can take different forms:

> They think that the Brexit Bill will get *lost in a House of Commons crevasse or buried....* They think that we will simply despair of *finding the way out of the EU* and *sit down on the floor and cry - like some toddler lost in the maze at Hampton Court.*[46]

Here 'constraint' is like being trapped in a crevasse and then being lost in maze; the sense of unjust of entrapment leads to the ultimate enactment of embodied emotion, when feelings of frustration lead to just sitting down and crying. It is the visceral and embodied nature of these metaphors that evokes responses from his readers such as laughter. Later in the same article the embodied simulation increases in intensity when the metaphors are mixed:

> It was about *trussing the nations together in a gigantic and ever-tightening cat's cradle of red tape.*[47]

Here we have a cat's cradle—a game played by children in which string has the pattern of a cradle; this is blended with the idea of red tape, that which was originally bound around Civil Service documents and has become a symbol of unnecessary bureaucracy: moral intuitions based on the Liberty/Oppression foundation are not always reasoned out but arise from repeated framing over time. This more elaborate mixing of metaphor, like multimodality, enforces simulation so that we experience physically a sensation of painful entrapment. The level of pain became increasingly intense in Boris's allegory of entrapment during the 3-year period (2016–2018) as the withdrawal process proved increasingly complex, and especially following the publishing of the Chequers Withdrawal agreement that Theresa May was offering as the only way to withdraw from the EU. Boris was strongly opposed to this, and in a lengthy article summarised his views with a powerful metaphor:

> But in case the Government continues to brazen it out, let me tell you roughly what that advice says - namely, what every lawyer can see: *that this 175 page backstop is a great steel trap that is about to clamp its jaws around our hind limbs and prevent our escape.*[48]

The level of intensity has increased, we are no longer in the world of being locked in car, a child's game or in a lavender-scented embrace, we have become an ensnared animal in a great steal trap: the visceral character of Boris's metaphors enforce the moral intuitions such as Harm and Oppression that characterise the allegory of entrapment and invite a simulated embodied response. In terms of moral reasoning: the greater the dangers of Britain not exiting the EU without constraints on its future trading relationships the more intense the level of pain caused by the entrapment that prevents such a withdrawal. Consider how he continues later in the article:

> *Whatever we do, and no matter how much we struggle, we will feel the teeth of the trap biting deeper into our flesh.*[49]

Britain has now become a runaway slave, a poacher, an outlaw or a criminal who has been caught in giant mantrap: it is the embodied and visceral nature of Boris's metaphors of entrapment that narrate an allegory based in the moral intuitions of Harm and Oppression with a powerful moral argument: we should break free of these entrapments by restoring Care and Liberty—even by withdrawing without a deal. This is better than staying permanently *trapped* in a customs union and in the single market. The self-righteousness is visceral and is grounded in the Liberty/Oppression moral foundation.

Occasionally Boris offers some glimpse of what release from entrapment might look like, for example in the following—space exploration is used as a symbol of successful technology and science that he frames as offering Britain a way forward (and upward) and employs the metaphor of space exploration:

> So here we go. After nine months on *the launch pad*, Britain finally engaged the *most famous ignition sequence* in diplomatic history. At 12.29 pm London time, the Prime Minister's Article 50 letter was delivered in Brussels and *the countdown began*. After nine months of meticulous legal, technical and political preparation, the *engines switched on* and are today *firing in an irreversible crescendo*. The negotiations are now under way, and when they are complete *this country will have lift off - blast off - for an extraordinary voyage.*[50]

The Reganesque extended metaphor takes us through the stages of a space launch: there is the anticipation of the countdown during which in embodied terms the adrenalin increases, this continues with an 'irreversible velocity' and 'lift off'—the orgasmic moment of release of all the pent up and tedious technical planning. Once again Boris relies on embodied simulation to recreate those emotions of excitement using the source domains of pressure and speed. Sometimes this manifests itself using science-based metaphors:

> We were told that goods would start pinging around the EEC as if in some *supercharged cyclotron*.[51]
> the best minds from across the world are meeting in some of the best pubs and bars and nightclubs like subatomic particles *colliding in a cyclotron* and they are producing those *flashes* of innovation that are essential for long term economic success.[52]

It is important to Boris's image to sustain a self-representation as being free from entrapment, and it is a theme to develops in his speeches with the idea of rejecting the concept of 'fortress Britain':

> ...especially young people who may feel that this decision involves somehow *pulling up the drawbridge* because I think the very opposite is true.[53]
> People believe that *we have thrown up a figurative drawbridge*, made it less easy to live, study, work abroad; and decided to sacrifice the European-ness in our identities.[54]
> We do not want to *haul up the drawbridge*; and we certainly don't want to minimise the wonderful contribution they have made...[55]

The corollary of his argument that the EU is a force of unjust form of entrapment, based on CONTAINERS ARE BOUNDED SPACES, is that the UK is not. But, his desire to emphasise this shows how much images of entrapment frame his thinking and derive from the moral foundations of Care/Harm and Liberty/Oppression.

We may wonder why it is that Boris's dominant metaphors for Britain's relationship with the EU is one of unjust entrapment? Could it be that it is a transfer of his own personal fears, and moral intuitions, about entrapment onto the body politic? Trying to escape from an external force seems to be a key theme in his personal life: he has found personal relationships highly constraining: his marriage to Allegra broke down as he did not seem well equipped for the expectations of a marriage, as she noted: "When we got married, that was the end of relationship, instead of the beginning".[56] His first job with a management consultancy (LEK) involved "grinding numbers, detailed analysis", he walked out after one week and his biographer notes that "It is difficult to imagine a job description less suited to a free spirit with a dislike of detail and team playing". But he also felt constrained by some of the demands of journalism, such as keeping to deadline, a former colleague notes: "Getting copy from Boris was like blood out of a stone"[57] or even keeping to the truth. He lost his first job in journalism for *The Times* after falsely attributing a quotation concerning Edward II and Gaveston to his godfather—an established academic Dr. Colin Lucas—who had to take action by contacting the editor because it was not only falsely attributed but also historically inaccurate. He was not well suited to the constraints of high political office as Foreign Secretary either. For Boris language has been a source of liberation from the constraints of personal relationships and, sometimes, from the constraints of journalistic truth: from the detail and nurturance that both require. In this regard his style, reliant on moral intuitions rather than worked arguments, resonates with the anti-elite discourse of populism.

Boris Johnson's Political Frames

As a politician, rather than as a journalist, Boris naturally absorbs the political frames that I have argued in the previous chapters were central to "Leave" discourse: Patriotism and the Nation, Distrust and Betrayal and War and Invasion. In an article for *The Telegraph* he developed his ideas of national identity by contrasting loyalty to the European Union with loyalty to Britain as if these were *rival* identities rather than complementary ones (the view of many Remainers). He refers to 'people's natural feelings for their own country' and contrasts this with the 'tub-thumping nationalist'—he believes that pride in one's own country is threatened by 'transnational sense of allegiance'[58]: This is the familiar territory of his Middle England readership. Drawing on the frame of Distrust and Betrayal he is constantly fearing that Brexit supporters will be 'cheated' of their success in the referendum:

That means in a very practical sense that we will fail *to take back control* of our borders - and *thus cheat the electorate of a major promise* at the referendum.[59]

While subscribing to both War and Invasion scenarios depending on readership, Boris generally preferred the Invaded Nation one. We saw this already with reference to 'punishment beatings' being inflicted by the EU and his declaration before the referendum that 23 June could be "Britain's Independence Day". In his letter of resignation he wrote: 'In that respect we are truly headed for the status of colony - and many will struggle to see the economic or political advantages of that particular arrangement'. As a former imperial power Britain has always had a somewhat ambiguous relationship with the concept of freedom. Britain's positive self-image as the bastion of democracy has been constrained by its status as an imperial power. In a televised debate at the Wembley arena David Cameron addressed Boris's claim, publicly stating; "the idea that our country isn't independent is nonsense. This whole debate demonstrates our sovereignty".[60] 'Independence' implies invasion and colonisation and Boris sought to free the nation from the feelings that it was constrained by its colonial past by offering an image of liberation from that past that appealed to English nationalism. It is metaphor that provided him with the necessary release from constraint, just as it offered release from literal language. It derives from the moral foundation of Liberty but interlinks at times with Harm, Cheating, Subversion and Degradation.

Other evidence of the Invaded Nation script is in an interview *The Daily Telegraph* in May 2016: "Napoleon, Hitler, various people tried this out, and it ends tragically. The EU is an attempt to do this by different methods".[61] This contributed to a scenario that was reinforced rhetorically by his stance on Islam. *The Daily Telegraph* published Boris's article on the Danish face veil ban. Boris argued against any ban on the burqa or nikab but suggested that such garments make the wearer resemble a "letter box" or a "bank robber". In September 2018, he wrote: "We have opened ourselves to perpetual political blackmail. We have wrapped a suicide vest around the British constitution – and handed the detonator to Michel Barnier"[62]; he was criticised by senior members of his own party but the increase in the intensity and rhetorical force of his metaphor reflects an increasing shift to the political right that corresponds with the level of intensity in the allegory of unjust entrapment: increasing linguistic intensity reveals a shift in political alignment— especially when physical force is implied by the CONTAINERS ARE BOUNDED SPACES conceptual metaphor and the moral foundation of Harm. Right-wing discourse exploits the emotional potential of a metaphor schema in which there is a build up of pressure, and more extreme right-wing or racist discourse refers to critical junctures—such as the explosions of terrorists implied here—at a time when he feared the 'betrayal' of Brexit.

In Chapter 7 we will find that the political framing the European Union as a 'happy family' argued for a closer relationship and explains why Brexiteers such as Boris *avoided* family metaphors altogether when describing the UK relationship with the EU. Boris only used family metaphors to refer to people *within Britain*, or the people who would like to *ally closely with*:

> They are all wrong, and I have seen how championing Global Britain is in the financial interests of every family in this country. British embassies are the vital *beach-heads* for the promotion of British trade, culture, and interests. If you go to them you will see the pulling power of the UK - crowds buzzing with local cabinet ministers and all the bigwigs. And dotted throughout the party are the representatives of *the wider family* of Global Britain.[63]

Here the first mention of 'family' is a literal one, but he shifts to metaphor with the Invasion scenario of 'beach-heads' to introduce the second use of 'family' as a metaphor referring to the 'family of the Commonwealth'; he elaborates on the close and valued relationships with the Commonwealth in some detail in an article for *The Sunday Express*:

> I hope this will be a uniquely memorable gathering, showing just how much importance Britain attaches to the Commonwealth. And I believe that our faith is amply justified. As we celebrate Commonwealth Day

tomorrow, the Commonwealth's 53 members …are joined with us by ties of history and friendship and the English language. They share our values of democracy, human rights and the rule of law.[64]

For Boris 'family' entails mutual obligations and deeper emotional commitments than 'friends' and 'global Britain' extends the family frame to embrace the Commonwealth. While the Commonwealth nations are 'family', the nations in the EU are only 'friends'; for example, in his press articles authored during the 3-year period he uses either the phrase 'European friends' or 'EU friends' 15 times. Once negotiations for the departure of the UK from the EU were underway, he employs 'friends' more than 'family' thereby subtly reframing the relationship as close—but no longer family. He sometimes uses the term 'my friend' ironically—for example when referring to known rivals, but he also personalises his article by using 'my friends' when addressing his readers. He views his 'friends' broadly to include readers across the full social gamut of the British press:

My friends, I must report that there are at least some people who are woefully underestimating this country. They think Brexit isn't going to happen. (*Telegraph*)[65]

Like an unstoppable express, we are heading for Brexit and, frankly *my friends*, we can't arrive soon enough. (*Express*)[66]

A deal - and at long last we will leave the EU, and fulfil the mandate of the June 2016 referendum. Won't we? Alas, *my friends*, we will not. (*Sun*)[67]

The insertion of an address term of endearment in subordinate clauses adds rhetorical weight to the point he is making by delaying actually making it: it's a trick of spoken language to add emphasis by deferring an evaluation.

As a former Foreign Secretary Boris is skilled in the nuances of naming and the hidden definitions that names express: clearly the UK's relationship with the EU is framed as a transactional one. Friends may assist and co-operate with one another but the emotional loyalties of family may be absent; our family is clearly defined and limited in size but, as Facebook has demonstrated, the notion of 'friend' is so loose as to include anyone else in the world. For Boris there are degrees of friendship and friends anyway are only for doing business with:

> We need a new partnership and a new deal with *our friends in the EU,* based on trade and cooperation, but without this supranational apparatus that is so out of date and is imitated nowhere else.[68]

The notion of friendship always implied gritted teeth and the 'nation as family' frame has dominated his rhetoric, even to the extent of including Remainers in the family:

> There were more than 16 million who wanted to remain. They are our *neighbours, brothers and sisters* who did what they passionately believe was right. In a democracy majorities may decide but everyone is of equal value.[69]

He may be alluding to the divisions within his own family, as for example in September 2019 when his brother Jo Johnson resigned from the Cabinet in support of fellow Conservatives who had been thrown out of the party. For Boris departure from the EU was not the end of a marriage but simply the re-alignment of a friendship group to include a wider social network. Typically, Boris combined 'friends' with the more businesslike 'partners':

> That means we can start next year's Brexit negotiations with confidence in our ability to weather any short-term uncertainty - and in Britain's enormous value as a vibrant *trading partner* to our *European friends.*[70]

The combination implies a transactional view of friendship—one that extends beyond trade to security and immigration. Boris made a number of references in his press articles to the idea of Britain having a 'deep and special partnership' with the EU, and attributes the origin of the phrase to Theresa May:

> What we are looking for is not a divorce, not a dissolution of the emotional and psychological bonds between Britain and our European friends, but a transition to a new relationship. The PM calls it a *"deep and special partnership"*, and I believe that concept should be overwhelmingly appealing to the vast majority of people both in this country and on the continent.[71]

The phrase alluded to the 'special relationship' that historically Britain claimed to have with the USA but was probably viewed by EU negotiators as indicating a desire to continue to benefit from its relationship with the EU without making a financial contribution. It is worth noting that Boris quotes the Prime Minister as the source of the metaphor thereby dissociating himself from its authorship claims: it is a third person perspective on how *others* might view the relationship rather than how *he* views it. His model for the relationship between the UK and Europe is a 'partnership'—but very definitely not as part of the same family: relationship metaphors play a crucial role in the framing of political positions as we see in the next chapter.

Even for Boris, after the referendum Europe was no longer to be considered 'the enemy' as metaphors of friendship and neighbourliness were more likely to get a better 'deal' in the negotiations. But when withdrawal negotiations were not going well 'partnership' metaphors were replaced by 'bullying' ones that activate the moral foundation of Liberty and Oppression. Boris quite often talks about 'bullying'—a word that no doubt forms part of the lexicon of his Eton and Oxford pedigree:

> We get an unending and intensifying diet of fear. *We are being bullied* and brow-beaten into remaining in this failing system - and I think the public can see through it.[72]
> ...the experience of Greece alone is a lesson in the absolute insanity of any country allowing itself *to be bullied* by EU negotiators.[73]

Boris was not a leading critic of the EU in relation to the Greek crisis at the time, and yet clearly the memory of a history of bullying is something that he believes necessary to draw on when it is Britain that is being 'bullied' since bullying is indeed a form of oppression.

With the exception of his time as Mayor of London, 'team' is not a word that Boris uses very much and when he does it is as if he were *not a member of that team*; for example:

> But with undimmed energy and enthusiasm, Theresa May and her *team* are determined to get on with the job.[74]

At a time when he was Foreign Secretary it is significant that he refers to 'her' team rather than 'our' team. His biographer notes that in spite of his personal charm and success in building highly prestigious social networks he was neither a team player nor enjoyed clubs—frequently distancing himself from male company. In his articles on Brexit, references to 'clubs' provided a frame for moral reasoning, but Boris always refers to himself or his country as being *outside the club*. He refers to the EU as: 'this club of soi-disant liberal western nations'.[75] Then just four days before the Referendum he asked:

> I believe it is an *unshackling* of Britain. We have now got four days *to take those chains off. If this was a club and you were being asked to join now would you dream of doing it?* The answer is no. So why stay in?[76]

For Boris the idea of teams and clubs, and perhaps marriages, are that they are constraining forces on the individual freedom that he values so highly (except of course the Bullingdon Club); real relationships are those with family alone: all others are for personal advancement. There is therefore conflict between the moral foundations of Loyalty/Betrayal and Liberty/Oppression.

The Nation-as-Body Frame

Politicians often frame international relationships in terms of a competitive race. In a previous study[77] I described how they communicate their will to power by framing international affairs as a race (expressions such as 'global race' or 'race to the bottom') in which countries are equated with runners in a race in which there are only winners and losers. The competitive race metaphor is not one that necessarily has to be applied to nations as a whole: a frequent metaphor used in relation to the pro-Brexit in poorer parts of the UK was that it was a reaction of the 'left behind' parts of the country. The metaphor 'left behind' implies some sort of a race in which there are winners and laggards. Given his highly competitive, individualistic nature and his strong free market ideology it is not surprising that Boris frames the nation of Britain as in a competitive race with the EU:

> ONCE Britain was known as the *'sick man of Europe'*. Now our nation is *racing ahead* economically and has no need of the failing European Union.[78]
>
> She transformed the idea of Britain, the *schwerpunkt*, the *mission statement* – from *sick man of Europe* to *bustling* and dynamic *entrepot*.[79]
>
> In exports *we are thrashed* by other Europeans - France, Germany and Spain.[80]

Britain's quest to withdraw from the EU is viewed as a struggle to win a prize in a competition:

> That was the vision of Brexit we fought for; that was the vision the Prime Minister rightly described last year. That is *the prize that is still attainable*.[81]

The Competitive Race frame activates individual, rational self-interest and argues against values of solidarity and co-operation. The frame accommodates evolutionary psychological views of inherent, biologically determined, male aggression and the 'naturalistic fallacy' that nature is inherently competitive and that humans are driven to self-perpetuate their genes.[82] Since DNA is part of this ideology, politicians that adopt this frame are themselves often members of large dynastic families—as is the case with Boris: family loyalties overriding other types of social relationship. Health metaphors are closely related to embodied simulation because imagining a diseased body invites a simulation of what it would be like to be diseased. The nation as a body metaphor has been summarised by Andreas Musolff:

The NATION-AS-BODY metaphor is lexicalized in English in the phrase body politic, which belongs to a whole field of expressions that refer to political entities in terms of bodily organs and functions, such as head of state, head of government, long arm of the law, organ (of a party), sclerosis or tumor (of the body politic) and others. The phrase body politic appears to have originated in the early 16th century as a loan translation from corpus politicum and was used to describe the political role of the king (as opposed to his physical identity, the "body natural") and by extension, the monarchical state in England. It is still employed today in British and US public discourse...[83]

When the body is ailing this frames a situation that requires some form of 'medicine' or 'surgery'. From at least 1993 onwards the perceived inefficiency of the EU has been described as 'euro-sclerosis'; this metaphor came to symbolise strongly anti-European sentiment for a section of the Conservative Party that later developed into the European Research Group that advocates a complete break from the EU. Boris regularly signals his alliance with this frame by using the same metaphor:

> It (the EU) *is sclerotic, opaque*, elitist: different nations bound together by a centralised bureaucracy that ordinary people can neither understand nor vote out.[84]

The metaphor allies Boris with an ideological framing of THE EUROPEAN UNION as an ILLNESS; this ideology views measures that seek to protect workers, and legislation favouring trade unions, as 'sclerotic' because they encourage government regulation and conflict with the Anglo-American business model with its competitively oriented values. As well as Care/Harm, this draws on the Sanctity/Degradation moral foundation because illness, especially when it is contagious, threatens the sanctity of the body. The metaphor scenario of the following article he wrote for *The Daily Telegraph* on September 28, 2018 is based around notions of embodiment; according to his argument, following Chequers, the British body politic had become increasingly an ailing one. The article commences and ends with reference to having 'the guts' in which Britain has attached itself to a sick body (the EU) and is suffering physical harm from which it must recover. All body related metaphors are in italics; those related to Illness are in bold and I have underlined a frame where loss of control is framed as loss of control over the human body resulting in poor body posture.

> They *saw a body* that has evolved far beyond the "Common Market" they were invited to join, a superstate with no real democratic control.
> In short, they saw a choice between an outdated and **sclerotic EU,** and the chance to do things differently;
> The result was that from the very beginning the British Government **exuded a conspicuous infirmity of purpose**
> It (Chequers proposals) was a further **symptom** of the utter lack of conviction with which the UK embarked on these talks that we so meekly accepted the sequencing proposed by the EU.
> That is a <u>*pretty invertebrate performance.*</u>
> But it is <u>*the UK's supine posture*</u> that has enabled the EU to get away with it.
> We must decide whether we *have the guts* to fulfil the instruction of the people - to leave the EU and truly take back control of our laws and our lives.[85]

In Boris's use of the Nation-as-body frame, we find the same progress that occurred in the allegory of unjust entrapment: as the negotiations became increasingly difficult during the withdrawal period—so the level of intensity of his metaphors, as measured by the level and nature of physical pain that is inflicted in his metaphors, grew. At first it is other bodies that are the victim of an aggressive and unsympathetic EU nurse:

> We have seen what happens when democracy *is elbowed* aside. The Greek people's decisions were ignored by Brussels, which *forced its economic medicine down their throats*, destroying the hopes of a generation and leaving more than half of young people there jobless.[86]

He clearly liked these forceful embodied metaphors because he repeated them the next day:

We have seen what happens when democracy is *elbowed aside*. Brussels ignored the Greek people and *forced its economic medicine down their throats*.[87]

The Greek body politic is no longer sacrosant and has been degraded. In 2017 there was still some hope for the British body politic:

A great, bright, warm six-million-strong *constellation* of British minds and British hearts, *a pulse in the eternal mind*, no less, giving somewhere back the thoughts by Britain given (as Rupert Brooke almost puts it).[88]

But by the summer of 2018 when negotiations were not going so well the metaphors of embodiment increase in their force and become an allegorical account expressing a high degree of pain:

We must try now, because we will not have another chance to get it right. It is absolute nonsense to imagine - as I fear some of my colleagues do - that we can somehow afford to make a *botched* treaty now, and then *break and reset the bone later on*.[89]

He repeated the same metaphor of 'breaking and resetting the bone' at the end of the article: a sure sign that it offers an allegory advising on the need to tolerate short term pain for long term gain: if we don't get the right deal now, then it will much more painful later on—so this is a sort of inversion of the Care/Harm moral foundation where Care requires inflicting immediate Harm in order to restore the sanctity of the body. Indeed pain was something he expressed views on in his party conference speech in October 2017:

Humanity will always have its afflictions in mind or body because without pain and doubt and anxiety there can be no pleasure and no triumph and no success.[90]

But by the end of November 2018 the negotiations with the EU were going so badly, with the UK's refusal to budge on the backstop, that Boris articulates the pain and suffering to be inflicted on the body politic of the UK:

In the protocol on Northern Ireland, there is a note almost of malice, as though *the EU is punishing us by the surgical severing of part of the UK.* From one convoluted paragraph to the next, you can follow the *plot to amputate Northern Ireland* and keep it in the EU - run by the EU, but with no influence in Brussels except via Dublin.[91]

Here, we have an allegory of unnecessary surgery, whether botched or otherwise, it is a surgery that is being inflicted on a patient who does not wish to undergo surgery and is therefore closer to torture breaking the rules of appropriate Care and infringing the moral foundation of Sanctity/Degradation. The nation-as-body frame in which in its milder form is just losing a race, ends up like a Henry More torso with a few flailing stumps for limbs: it is a body that is having its bones broken and its limbs amputated. The visceral nature of the moral reasoning in this frame therefore complements the same story that is told in the allegory of unjust entrapment, but it has become a medieval morality tale. Together his allegories of pain are viscerally expressive and quite unique to Boris's style of political communication and perhaps culminated in his claim of September 2019 that he would rather be found "dead in a ditch" than agree to a further extension of Brexit.

Summary

In this chapter I have argued that simulated embodiment helps us to interpret Boris Johnson' journalistic and political frames. As well as reinforcing typical Leave frames such as 'Distrust and Betrayal' and 'War and Invasion', the concept of enforced constraint by an oppressive EU leads to an Allegory of Unjust Entrapment in which an alien force—whether a foreign taxi driver or Nanny Brussels ensnares Britain within a container, following the CONTAINERS ARE BOUNDED SPACES conceptual metaphor, from which it is morally obliged to release itself. As well as offering humour and ribaldry, the embodied nature of his metaphors of constraint and release fits within a larger Nation-as-Body frame that includes frames for Darwinian competition, illness and allegories of pain and suffering. These derive from moral intuitions such as Care/Harm, Fairness/Cheating, Sanctity/Degradation and, above all, Liberty/Oppression, but are also employed in moral reasoning and include all the moral foundations identified by Haidt.

The embodied, visceral and fractured style of his allegories corresponds with the view of a leading Irish commentator who noted that the leaders of the Brexit campaign:

> …offer a jagged razor of incoherent English nationalism to distressed and excluded communities and say, 'Go cut yourself, it feels good'. It does feel good. It is exhilarating and empowering. It makes English hearts beat faster and the blood flow more quickly – even if it's their own blood that's flowing'.[92]

What is the origin of Boris's allegories and morality tales? What are the processes through which he creates empathy with his readers through embodied simulation? His biographer describes how Boris prepared for writing an explosive article:

> After locking his door, he could then work himself into a frenzy by hurling repeated four-letter abuse at a ragged yucca plant near his desk.… anyone passing ..could not help but be alarmed at the torrent of guttural roars and full volume expletives from the bay window above. His outburst spent he would settle down to his keyboard to dash off at hurtling speed – and with a violent fist-handed typing style – another brilliantly damaging and inventive thousand words.[93]

Presumably the basis for his invective was in embodied simulation: he would identify the topics that the 'gammons' might, based on their moral intuitions, feel frustrated about—Brussels diktats etc.—then verbally and physically re-enact the introspective states that he had acquired during experience of occasions when he had personally felt frustrated. By simulating the experience of his readers (which might have had quite different triggers from his genuine sources of frustration,) he was able to reach an embodied state based on moral intuitions that could create visceral allegory. This has similarities with boot camp training methods where shouting is used to trigger cognitive re-enactment that in turn triggers real emotions and their embodied responses: once the neural pathways are stimulated by physical shouting this allows the re-activation of episodic experiences hidden in personal memories. Similarly, actors prepare for roles by using physical movements and verbal actions because this allows them to suppress their own personality to simulate the emotions of a fictional persona. For a man who had born the scars of physical pain in the past, this was perhaps not so difficult. In writing of his prep school experience in the 1970s when masters could legitimately inflict pain on their charges he wrote: "I remember being so enraged at being whacked for talking at the wrong moment that it has probably given me a lifelong distrust of authority".[94] This makes one wonder how far those masters were responsible for contributing to the mental state of one of the fathers of Brexit: when penning his articles was he imagining himself delivering a sound thrashing, or enacting the verbal equivalent of kicking the cat?

Notes

1. *The Telegraph*, 29 January 2004.
2. Meeting, 25 February 2013.
3. This is explained in Chapter 9.
4. *The Express*, 4 October 2017.
5. *MailOnline*, 21 May 2017.
6. *The Daily Telegraph*, 8 February 2010.
7. Purnell, S. (2011), p. 156.
8. *The Daily Telegraph*, 20 June 2016.
9. Speech, 2 October 2018.
10. *The Sunday Times*, 18 June 2017.
11. Purnell, S. (2011), p. 162.
12. gian paolo accardo @gpaccardo, 20 Jun 2016.
13. Tom Spilsbury @TomSpilsbury, 22 Jun 2016.
14. Anna Chen @MadamMiaow,22 Jun 2016.
15. BBC News (UK) @BBCNews, 21 Jun 2016.
16. Purnell, S. (2011).
17. *The Daily Telegraph*, 25 April 2016.
18. *The Telegraph*, 13 December 2007.

19. *The Daily Telegraph*, 27 August 2018.
20. *The Express*, 4 October 2017.
21. Purnell, S. (2011), p. 262.
22. Purnell, S. (2011), p. 282.
23. https://www.theguardian.com/politics/2008/may/01/boris.livingstone.
24. https://www.telegraph.co.uk/news/uknews/1557548/Boris-Johnson-in-quotes.html.
25. *MailOnline*, 21 May 2017.
26. *The Sunday Times*, 18 June 2017.
27. *i-Independent*, 9 August 2018.
28. *The Daily Telegraph*, 3 September 2018.
29. Gibbs, R.W. (2015), p. 266.
30. *Telegraph*, 28 October 2018.
31. Boris Johnson, Remarks, 18 January 2017, https://www.politico.eu/article/boris-johnson-to-france-no-punishment-beatings-over-brexit-hollande/.
32. *The Daily Telegraph*, 6 June 2016.
33. Ibid.
34. Ibid.
35. *The Daily Telegraph*, 20 June 2016.
36. *Telegraph.co.uk*, 28 October 2018.
37. Resignation Letter, 10 July 2018
38. 30 May 2016, https://www.facebook.com/borisjohnson/posts/yes-indeed-let-us-talk-about-economics-lets-look-at-the-real-economic-impact-of-/10153725173711317/.
39. *The Daily Telegraph*, 28 September 2018.
40. *Telegraph.co.uk*, 25 November 2018.
41. Resignation Letter, 10 July 2018.
42. *The Sun*, 23 June 2018.
43. *The Daily Telegraph*, 22 February 2016.
44. Ibid.
45. *The Sun*, 3 March 2016.
46. *Telegraph.co.uk*, 15 September 2017.
47. Ibid.
48. *Telegraph.co.uk*, 2 December 2018.
49. Ibid.
50. *The Daily Telegraph*, 30 March 2017.
51. Speech, 9 May 2016.

52. Speech, 2 October 2016.
53. Speech, 24 June 2016.
54. Speech, 14 February 2018.
55. Ibid.
56. Purnell, S. (2011), p. 98.
57. Ibid. 109.
58. *Telegraph.co.uk*, 15 September 2017.
59. *Telegraph.co.uk*, 28 September 2018.
60. David Cameron, https://www.theguardian.com/politics/2016/jun/22/brexit-independence-day-claim-nonsense-says-david-cameron.
61. https://www.telegraph.co.uk/news/2016/05/14/boris-johnson-the-eu-wants-a-superstate-just-as-hitler-did/.
62. https://www.independent.co.uk/news/uk/politics/brexit-boris-johnson-suicide-vest-theresa-may-chequers-a8529436.html.
63. *The Daily Telegraph*, 16 July 2018.
64. *The Sunday Express*, 11 March 2018.
65. *Telegraph.co.uk*, 15 September 2017.
66. *The Express*, 29 March 2018.
67. *The Sun*, 15 November 2018.
68. *The Daily Telegraph*, 29 February 2016.
69. *The Daily Telegraph*, 27 June 2016.
70. *The Daily Telegraph*, 29 November 2016.
71. *The Daily Telegraph*, 30 March 2017.
72. *The Daily Telegraph*, 13 June 2016.
73. *The Daily Telegraph*, 27 August 2018.
74. *The Daily Telegraph*, 22 June 2017
75. *The Daily Telegraph*, 18 April 2016.
76. *Daily Star Sunday*, 19 June 2016.
77. Charteris-Black (2017).
78. *Express Online*, 22 June 2016.
79. Speech, 27 November 2013.
80. Speech, 28 May 2018.
81. Speech, 19 July 2018.
82. Goatly, A. (2007) *Washing the Brain—Metaphor & Hidden Ideology* (p. 159). Amsterdam and Philadelphia: John Benjamins.
83. Musolff, A. (2014).
84. *The Daily Telegraph*, 13 June 2016.
85. *The Daily Telegraph*, 28 September 2018.

86. *Mirror*, 21 June 2016.
87. *Daily Mirror*, 22 June 2016.
88. *Telegraph*, 15 September 2017.
89. *Daily Telegraph*, 19 July 2018.
90. Speech, 3 October 2017.
91. *Telegraph.co.uk*, 18 November 2018.
92. O'Toole, F. (2018), p. 132.
93. Purnell, S. (2011), p. 123.
94. *The Telegraph.co.uk*, 26 October 2009.

References

Charteris-Black, J. (2017). Competition Metaphors & Ideology: Life as a Race. In R. Wodak and B. Forchtner (Eds.), *The Routledge Handbook of Language and Politics* (pp. 202–217). London and New York: Routledge.

Gibbs, R.W. (2015). The Allegorical Characters of Political Metaphors in Discourse. *Metaphor and the Social World* 5, 2: 264–282.

Goatly, A. (2007). *Washing the Brain: Metaphor and Hidden Ideology*. Amsterdam: John Benjamins.

Musolff, A. (2014). The Metaphor of the "Body Politic" Across Languages and Cultures. In F. Polzenhagen, Z. Kövecses, S. Vogelbacher, and S. Kleinke (Eds.), *Cognitive Explorations into Metaphor and Metonymy* (pp. 85–99). Frankfurt: Peter Lang.

O'Toole, F. (2018). *Heroic Failure: Brexit and the Politics of Pain*. London: Zeus.

Purnell, S. (2011). *Just Boris: The Irresistible Rise of a Political Celebrity*. London: Aurum Press.

7

Happy Families and Special Relationships

The Family Frame

In this chapter I explore the extent to which the moral and political issues underlying Britain's decision to leave the EU were communicated through metaphors deriving from the family and other types of relationship such as being a 'friend' or 'partner'. Drawing on the 'nation-as-person frame', knowledge of interpersonal relationships provided the grounds for metaphors to discuss moral issues arising from Brexit. When a nation is framed as a person it implies that its relationship with other nations are like interpersonal relationships: just as a person can get married, so an outward looking alliance with another country can be described metaphorically as a 'marriage' bringing in various moral foundations. This frame takes its origin in the way that sovereign rulers—medieval kings, queens, princes and princesses—resolved political tensions, or guarded against invasion, by marrying a symbolic figure from a rival sovereign power: war could be prevented through such symbolic acts. The argument of the 'nation as person' frame is that two nations can become, metaphorically, a family by creating a symbolic link through their royal families; this frame embraces

© The Author(s) 2019
J. Charteris-Black, *Metaphors of Brexit*,
https://doi.org/10.1007/978-3-030-28768-9_7

international relationships with other nation-persons wishing voluntarily to make a family together. The body politic is sustained through the body of the head of state.

But there is a second frame in which the nation as a whole is framed as a family. This metaphor has a different argument because it implies that a shared sense of belonging is best found through the idea of a family *within the nation*. I will refer to this as the 'nation as family' frame. It is one that motivates words such as 'fatherland' or referring to people as 'brothers and sisters' because they are from the same nation and share a common history. The 'nation as family' frame overcomes divisions within a group of people and is inward looking and tribal in nature and relies on the moral foundation of Loyalty among and towards family members. By contrast, when a group of nations refers to itself metaphorically as a 'family' it draws on the moral foundation of mutual Care and implies that our shared sense of identity reaches out across national boundaries. It is outward looking and can overcome tensions and conflicts between sovereign nation states by rejecting blood-based tribalism because of the harm it causes.

Although the 'nation as person' frame is apparently more individualist it creates the potential for a sense of a shared common identity as being human rather than simply British. People who rely exclusively for their sense of identity using 'nation as family' are those who define themselves in terms of geographically based sovereignty, whereas those who reject this metaphor as inadequate for working out relationships with people from *other* groups prefer frames that allow them to feel human *anywhere*. Whether offering a model for understanding the relationships just *within* a nation, or those *between* nations, the family frame is highly potent because it draws on what most people experience as their first social unit: where they learnt how to feel and where they learnt the difference between right and wrong. Some insight into the tension between the 'nation as person' and the 'nation as family' frames can be shown by a YouGov poll conducted in 2011 showing that 62% agreed with the statement: "Britain has changed in recent times beyond recognition, it sometimes feels like a foreign country and this makes me uncomfortable"[1]: if Britain now felt like a foreign country then this indicated it no longer felt like a family. With the referendum result going their way, Leave politicians now referred to European nations using other types of metaphor such as 'friends' and 'neighbours'. These politicians relied on the 'nation as family' frame since it provided the basis for an outlook based on national identity: if Britain didn't feel like a family it certainly should do. I will also suggest that in their desire to seem patriotic many Remain supporters inadvertently followed them in adopting the tribal 'nation as family' frame based on the morality of Loyalty and Betrayal.

The historical practice of establishing power relationships between nations as if they were individual people reinforced the potential for both frames to ensure the legitimacy of the head of states. The 'family as nation' frame allowed rulers to take on the authority that 'parents' naturally have over their citizen 'children' and so also relies on the moral foundation of Authority. Many national leaders have been given the official or unofficial title of 'father of the nation'; this title derives from the Latin expression *Pater Patriae* and was bestowed in Rome by the Senate on those deemed worthy of the title. In some cases the honorific title has been bestowed on women, when Queen Victoria was known as the 'grandmother of Europe' after nine of her children married into Royal families across Europe—this implied a group of nations were a family; similarly, the current German Chancellor is nicknamed Mutti or 'mama' but she is as much mother of Europe as she is of Germany (a metaphor that somehow escaped the British Prime Minister Theresa May). The founders of the USA are known as the 'founding fathers' and the leaders of many newly independent nations adopted the title 'father of the nation'. Such leaders sought legitimacy with reference to the social unit of the family, since this entailed a reciprocal moral obligation between the citizens and the leader of the newly formed nation: in exchange for care and protection they demanded loyalty and authority.

I would like to provide evidence of how the family frame has dominated Brexit by considering kinship terms in the press. In the three-year period prior to 1 January 2016 there was not a single press article that contained both the words 'Brexit' and a kinship term in its headline, however in the three year period 2016–2018 there were 456 press articles that included 'family' and 'Brexit' in their headline and 542 articles that included 'Brexit' and another kinship term in their headline. The most frequent term 'brother' occurred in 95 articles with some reference to Boris Johnson, many alluding to different views on Brexit within the Johnson family (particularly his father's decision to join his son's pro-Brexit position), 24 included a reference to David Cameron and 20 a reference to Nigel Farage. The media had clearly identified the cast for a British family drama that was to run and run arousing passions and reflecting a debate characterised by the emotions aroused by family rows: the press offered numerous stories on how opposing stances on Brexit led couples to divorce.

While family metaphors were highly popular in the media and on social media because of their potential for arousing powerful emotions, politicians supporting Leave, such as Boris Johnson and Jacob Rees-Mogg, were cautious about using such metaphors in their official statements in the period after Britain's withdrawal. The metaphor of 'the European family' had long been used by the European Commission as way of expressing a shared identity. This frame was a response to the social identities based on the 'nation as family' frame that had caused two World Wars: if the family were Europe, rather than the nation, then EU nations had the same sorts of moral obligations and reciprocal responsibilities towards each other—for physical protection and financial support—as do members of a family. The organisers and leaders of Leave wanted to reserve the powerful emotional resonance of 'nation as family' exclusively for feelings about the homeland and therefore preferred to think of other European countries as 'partners' rather than as 'family'. It was essentially this shift in metaphors that created the political distancing from Europe that was fundamental to their goals. More than just rhetoric, metaphor *actualised* the types of relationship on which they modelled the future. Brexiteers strongly advocated that Britain would continue to be a close 'friend' or 'partner' of the EU—but reserved the term 'family' either for members of the British nation, or for other Commonwealth nations where English was spoken. Ironically, the British family has turned out to be a curiously dysfunctional one, characterised as much by Betrayal as by Loyalty!

As well as discussion of financial matters and the legal intricacies of Britain's departure, there is another deeper role for family metaphors in the discourse of Brexit: this is discussion of moral issues and obligations. For these reasons I agree with George Lakoff that 'family' metaphors contribute to an ideologically based worldview of political morality in which individuals take on moral responsibilities by virtue of their parenting style.[2] In a way that was also used by Haidt in his work on moral foundations and the righteous mind, Lakoff employs what he refers to as a 'model' or 'worldview' based on the family to account for differences between political affiliation: he associates a Conservative worldview of politics as deriving from a model based on 'strict father' morality and a Liberal worldview of politics as deriving from a model based on 'Nurturant Parent' morality.[3] The 'Strict Father' worldview is based on an assumption of the inherent badness of human nature, and so the moral responsibility of the father is to foster individualism and self-discipline to overcome this; by contrast, the Nurturant Parent worldview derives from a belief in the inherent goodness of human nature that needs to be brought out by a parent who does not enforce traditional roles. Developments of this approach distinguish between those that keep to one or other of these moral stances on parenting, and 'biconceptuals' who shift their stance according to the particular topic, so parents may be Strict Fathers in their attitude to crime and debt, but Nurturant Parents in their attitude to the environment or same sex marriage.[4] Another possibility is that such biconceptuals may oscillate between stances depending on the political topic. In the case of Brexit for example, someone may have a Strict Father view in relation to immigration and crime but a Nurturant Parent one in relation to European social policies.

However, as with Haidt's moral foundations model, the purpose of Lakoff's model was to describe differences between Conservative and Liberal worldviews within a single country—The United States—and was not intended to offer an account of international relationships. Brexit was remarkable in that affiliations did not reflect whether people were politically oriented to the 'left' or the 'right'. In the Brexit debate the binary choice of Leave or Remain did not correspond with Lakoff's Conservative and Liberal worldviews and nor did it relate to national political considerations. As a result family metaphors, while still highly moral, have to be modified in various ways when discussing international relationships. For example, Lakoff's 'Strict Father' and 'Nurturant Parent' model does not discuss the stages in a relationship through which families go in divorce and the emergence of new types of relationship: it is essentially static. Lakoff's model is concerned with how political outlooks reflect parenting styles. But Brexit was not about parenting styles, it concerned relationships between metaphorical 'brothers', 'sisters', 'lovers' and 'partners', and *which* people were considered to be in one's own group. In this chapter I suggest that the position on Brexit determined whether agents (Twitter activists, politicians etc.) persisted with 'family' metaphors or replaced them with less emotionally resonant metaphors such as 'partner' or 'neighbour'. I demonstrate how metaphor choice defined political stance and how these contested positions are better understood as 'relationship frames'. I also compare how Leave and Remain politicians and opinion formers employ family frames and other relationship frames such as 'enemy' or 'club'. I explain how those who advocated leaving the EU reframed Britain's relationship with Europe in terms of 'friendship' or other relationship metaphors that imply a different set of moral obligations from family ones. In the following chapter I will then explore how the relationship frame provided basis for thinking of Britain's relation as a marriage that had ended in a divorce.

Relationship Terms

Relationship terms include 'partner', 'friend', and 'neighbour' that all have the potential to express a relationship as being more or less close in emotional terms: 'blood is thicker than water' because family relationships are idealised as being emotionally closer than friends and certainly entail a higher level of moral and legal responsibility. 'Partner' does not specify the nature of the relationship, other than from context; for example a business partner may not be someone we are close to, but 'partner' can also refer to an emotionally and sexually intimate relationship that does not necessarily entail marriage. People often use the term 'partner' when they seek to avoid having to specify either whether or not they are married or whether or not they are in a same sex relationship; so 'partner' is potentially ambiguous regarding the emotional closeness it expresses—it is a phrase that people use when viewing their relationship from an external perspective. 'Neighbour' is more distant emotionally as it is spatially defined: someone who lives next to us but is separate from us as in the proverb 'Good fences make good neighbours'. We choose our friends and partners but not our neighbours—although we don't choose most of our family either! I will illustrate how variations as to whether other European nations were described metaphorically as part of the same 'family', 'friends', 'partners' or 'neighbours' became an important marker of political stance and reflected shifting political viewpoints.

I compared five relationship terms on Twitter and in newspaper headlines in the three-year period from 1 January 2016 until 31 December 2018. My purpose was to establish how far such relationship metaphors were used to frame a story on Brexit based on considerations whether they were used on social media or in the press and how far political outlook influenced metaphor choice. The phrases I examined can be sequenced in terms of the emotional closeness, so a family metaphor conveys a higher level of intimacy than a friendship metaphor, which in turn conveys a higher level of intimacy than 'partner' or 'neighbour' metaphors. The more a relationship is thought of as a family one, the more intense the moral intuitions, based on the Loyalty, and even the Sanctity, of the family are aroused. The phrases I searched were 'European family', 'family of nations', 'European friends', 'European neighbours' and 'European partners'. I also looked at other relationship metaphors such as 'enemy' and 'club' in addition to kinship terms such as 'father', 'mother', 'brother', 'sister' and 'child'.

I searched the 3-year period in 6 blocks of six months each, noticing how far the use of a particular metaphor increased or decreased according to the overall context of the political events of the campaign, the Referendum itself and the subsequent negotiations to leave the EU. For Twitter I searched the relationship phrases under the hashtags #Brexit; #Remain and #Leave. I also wanted to establish whether there were differences in how the 'Remain' and 'Leave' supporters framed their stories on social media as compared with the press. Using the Nexis database I undertook a search of all articles in this period that had 'Brexit' in the headline alongside one of the five relationship-related phrases in the main text of the article. The primary purpose of newspaper headlines is to engage readers' interests so as to encourage them to read the article; they often do this by triggering a particular frame of interpretation that corresponds with readers' anxieties, concerns, interests and moral foundations. This allowed me to establish the how the pro-Brexit and pro-Remain press framed the relationship between the UK and the EU and identify any differences from how it was framed on Twitter. The numerical findings for the analysis of both Twitter and the press are shown in Tables 7.1 and 7.2.

All five 'relationship' metaphors are used frequently throughout the period in the press and on Twitter. 'European partners' was consistently the most frequent in press headlines, followed by 'European neighbours'; by contrast, the emotionally warmer 'European friends' was the most frequent on Twitter—especially in the campaign period and again in 2018 when pro-Europeans took to Twitter in their quest for a people's vote. In both mediums those who wanted to express emotional proximity to Europe referred to their 'European friends' whereas those seeking a more emotionally detached political alignment used 'European partners' and both phrases were more common on Twitter in 2018 as compared with 2017. 'European friends' was used frequently on Twitter in the campaign period whereas 'European neighbours' occurred consistently throughout the period and was less likely to be used on social media by Remain activists. Following the campaign result 'European friends' served as a more general relationship term without the emotional coerciveness of family metaphors and in keeping with the broad, and sometimes meaningless sense, in which it is used by Facebook (surely having met someone is a prerequisite for friendship but I still get 'friends requests' from people whom I have never met). In particular, Leave supporters saw the phrase as a strategically important metaphor for maintaining relationships with the EU—even if they were not as close as previously. An overview of how relationships are expressed using metaphors based on spatial relationships is shown in Fig. 7.1.

When the EU is referred to as part of the self (as when someone says 'I feel more European that I do British') this expresses the highest level of emotional engagement and metaphor is not used. But when the EU is referred to as a 'family' member this expresses a higher degree of

Table 7.1 Relationship metaphors on Twitter: January 2016–December 2018

	January–June 2016	July–December 2016	January–June 2017	July–December 2017	January–June 2018	July–December 2018	Total
'European friends'	96	39	44	42	84	64	369
'European partners'	77	38	43	35	81	65	339
'European neighbours'	41	30	38	38	42	40	229
'European family'	83	14	32	23	24	29	205
'Family of nations'	13	15	14	16	18	12	88
Total	310	136	171	154	249	210	1230

Table 7.2 Relationship metaphors in press headlines: January 2016–December 2018

	January–June 2016	July–December 2016	January–June 2017	July–December 2017	January–June 2018	July–December 2018	Total
'European partners'	272	283	424	132	115	105	1331
'European neighbours'	190	163	135	103	100	67	758
'European friends'	62	151	53	69	25	30	390
'European family'	25	4	58	6	7	9	109
'Family of nations'	7	36	12	4	5	9	73
Total	556	637	682	314	252	220	2661

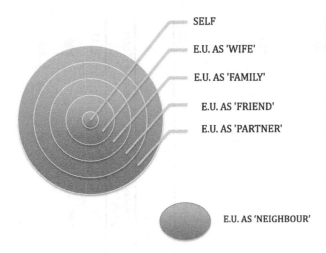

Fig. 7.1 Relationships as spatial proximity

emotional engagement than when it is referred to as a 'friend', which in turn expresses an emotionally more proximate relationship (we feel 'closer' to it) than when it is referred to as just a 'partner'. When the EU is referred to as a 'neighbour' it is no longer part of *our* group and is only geographically proximate rather than emotionally close.

The 'European Family' and the 'Family of Nations'

Metaphors that referred to Europe as a family were mainly in tweets and in pro-Remain press headlines that advocated Britain's continuing membership; framing the European Union as a family argued that there was a stronger and more intimate relationship than one based on friendship alone. Although family metaphors were less frequent in both mediums than other relationship metaphors, 'European family' served as a unifying slogan for those who supported 'Remain', and this filtered through to the press in the first part of 2017. 'Family of nations' peaked in press headlines following the Referendum to reflect support for internationalist sentiment based in the moral foundation of Care.

There were some interesting fluctuations; for example 'European family' was used on Twitter much more during the referendum campaign. The metaphor declined in the period immediately after the result but then revived again from January 2017. The metaphor always implied a strongly pro-EU position and many quoted a speech from Churchill's in September 1946 that was organised around the 'European family' metaphor in which he set as a goal: 'Our constant aim must be to build and fortify the strength of the United Nations Organisation. Under and within that world concept, we must re-create the European family in a regional structure called, it may be, the United States of Europe'. Many across Europe viewed this as a mission statement for the formation of a European Union—although it was not clear what Britain's role would be as Churchill went on to say: 'In all this urgent work, France and Germany must take the lead together', Britain and America's role was to be: 'the friends and sponsors of the new Europe'. So while Churchill advocated a 'European family', based on the nation as person frame he viewed Britain as a friend rather than as a family member. In spite of this strong advocates of Remain preferred 'family' to 'friend' metaphors:

> If Europe is to be saved from infinite misery, and indeed from final doom, there must be an act of faith in the *European family* - Churchill (45 retweets)[5]

The 'European family' metaphor served as a rallying cry for those who could not accept that the UK had left the European family. Strong pro-Europeans continued to allude to Churchill's metaphor including the EU's Brexit negotiator Guy Verhofstadt who viewed it as rhetorical appealing to young people:

> "There will be a young man or woman who will try again, who will lead Britain again into the *European family*...and a young generation that will see Brexit for what it really is," Guy Verhofstadt, the European Parliament's Brexit negotiator, said.[6]

In terms of the Brexit negotiations, the metaphor was one that could be deployed to argue for the continuation of the 'European family' after

Britain's departure, but also the hope that it would not be a permanent situation and since one can never really leave a family, highlighted the option of a return:

> There are no winners from #Brexit. The departure of the U.K. from the EU is a failure for everybody. Let us make the best of it, knowing that in the near future, there will be a new generation in Britain who will decide to come back into the *European family*. #IamEuropean. (3100 retweets)[7]

Others viewed Britain's departure as strengthening the surviving family—like bereavement, it would bring the surviving 'family members' closer together within the comforting bosom of the family:

> Joseph Muscat, prime minister of Malta - which holds the EU's rotating presidency - said the bloc had never been more unified than in its policy towards Brexit. I spoke and visited basically all other 26 member states and there's a... convergence on the attitude towards Brexit. I have never seen such a convergence within the *European family*.[8]

The appeal of the 'family' metaphor is based on the moral foundation of Loyalty. A phrase that extended the metaphor into a more fully formed political slogan was 'the European family of nations'; a Remain activist exhorted his followers to demonstrate support for the EU by appealing to their sense of family membership:

> For our place in the *European family of nations*, for your country, for your community, for your family, for your enlightenment values, fight #Brexit. Talk to your family, neighbours and work colleagues, we can win this! It's up to us! (36 retweets)[9]

Notice how he avoids mentioning the opposition (apart from the hashtag) and frames the appeal of the European union entirely in positive concepts such as 'enlightenment values' that invite solidarity. This is in contrast to other tweeters who—while still using the same metaphor—do so in a tone that is angrier and expresses negative feelings towards Leavers:

Tired of #Leavers *bleating* on about EU being difficult. The UK is being driven from *the EU family* of 500m by a minority of 17m. Why should the EU *kowtow* to an unrepresentative few? It looks after the interests of all, including we Remainers and those who didn't vote for a change. (208 retweets)[10]

Here 'bleating' is a metaphor that implies that Leavers are sheep, and 'driven' implies physical force, rather than the outcome of a democratic process; 'kowtow' emphasises a relationship of servitude, the moral appeal is on the basis of Betrayal rather than Loyalty. The risk is that these words will have the opposite of their intended effect by antagonising those who voted 'Leave' rather than appealing to them, thereby strengthening their opposition to Remain on the basis of counter-loyalties and reinforcing the 'Remoaner' stereotype coined by the pro-Brexit press.

A staunch Remain activist, Graham Simpson, only employs negative language to target symbols of Brexit rather than people who voted Leave. Linking to a photo he contrasts the solidarity symbolised by of Macron and May standing side by side alongside an isolated Theresa May. The accompanying text reads:

One confident, assured, backed by the *European family of nations*. The other, in office but not in power, complicit in the weakening of her country, economically, diplomatically and socially. #Brexit reality. (299 retweets)[11]

A corollary to the more united Europe invited by Brexit was that Britain would be excluded from, and even ostracised by, the European family to its own detriment. *The Observer* quoted David McAllister, a German MEP:

No one, he says, "wants to be nasty" to the UK, but it is the one which has asked to leave. "We didn't ask for this divorce. Sorry. But we are members of a *family of nations* and were happy to have our British *neighbours, friends, allies in our family.* But they have asked to *leave the family.* They have got to sort this out."[12]

In press articles the phrase 'EU family' usually referred to negotiations surrounding the many families from the EU that lived in the UK and visa versa. However, the EU employed the phrases metaphorically on the national days of EU member states:

> Happy National Day, Spain! ¡Feliz Fiesta Nacional, España!
> Spain *joined the EU family* in 1986, committed to the European project
> #12octFiestaNacional (1400 retweets)[13]

The tweet includes images of the Spanish and EU flags and a party popper. Identical messages were posted for more nations such as Sweden and Denmark on their national days. The metaphor of the European family at times served as a propaganda tool by those who were opposed to Brexit and official representatives of the European Commission. Fear of exclusion from such a family and becoming an outcast was viewed as a powerful argument to prevent Brexit. Only as a last resort would someone voluntarily seek to leave a family, to become an orphan, and only when the relationships were highly damaging. However, given the disruption caused by Brexit, and the evident lack of unity within Britain, the type of family that has emerged appears to be a highly dysfunctional one. Issues of degrees of citizenship have raised difficult questions of what constitutes membership of the 'British family': for former Commonwealth citizens, for Muslims as well as for those who originate from European countries. Consider the following tweet by Ravi Singh:

> My father served in British Navy & was a POW in Singapore.
> Sad to see so much racist rhetoric in #Brexit campaign> (+ link to a sikh holding up a handwritten sign that reads: 'I AM AN IMMIGRANT DON'T USE PEOPLE LIKE ME TO JUSTIFY RACIST POLITICAL AGENDAS!!!! RAVI SINGH' (149 retweets)[14]

It reminds us that many immigrants had come to view themselves full members of the British family by virtue of their rights as Commonwealth citizens who had fought for Britain—a different family of nations. There were considerations of shared language and shared history that were not fully accommodated by either the notion of

Britain or the EU as 'family' but which some Eurosceptics employed to argue for the Commonwealth as offering an alternative 'family' to the European Union on the basis of an appeal to the moral foundation of Loyalty. These were examined in the last chapter on Boris Johnson.

Family metaphors in general are potentially coercive because of their potential to arouse explosive emotions by ideas of betrayal, which is probably why there has been a shift over to the less emotionally intense metaphors of European 'friends' and 'partners' as the withdrawal period has progressed. This may also be why some Brexit supporters showed awareness of the propaganda value of the 'European family' metaphor by using it ironically:

> Sure aren't we all just one *big happy European Family*? Oh yeah #Brexit![15]
>
> Jokes aside. The EU isn't happy about #Brexit not because it loses a member of a "*big European family*". The EU gets from us more than we get from them. The sooner we leave, the better. (14 retweets)[16]

Supporters of Brexit often tweeted 'father' literally as a form of emotional appeal based on their father's war record

> Happy Father's Day - I shall think of the freedoms my old man and the other lost dads fought for when I #VoteLeave (173 retweets)[17]

Other highly coercive posts were evidently far right propaganda:

> No good father can sit quietly while a mass invasion of anti-western muslims are coming to destroy our culture and country. #Brexit #MAGA (21 retweets)[18]

This is based on an appeal to the moral intuition of the Sanctity of a homogeneous, white Christian culture which is degraded by muslim immigration. In a search to activate the Loyalty/Betrayal moral foundation, Tweeters on both sides used the metaphor 'father of Brexit' and 9 different politicians were identified in this role including: Nigel Farage (7); Tony Benn (7) and Boris Johnson (5). The most retweeted 'father of Brexit' by a pro-Remainer was:

Boris Johnson had a nice meeting with his friend Joseph Mifsud, the mysterious Maltese professor at the heart of the #TrumpRussia investigation. (+ link to an Observer article on this connection). Keep in mind that Johnson is, if not the father of #Brexit, at least its fairy godmother. (209 retweets)[19]

The humorous gender switching in the second part is in keeping with Twitter style. On the pro-Leave side an account named 'Brexit Britain' posted a number of tweets that argued that Tony Benn was the founding father of Brexit:

GREAT #TonyBenn *the Founding Father* of #Brexit! On #Democracy in #Europe! #Labour #Brexit #VoteLeave #EUref #BBC #EU (83 retweets)[20]

There were six separate tweets posted in the period that all referred in some way to Tony Benn as the 'father of Brexit' and this, along with the multiple hashtags, suggests that they were part of a funded propaganda campaign targeting older Leave voters in working class communities. There were only 21 references in the press during 2016–2018 to 'father of Brexit' of these 9 were to David Cameron because of his decision to have a referendum and 9 were to Boris Johnson—often satirically alluding to his paternity of children by different women. There were no references to 'mother of Brexit' during this period.

After 'father' the most frequent kinship term on Twitter was 'brother' and it was commonly used as a metaphor that sought to overcome the fear that if Britain voted for Brexit it would become an outcast from the European family by emphasising that there were still family type relationships with nations outside the EU. The Leave campaign were more effective in exploiting the emotional appeal of family metaphors; 85% of tweets in the first six months of 2016 that referred to 'brothers' and 'sisters' advocated Leaving the EU. There were around 40 tweets that contained both 'brother' and 'across the pond' and these tweets occurred in the days leading up to the vote by those who were not going to themselves vote because they were not British:

I truly hope that our British *brothers* and *sisters* have the courage to lead again and #VoteLeave. Britain is more than a state #LeaveTheEU (18 retweets)[21]

My *brothers* and *sisters* across *the pond*: The UK was once the financial center of the world. Your kingdom will rise again. Congrats. #Brexit (22 retweets)[22]

Kudos to our *brothers* and *sisters* across *the pond* voting out the corrupt, manipulative EU. #DemocracyWins #Brexit (25 retweets)[23]

Evidently agents outside the UK with their own political objectives were seeking to influence the outcome of the referendum by emotive family based appeals; they sought to counter the appeal of the Europe as family frame by offering alternative family loyalties. However, this was not solely on the basis of emotion but also grounded in the moral intuition of nativist populists in the US, Australia and elsewhere that although geographically distant, the Leave movement in the UK shared their own values and ideology—for example a distrust of experts and a desire for freedom.[24] Twitter provided the ideal vehicle through which such moral alignments could be communicated by metaphor.

'Friends'

If the family was not considered an appropriate metaphor for Britain's relationship with the EU then an alternative metaphor for describing this relationship was 'European friends'. Just to recap, from Table 7.1 we see that the most frequent use of 'European friends' on Twitter was in the 6 month period leading up to the referendum because it was a metaphor employed by supporters of Remain as a campaigning strategy. At its simplest level 'European friend' was an appeal on Twitter to broader feelings of international solidarity that had characterised Britain's original referendum in 1975. During the Referendum campaign this idealistic appeal was viewed as especially attractive to young people who Remainers viewed as their voting base. Typical uses of the metaphor were multimodal and included an image of a young person:

A little message from a few of our younger *European friends* in #Durham today #StrongerIn #VoteRemain (+ link to video of a group of schoolchidren holding a Vote Remain placard). (20 retweets)[25]

The following tweet showed a young man holding a placard on which were written in handwriting the verbal statement that formed the text part of the tweet:

'We love our *european friends*, housemates and partners. We are voting in' #Yes2EU #VoteRemain #WeAreIn (6 retweets)[26]

There is no doubt that this idealism and sense of international compassion motivated the formation of the People's Vote campaign in April 2018. The metaphor therefore peaked again after its launch sometimes to appeal to European leaders to assist in resisting a 'no deal' Brexit that was viewed—even by some who had voted Leave—as potentially economically disastrous:

Delighted to see President Macron backing efforts to stop a far right no deal #Brexit. We need all the help we can get from our *European friends* to #StopBrexit (23 retweets)[27]

By comparison, in press headlines 'European friends' occurred most often in the six months directly *following* the referendum in quotations from politicians of both sides of the debate who were seeking to establish a satisfactory future relationship with Europe. Theresa May was widely quoted in the press:

"I have been clear that Brexit means Brexit. But I also want to be clear here today, and across Europe in the weeks ahead, that we are not walking away from our *European friends*. Britain will remain an outward-looking country and Germany will remain a vital *partner* and *a special friend* for us."[28]

Central to these more rational deliberations—in contrast to the emotional reactions of individuals on Twitter—was a wider concern with the impact of Britain's possible departure from the EU on international security. The expression 'European friends and allies' occurred in 86 headlines in articles on Brexit during the 3 year period—nearly a quarter of the total—uses of the 'European friends' metaphor indicating a notion of friendship that involves mutual protection from enemies. It also invokes historic memories of duty and loyalty as implied by the War and Invasion frame. Jacob Rees-Mogg when deliberating on the citizenship rights of EU nationals adds emphasis to the expression by reversing its normal sequence:

> We are dealing with *allies and friends*, so this should never have been a topic of negotiation. We should simply have set out our stall and said what we would do. I am glad that it is now clear that in the event of our leaving on WTO terms, we will protect the rights of EU member state nationals who are living in this country.[29]

The need for mutual protection, against the threat of Russia, criminals and terrorists was a preoccupation of government more than of individuals. This is why the 'friends and allies' metaphor tended to dominate in press headlines as a means of expressing concerns of politicians (as reflected in their public statements) about the implications of no longer being part of the European family. So, effectively, in the press 'European friends' was more premeditated and oriented to the moral reasoning of the 'head', while on Twitter the metaphor was more affective, less strategic and more oriented to the 'heart' and grounded in the moral intuitions of Care and Fairness. Emotional appeals on Twitter were often expressions of remorse for Leave campaign strategies that were seen as a threat to friendship status:

> As the #Brexit campaign reaches a new low, our *European friends* look on, wondering why a smart nation is allowing this disgraceful rhetoric. (35 retweets)[30]

This tweet included some of the more controversial Leave supporting images from media tabloids and its author, Jüergen, Maier is the Chief Executive of Siemens UK and is of British-Austrian background, for whom there is a close integration of personal and social responses to Brexit.

Following the result many took to Twitter to express their remorse in emotionally charged and very personal language:

> It's a sad, distressing day to be British. Good bye *European friends*, Hello recession. I am shocked, appalled & very, very worried (+ emoticon).[31]

Feelings were especially intense for those who had friends in Europe, or whose families crossed European national borders. If EUROPE IS A FAMILY, then a political decision such as leaving the EU could be interpreted at a more emotional level as a threat to people's broader sense of identity, as human beings, as brothers and sisters in a European if not universal family. In a spirit of solidarity, non-British people also expressed empathetic feelings of regret:

> My heart is with all British *European friends* and all Hungarians in UK, esp those trying to find a safe harbour for their kids #Brexit shock[32]
>
> Talking to other *European friends* about #Brexit we all feel the same: deeply wounded & yet sorry for UK & the huge number of Remain voters.[33]

In the month following June 23rd a large number of Remain supporters took to Twitter to apologise for a national decision that they viewed as both a personal insult—an actual rejection of friendship based on the EUROPE IS A FAMILY metaphor—and a form of personal shame:

> Devastated by the country's choice to #Brexit Reaching out this morning @aosdanaiona to all our *European friends* across the world, sorry.[34]

However, although predominantly a pro-Remain appeal, the 'European friends' metaphor was contested by Brexit supporters who also used it during the referendum campaign as a strategy to argue that rejection of EU membership did not equate to rejecting friendship with people from Europe:

> The argument is not about our *European friends*, it is about the anti-democratic monster called the EU. #Brexit #LeaveEU (12 retweets)[35]

Such tweets question the EU IS A FAMILY metaphor by arguing that the institution of the EU is not equivalent to the people from Europe that its claims to represent. Other pro-Brexit tweets had the colour of propaganda by employing 'friends' in a way that explicitly contests its adoption as a pro-Remain meme:

Lesley Miller Retweeted Brilliant_Brummie
All our *European friends* are supporting UK and hoping that we deliver #Brexit - lets not dash their hopes. (10 retweets)[36]

However, Pro-Remain activists continued to appeal to international 'friendship' across European borders after the referendum result:

I hate the things May is saying to our *European friends* about how we've never felt at home in the EU. Don't believe her! #Brexit (1130 retweets)[37]

Notice here how a tweeter who employed the European family metaphor when garnering support for the People's Vote campaign, shifts tone by using the milder 'friends' metaphor when speaking to a broader audience who are not necessarily activists. Strategically, it was more effective for supporters of the official 'People's vote' campaign to make less emotionally coercive appeals to European friends, especially when these friends were known to have a British following. Part of the People's Vote strategy was the celebrity endorsement:

This is superb from Jurgen Klopp on #Brexit
I increasingly think many of our *European friends* care more about the future of us Brits, than we do. We need to #ExitFromBrexit (+ link to article in which Klopp questions Brexit) (188 retweets)[38]

Here the appeal is to pathos rather than logos as the generally popular German coach of Liverpool FC, Jurgen Klopp, is known to be an extremely passionate man and the idea of others caring more for 'us' encourages international altruism grounded in the moral intuition of Care. Here a non-family member who is represented as an ideal friend who cares as much, if not more, about his friend than he does himself.

Other Remain supporting tweeters circulated endorsements for their position by linking to statements by public figures such as John Major:

> *European friends,…*: "We are all urged to be "patriotic" and get behind #Brexit. But it is precisely because I am patriotic that I oppose it". One of the few decent politicians left standing in Britain. (link to text of a speech by John Major in the Mirror, 1 March 2018). (40 retweets)[39]

The argument of the tweet and the article could be summarised as follows:

> **Major Premise**: Patriots are urged to support Brexit.
> **Minor Premise—Implied**: Brexit presents many threats to the nation.
> **Conclusion**: So it is patriotic to oppose Brexit.

The tweet is designed to reject a populist argument that it is more patriotic to support Brexit and it is worded as an enthymeme because the arguments for the dangers of Brexit are not made explicit in the minor premise (though they are elaborated in the speech by John Major). The tweeter therefore challenges a view of the world based on the patriotism of separate nation states by following John Major in claiming that the only truly patriotic position is to remain in the EU. This is an effective argument because it attacks the claim that patriotism necessarily leads to a pro-Brexit position. It seeks to reconcile the tension between the 'nation as person' and 'nation as family' frames by construing shared identity in a more complex way so that being a member of the British family does not curtail *also being part of a European family*. In terms of moral foundations, Care is not necessarily in opposition with the other moral foundations of Fairness and Loyalty.

The predominant feelings of remorse, regret and sadness at the referendum result has continued to characterise those who use the metaphor:

> The Union Jack is flying alongside our *European friends* for now. An important, poignant but sad visit to the #EuropeanParliament today in Strasbourg. A real sense of the tragedy of #Brexit from our guide and fellow Europeans around us that *our bond has been broken*.[40]

With the metaphor of the 'broken bond' this tweet acknowledges a shift away from the 'Europe as family' frame towards the more emotionally distant relationship of Europe as friend.

In the press the 'Europe as friend' metaphor was gradually adopted by Brexit supporters, for example the Brexit supporting owner of Wetherspoons, Tim Martin is quoted:

Our *European friends* are being *dragged down* by Brussels' bureaucracy.[41]

The Brexit secretary Dominic Raab:

Until we've made a big-hearted positive offer to our *European friends*, you won't start to see a reaction from Brussels that is anything other than *cold*.[42]

Essentially the notion of friendship shifted after the referendum from being a powerful expression of emotional affinity with 'European friends' to something more transactional—more the type of friendship implied by 'Facebook friends'—someone who I continue to want to be associated with, and to deal with—but for whom I don't necessarily have any strong emotional attachment. We also saw this essentially transactional view of friendship in Boris Johnson's metaphors in Chapter 6.

'Enemies'

The word 'enemy' instantly triggers the Care/Harm moral foundation. We saw earlier how the dominant war frame for fighting the Referendum employed 'enemies' and how in a 'Them' and 'Us' struggle the identity of 'Our' side was established with reference to the 'enemy'—that could either be the European Union or its traitorous supporters within Britain. However, the phrase 'European enemies' only occurred 3 times in 3 years on Twitter but was much more evident in relation to the 'enemies within' after *The Daily Mail* published a

'Wanted dead or Alive' poster with images of three High Court Judges alongside the headline 'enemies of the people'; this was because of their ruling that the government would require the consent of Parliament in order to give notice of its intention to leave the European Union. Many viewed this as a form of 'hate speech' that vilified a professional group and The Independent Press Standards Organisation received over 1000 complaints about the front page. It is worth noting that out of 60 uses of 'enemies of the people' on Twitter, 54 were posted by Remain supporters: it was Remain supporters who saw the use of an inflammatory metaphor grounded in the moral intuitions of Harm and Betrayal as more likely to serve their rhetorical goals. The most widely retweeted alluded to the type of discourse that had contributed to the murder of the young Labour MP Jo Cox:

> Steve Bannon encouraging people to "rise up" & "fight to take their country back," Tory MEP suggesting Treason Act be updated to deal with those showing "extreme EU loyalty," public being called "Saboteurs," judges labelled "**enemies of the people**." Remember Jo Cox? (1900 retweets)[43]

The expression 'enemies of the people' appeared to reflect totalitarian values deemed inappropriate in a democracy and gave the opportunity to Remainers to publicise other threat to democracy:

> In a free society, people should also be able to criticise #Brexit without being called traitors, **enemies of the people** or being against democracy. But you don't like people criticising brexit do you Nigel? (106 retweets)[44]

No tweets by supporters of Leave that include 'enemies of the people' were retweeted more than 100 times and the few that were retweeted represent far right propaganda:

> The left wing would rather destroy this country than see it go down an alternative path. They are the true **enemies of the people**. #brexit (71 retweets)[45]

I also searched tweets that included the words 'European' and 'enemies' and found, surprisingly, that out of 40 only 20% were posted by Leave supporters. Remain supporters referred to supporters of Brexit or politicians such as Trump or Putin that they believed were fostering Brexit from afar as 'enemies'.

> #Brexit and #Trump were entirely funded by our **enemies**, who wish to see the end of USA/**European** military dominance, so that Russia can become dominant.[46]

It could be argued that the use of 'enemies' and 'European' in the same tweet reinforces the frame of Brexit as a war scenario in which two sides are engaged in a life and death struggle reminiscent of the Cold War. Rather than employing a new frame it reinforces the dominant war frame established by the Leave campaign that relied strongly on Loyalty/Betrayal morality. This was noticeable in the more skillful and ironic use of 'enemies' by Leave tweets half of which included the ironical phrase: 'With friends like these: Who needs Enemies?'. But this meme was picked up by more suspicious posts that lack credibility because of the their explicit propaganda content:

> Victor Davis Hanson: Macron Wants 'European Union Army,' Can't Make NATO Payments. With allies like these, who needs enemies. @realDonaldTrump #MAGA #France #Brexit[47]

Notice the number of hashtags attached (I have not included all) to what is known to be an emotive issue for voters—the threat to the status of the British army presented by the prospect of a European one.

'European Partners' and 'European Neighbours'

The phrase 'European partners' was easily the most frequent relationship metaphor used in press headlines and the second most frequent was 'European neighbours'. 'European neighbour' implies geographical location but does not do so in a way that implied strong obligations or strong affection. Its use was relatively constant on Twitter suggesting that it was viewed as emotionally more neutral than references to 'family', 'friends' or 'partners' and this may explain why there were no particular peaks during the 3-year period. However, 'European partners' peaked in the press in the first six months of 2017 especially in articles on the negotiations for the British withdrawal. It was used mainly by the Leave supporting press to emphasise that in spite of leaving, Britain wanted to maintain a close relationship with the EU; commonly it was used alongside other non-kinship metaphors:

> I want us to be a truly Global Britain - the *best friend and neighbour* to our *European partners*, but a country that reaches beyond the borders of Europe too. A country that goes out into the world to build relationships with *old friends* and *new allies* alike.[48]

However, when negotiations were not going well, then questions were raised as regards the nature of the relationship. In the following *The Daily Telegraph* uses scare quotes around 'partners' and reverts to more familiar war metaphors, which though not mentioning 'enemy', clearly imply that the EU is 'the enemy':

> There is now less than a month remaining of the Brexit phoney war; a month in which Theresa May will ask the British people to arm her with a thumping Westminster majority with which to do battle with our *European 'partners'* (as we used to call them, and hope to still).[49]

Leave supporters used the partnership metaphor to demonstrate how reasonable they were in the negotiations and their desire for a collaborative arrangement after Brexit:

> The truth is that this country's negotiators have bent over backwards to be reasonable to our *European partners*. They've offered firm guarantees to uphold the rights of EU citizens settled in Britain, while putting forward sensible proposals for keeping the Irish border free from physical barriers.[50]

The pattern "With x like these: Who needs Enemies?" was also used with 'partners':

Just watching @SkyNews and these #Brexit speeches are hilarious. Notice how the remainers in the cabinet keep saying *"European partners"*.

1. The #EU is NOT the whole of #Europe. These eurocrats represent only the EU.

2. With *"partners"* like this, who needs *enemies*??[51]

The tweets is quite logically laid out and its argument is as follows:

Major Premise: The cabinet refers to the EU as "European partners".
Minor Premise—Implied: A good partner would help Britain.
Conclusion—Implied: The EU is an enemy.

The minor premise and conclusion both rely on inference and so it has the conflated, but highly effective structure of an enthymeme that invites the reader to work out the meaning. It is obviously much more subtle and effective than the widely condemned 'enemies of the people' *Daily Mail* front page. A similar contrast between 'partners' and 'friends' occurs in a speech by the leader of the strongly pro-Brexit European Research Group Jacob Rees-Mogg:

It (the 'red book') states that there will be years of uncertainty, but that assumes that our *partners in Europe* will lie and cheat. *But they are our friends,* or so the Government will have us believe, and article 50 of the treaty on the functioning of the European Union provides for a very straightforward two-year process for extracting ourselves...[52]

Notice how 'partners' here collocates with dishonest practices and is contrasted with 'friends' who avoid such practices—though in line with his anti-European position Rees-Mogg hedges the suggestion that Europe are our friends. As the concerns about a hard Brexit grew, increasingly, even pro-Remainers substituted the more emotionally distant 'partners' metaphor for the more intimate 'friends' metaphor:

For Britain's future prosperity, it is vital that close economic cooperation with our *European partners* is secured and sustained.[53]

A similar pattern occurs on Twitter where the emotionally detached 'partners' came to be used by Remainers who were anxious about the future relationship:

> We've become an isolated & weak country, weighed down by a buckling economy. #Brexit has left the UK with fewer friends & less power & without the valuable relations we've built with our *European partners,* the influence & credibility of the UK will also crumble. #BollocksToBrexit (662 retweets)[54]

The increasing use of 'partners' by the Remain side indicated that they had already accepted the outcome of the Referendum and were taking a pragmatic stance in seeking to avoid a 'no-deal' Brexit: gradually the moral intuition of Loyalty was replaced simply by that of Fairness. There were twice as many references to 'European partners' on Twitter in 2018 as compared with 2017 suggesting that this more pragmatic future oriented position was coming to be accepted even by those who hoped that Britain would not be leaving.

I classified a sample 100 instances of 3 relationship metaphors (European family, European friend and European neighbour) in press headlines and found that 'European neighbour' occurred around twice as often as the other two expressions combined. I then examined them according to whether they were from pro-Leave or pro-Remain newspapers. Both the pro-Leave and pro-Remain press preferred 'European neighbours' over the emotionally warmer alternatives. The pro-Remain press tended to avoid reference to 'friends' whereas *The Daily Telegraph* used 'friends' the most; and in the pro-Remain press only *The Independent* used the phrase 'European family'. This suggests that support for Remain was fairly lukewarm across the press at the affective level.

The Club

Another type of relationship metaphor that contributes to moral reasoning is based on the rights and responsibilities entailed by club membership that derive from the moral foundations of Fairness/Cheating and Loyalty/Betrayal. David Cameron introduced the club metaphor into the Brexit negotiations in a speech on immigration, given at a time when he was seeking to establish constraints on the entitlement of migrants to claim benefits in the UK:

> This is about saying: our welfare system is like a *national club*. It's made up of the contribution of hardworking British taxpayers. Millions of people doing the right thing, paying into the system, generation after generation. It cannot be right that migrants can turn up and claim full rights to this *club* straightaway.[55]

Here the 'club' metaphor was used to develop the moral intuition of Fairness/Cheating that imply that you should only be permitted to access financial benefits from systems into which you had contributed. Although 'club' metaphors have roots in the co-operative movement, and working men's clubs where mutual benefits were assured to contributors, this doesn't seem to be the sort of club that Cameron had in mind, which was perhaps more like a golf club or a Conservative club. The 'club' metaphor subsequently became much more common after the referendum result as a heuristic for the 'EU as a club' and if Europe was a club then Britain was leaving the club. This metaphor framed the moral reasoning that provided the basis of the withdrawal agreement and the type of losses or gains that might accrue to Britain on its departure. Jean-Claude Juncker said: "The EU is not a golf club that could be easily joined or left"[56] the 'club' metaphor continued to frame withdrawal as a cost-benefit analysis that drew on people's knowledge of the responsibilities of club membership—especially the requirement to pay a fee for membership—and the types of advantage that accrue from being a member. Brexiteers argued that when one leaves a golf club, one should stop paying the direct debit and avoid paying for another round of green fees. But in co-operative movements the basis for withdrawal is on need and this continues over time.

A survey I conducted of all tweets with the word 'club' during the 3-year period showed they were equally distributed between pro-Remain and pro-Leave supporters. The following tweet summarises the arguments on both sides in the form of a dialogue:

UK: We want to *leave the club* but retain all the benefits of membership.
EU: I'm afraid that's not possible if you chose to *leave the club*.
UK: Be more CREATIVE.
EU: We are being realistic. You can't *benefit from the club* and not be a member.
UK: STOP PUNISHING US! (+ crying emoticon) #Brexit (327 retweets)[57]

This tweet highlights the inconsistency of the Brexit position and implies the same moral ambiguity derived from intuitions about Fairness and Cheating that was identified in 'having your cake and eating it' metaphor discussed in chapter one. Understanding the tweet relies on interpreting the relationship metaphor frame so that the rules that apply to club membership also apply to EU membership. But pro-Leave tweets also explored moral reasoning through the frame offered by the 'club' metaphor:

> To *join a club* you pay an entrance fee. Whilst a member you pay a membership fee. Nobody *leaving a club* pays an exit fee! #Simple. #Brexit (83 retweets)[58]

This tweets develops the moral reasoning behind the original 'club' metaphor in relation to the idea that Britain owed 'membership fees' by framing it in terms of normal club rules on departure. Its argument is as follows:

Major Premise: You pay a fee when joining a club.
Minor Premise: You continue to pay while being a member.
Conclusion: You don't pay a fee when leaving.

Since there is no reference to the EU or to Britain it relies on the reader to interpret the relationship frame based on the metaphor THE EU IS A CLUB. We might question the relevance of the club metaphor because there were no clear rules when the EU was formed regarding what exiting members should pay. This situation had never been envisaged when the treaties were originally signed and so the question of the financial settlement needed to be resolved by negotiation rather than by metaphor. But metaphors offered highly effective frames for moral reasoning about the amount Britain should pay (if anything) for leaving the EU and aroused moral intuitions regarding Fairness and Cheating. The club frame reminds us of Musolff's metaphor scenarios. Here we have a general scenario in which a community of club members share the same rules of membership. However, on departure from the club they interpret these rules differently according to which 'club' scenario they bring to bear—is it a sports club with written rules for obligations on leaving? Or a political club with no codified rules for departure? Interpretation of correct ethical behaviour on the part of the departing member depends on which 'club' scenario is applied. For example, Remain tweets reinforced the apparent logical inconsistency of the position of leaving while continuing to benefit from membership:

> Science Minister complains that #Brexit means #Brexit. Not very clever these ministers are they. If you *leave the club* you no longer get to use the facilities. Not difficult. (289 retweets)[59]

Notice that these tweets allude to a sports club that has facilities—drawing on the deeply rooted love of sports—and their institutional structures—that characterises British culture. The following pro-Remain tweet makes the same argument in the form of a written reply from a club committee to a resigning member:

> Dear resigning *club member,*
>   Your letter states
>   You 'expect' to fully *leave the club* in 2021,
>   You want 'frictionless' *access to all club facilities* after that date, but
>   You don't want to obey all of our rules.
>   The committee will decide on your proposal, when we get it.
>   #Brexit (140 retweets)[60]

The moral reasoning looks something like this:

Major Premise: You want to continue using the facilities after leaving but don't want to follow the rules.

Minor Premise: Club members have access to facilities and obey rules.

Conclusion—Implied: Your position is inconsistent.

However club membership can be a rather authoritarian way of framing an issue because it implies a committee, a chairman, a set of rules and other institutional paraphernalia and this is why some Remain supporters rejected the 'club' frame as an appropriate frame for the relationship within the EU:

> I placed #fbpe into my name to show support and connect to other pro EU people. That is it. Its not a **club**. There is no doctrine. We come from all walks of life. There are working class to the elite.
> Connected by one thing only. To stop brexit. (369 retweets)[61]

This tweeter rejects the 'EU as a club' metaphor scenario as an appropriate way of framing and embraces a more inclusive social identity, which—judging by the number of retweets—was broadly held by pro-Remain supporters.

Some pro-Leave Tweets followed the line taken in the quote of Groucho Marx: "please accept my resignation - I don't want to belong to any club that will accept people like me as a member" by negatively evaluating the European club as socially exclusionary:

> This sums up the hardcore Remainer attitude perfectly; ignore the rest of the World in favour of the *Little Europeans Club*. Brexit is the chance to be a truly global leader. Wouldn't expect a petty little showman like Sadiq Khan to understand that. #brexit (81 retweets)[62]

This tweeter posted 6 tweets containing the phrase 'Little Europeans Club' arguing that Britain aspired to be the chairman of a global club. In a similar vein George Galloway questioned whether the EU was the right sort of club to be in:

> Don't Panic! If through EU perfidy we "crash out" of the *Bankers Club* in March, we have been there before. In fact it was our finest hour.

Britain can and will be an independent country. If we run out of Brie we can always eat cheddar. Let's have confidence in ourselves #Brexit (245 retweets)[63]

This tweet argues it is better not to be a member of any club rather than to be in a rich man's club: rather than an ordinary sports or football club the author, well known for his populist style, is framing the EU as an elite Gentleman's club with highly restricted access. Metaphors that highlight the exclusive nature of the EU club were popularised by the Leave EU campaign:

More Labour MPs advocate Brexit as the EU has become a *corporatist rich man's club* (146 retweets)[64]

LeaveEU, under its hugely wealthy founder Aaron Banks, saw populist anti-elitism as offering a persuasive political message grounded in the moral intuition of Fairness/Cheating.

Summary

In this chapter I have showed how our capacity to form all sorts of different social relationships served as the model for framing Britain's relationship with the European Union. I have distinguished between family metaphors such as 'father', 'brother' and the 'European family' and more emotionally detached metaphors such as 'partner' and 'neighbour' and showed how there was a shift in metaphor use. I have shown that family metaphors, though usually positive, can either draw on 'the nation as family' frame to produce nationalist frames, but can also draw on 'the nation as person' frame to argue for a more internationalist social identity. Both frames rely on intuitions regarding Care/Harm but have the potential for manipulative use of Loyalty/Betrayal morality; the 'nation as family' frame has greater potential to be emotionally coercive because it also draws on Authority/Subversion.

Between the two contrasting frames of the nation as family and group of nations as family are a set of intermediary metaphors that have varying levels of emotional intimacy ranging from 'friends' at the more intimate end of a scale to 'partners' and then 'neighbours' at the less intimate end. These metaphors are typically grounded in moral intuitions regarding Fairness and Cheating. I have demonstrated that variation in the use of such metaphors according to various aspects of the political context such as which 'side' the speaker was on, and whether the metaphor sought to establish a new type of relationship or harked back to an earlier one. Rich experience of all types of interpersonal relationships provided the roots for frames to flourish according to rhetorical purpose. When there was a need for transactional relationships with out-groups the 'group of nations as family' could be replaced by less intimate metaphors; by contrast, when there was a need to enhance in-group intimacy speakers would shift to the 'nation as family' frame.

Successful tweeters combined frames with moral reasoning that can be analysed as syllogisms or enthymemes, often combined with other rhetorical styles such as irony and humour. Ardent Brexiteers showed a highly strategic use of relationship metaphors by drawing on a range of relationship types and sometimes brought in scenarios of relationship betrayal and disloyalty as anticipated by the Loyalty/Betrayal moral foundation. Many Brexiteers framed the Commonwealth as an alternative 'family' to which Britain could return now that the EU were no more than 'neighbours' or 'partners'. Both sides employed the frame of the 'club' as a metaphor scenario for Britain's obligations (or otherwise) when withdrawing from the EU.

Notes

1. Cited in Goodhart, D. (2017) *The Road to Somewhere: The Populist Revolt and the Future of Politics*. London: C Hurst & Co.
2. See Lakoff (2002).
3. In the United States the term 'Liberal' refers to what in Europe is more commonly referred to as a 'left wing' political orientation with a higher degree of State involvement in areas such as education and healthcare.
4. See Lakoff and Wehling (2012).
5. Monty's Dog Nigel @montysdognigel, 21 Jun 2016.
6. *The Daily Telegraph*, 6 April 2017.

7. @guyverhofstadt, 29 Nov 2018.
8. *The Guardian*, 10 January 2017.
9. Graham Simpson, 16 July 2018.
10. Peter Timmins @petertimmins3, 18 Dec 2017.
11. Graham Simpson, January 18.
12. *The Observer*, 19 November 2016.
13. European Commission @EU_Commission, Oct 12.
14. @RaviSinghKA, 18 June 2016.
15. C.o.l.i.n. @Cynical_Colin, 11 May 2016 @BelfastTaxiMan.
16. @Ellie_the_Fairy, Aug 2.
17. Tony Parsons @TonyParsonsUK, 19 Jun 2016.
18. @MasterOfJediz, 19 Jun 2016.
19. @grantstern, 9 July 2018.
20. BREXIT BRITAIN Supporting BREXIT & #NoDeal! @ EUVoteLeave23rd, 18 Jun 2016.
21. MAGA Ian @IJCFilm, 21 Jun 2016.
22. MAGA REVOJUTION @Sheep2Wolves, 23 Jun 2016.
23. Summer Hawkes @SummerAnnHawkes, 24 Jun 2016.
24. See Bennet (2019) for a discussion of value, and Zappavigna (2019) for an analysis of how Twitter was used to display a moral affiliation with Gove's phrase 'We have had enough of experts'.
25. @NEStrongerIn, 19 Jun 2016.
26. @LivityUK, 20 Jun 2016.
27. @GrahameLucas, 19 Aug 2018.
28. *Express*, 20 July 2016.
29. Jacob Rees-Mogg, 10 September 2018.
30. Jüergen Maier @Jüergen_Maier, 15 May 2016.
31. Slinger @HelenSlinger, 23 Jun 2016.
32. Eszter Salamon @Esalamon, 24 Jun 2016.
33. @br_luigi_gioia, 24 Jun 2016.
34. @aosdanaiona, 24 Jun 2016.
35. HUGHES @JDHughes4, 30 May 2016.
36. Lesley Miller @LesleyMillercyp, 21 Jun 2016.
37. Graham Simpson @grahambsi, 22 Sept 2017.
38. Matthew Green #FBPE @MatthewGreen02, 1 Apr 2018.
39. @AgnesCPoirier, 1 Mar 2018.
40. @JoeWalkerUK, 13 Aug 2018.
41. *MailOnline*, 2 November 2016.
42. *Express*, 20 October 2016.

43. Dr Lauren Gavaghan DancingTheMind.
44. @remainer_stuart, 14 Mar 2018.
45. LIAR MPs @LiarMPs, 25 Jun 2016.
46. Claire's Outrageous Thoughts @claireOT, 18 Mar 2018.
47. Peachfuzz @CalamityPchfuzz, 13 Nov 2018.
48. Boris Johnson, *Daily Telegraph*, 18 January 2017.
49. Peter Foster, *The Telegraph*, 11 May 2017.
50. *Daily Mail*, 19 October 2017.
51. @Ash_Hirani, 8 Jun 2018.
52. Rees-Mogg, 16 March 2016.
53. *Guardian*, 6 June 2018.
54. Charlie Mullins OBE@PimlicoPlumbers, Oct 9.
55. David Cameron Speech, 28 November 2014.
56. Jean-Claude Juncker, Comment, April 2017.
57. @MadeleinaKay, 10 Jan 2018.
58. ROBert Kimbell #TimeForThePeople @RedHotSquirrel, 4 Mar 2017.
59. Peter Timmins @petertimmins3, 27 May 2018.
60. CathalMacCoille @CmacCoille, 7 Jun 2018.
61. @rocciabella, 16 May 2018.
62. Alexander Hall @AEHALL1983, Jan 2.
63. George Galloway @georgegalloway, 29 July 2018.
64. @LeaveEUOfficial, 10 Jun 2016.

References

Bennett, S. (2019). Values as Tools of Legitimation in EU and UK Brexit Discourses. In V. Koller, S. Kopf, and M. Miglbauer (Eds.), *Discourses of Brexit* (pp. 17–31). London: Routledge.

Goodhart, D. (2017). *The Road to Somewhere: The Populist Revolt and the Future of Politics*. London: C. Hurst.

Lakoff, G. (2002). *Moral Politics*, 2nd edn. Chicago and London: University of Chicago Press.

Lakoff, G., and Wehling, E. (2012). *The Little Blue Book: The Essential Guide to Thinking and Talking Democratic*. New York: Simon and Schuster.

Zappavigna, M. (2019). Ambient Affiliation and Brexit. In V. Koller, S. Kopf, and M. Miglbauer (Eds.), *Discourses of Brexit* (pp. 48–68). London: Routledge.

8

Are Marriages Made in Heaven?

Introduction

In this chapter I discuss the history of the 'marriage and divorce' frame to illustrate how influential metaphors, such as the 'divorce bill' originated in the media framing of British-EU relations. I demonstrate how the media framed the Britain's relationship with the EU as 'a marriage of convenience' from at least 1990 onwards and how therefore 'divorce' was always a possibility. I then consider the implications of the 'marriage and divorce' frame as the master metaphor for Britain's desire to leave the European Union.

If we think that moral reasoning arising from a master metaphor influenced Britain's decision to leave the EU this suggests that it was language that controlled social thought. If language governs how we think about the world and our beliefs, then language also prescribes our 'worldview'. When applied in a strong form this view is known as 'linguistic determinism' because language determines how we think. Since 44% of the couples that married in the UK in 1987 have since ended in divorce so framing Britain's relationship with the European Union as a 'marriage' also framed it as one that might end in 'divorce'.

© The Author(s) 2019
J. Charteris-Black, *Metaphors of Brexit*,
https://doi.org/10.1007/978-3-030-28768-9_8

Viewing international relationships using a marriage metaphor creates the potential for all the difficulties that married couples face to be applied to international relationships. If, like those 44% of couples, these difficulties cannot be resolved, divorce becomes inevitable. A 'divorce' metaphor adds drama and is attractive to newspaper editors because it triggers powerful cognitive scripts and moral reactions that carry implications for how we think and feel about international relationships. Nowhere are our intuitions aroused more than when we are commenting on close friends who are getting divorced—and usually sides are taken, and moral judgements made as to the guilty party.

When there is a strong emotional bond between two people they are in a much stronger position to overcome difficulties. Arguably this emotional element was missing in Britain's relationship with the European Union, partly because it had often been framed as a difficult marriage leading to a relationship characterised by haggling over the finances. Very often it is the children that keep a couple together and since Britain chose not to join the metaphorical child of the European Union—the Euro—there was an absence of that powerful emotional pressure. When millions of British people came to place their votes in the referendum in 2016 many voted with their hearts rather than their heads. Consider the following:

> #LOL Why #Brexit? Isn't *heart* more important than *head*? Isn't happiness more important than economy? Isn't honour more important than money?[1]

The head here serves as a metonymn for rationality since the brain is considered to be the seat of reason and thought, while the 'heart' is a metonym for the emotional and affective centre: the seat of our deepest loyalties and instincts: our love for our family and our group—our moral foundation of Loyalty/Betrayal. It is very common to contrast 'head' and 'heart' to bring out inner conflicts and unresolved tensions between different ways of thinking about a situation that actually take place in our brains.

I will argue in the next section that the story told by the media about Britain's relationship with the European Union was that it was a 'marriage of convenience'. And this echoed a widespread attitude: even the most ardent supporters of Remain frequently qualified their support with a comment showing some form of emotional disengagement with the EU—so there was a tendency to adopt a form of moral reasoning that was initiated by anti-European sentiment. The questions therefore have to be asked: did the marriage and divorce frame that predominated in the media *create* the conditions for Britain to leave the European Union? Or did it simply *echo* the feelings that many people had about Europe anyway? Just as a love affair originates in a fleeting imaginative exploration, so the 'marriage of convenience' script offered a narrative that naturally led to divorce. Even if adoption of the marriage and divorce frame by both pro- and anti-Europeans did not make Britain's departure from the EU inevitable, it certainly made it all the more likely. The frame did not *force* Britain to leave the European Union but it contributed to the moral reasoning that warranted its departure.

As early as 1994, in the post-Maastrict era which gave birth to the euro, metaphors of estrangement can already be found in media framing:

Prospects of closer union spur *thoughts of divorce*
DOWNING Street officials yesterday vehemently denied that John Major was *contemplating drastic surgery on* Britain's place in Europe. But what they could not deny was that deep in the Westminster *undergrowth*, some senior Conservatives are beginning to think the unthinkable and ponder a future *outside* the European Union.[2]

While the metaphors are mixed, the headline writer selects the most potent. Later in 1994 *The Independent* used the divorce metaphor to describe the relationship between Conservatives and the EU:

Tories face isolation in European Parliament; The Conservatives and their European allies are *heading towards a divorce.* The isolation of the Conservatives in Europe, and their internal divisions, are increasingly evident in the European Parliament....[3]

Once the idea had been introduced it was difficult to discard—until eventually 'divorce' became the normal way of referring to Britain's departure from the EU. Consider Table 8.1 that shows the number of newspaper headlines with both 'Brexit' and 'divorce' in 6 monthly periods from 2016 to 2018.

Table 8.1 Frequency of 'Brexit' + 'divorce' in press headlines 2016–2018

January–June 2016	July–December 2016	January–June 2017	July–December 2017	January–June 2018	July–December 2018	Total
26	99	288	515	97	100	1125

From less than 30 in the period before the referendum, the figure escalated reaching a peak of over 500 in the second half of 2017. Some of these articles were about literal 'divorce'—for example, custody arrangements for divorcing couples, or the increase in actual divorces as a result of a couple voting differently in the Referendum—but the majority were metaphors that framed Britain's withdrawal as a 'divorce'.

By framing international relations as a 'divorce' the press reminded their readerships of the 'marriage of convenience' script that had been well rehearsed over the previous 25 years because it triggered the moral foundation of Fairness/Cheating. Each stage of the script entailed moral intuitions: there are the causes of the marital problems: accusations of unfaithfulness (cheating), loss of sexual attractiveness, lack of emotional support, not pulling one's weight financially or agreeing about living room colours. There may be attempts to salvage the relationship with the assistance of discussion with other parties or marriage guidance counselling. At the divorce stage there are considerations of what constitutes a fair financial settlement and, where relevant, rights of access to the children. Often divorce lawyers are engaged, at great expense, and there are emotionally painful disputes over previously shared possessions. Divorce lawyers typically spend more time discussing money than children in such negotiations! All of these stages in the script offered potential for moral reasoning. A 'marriage and divorce' script frames the event in terms of an *expected sequence of events*. For this reason in this chapter I refer to the 'marriage and divorce *script*'. This is because what is salient is an expected series of events that happen in time sequence; I continue to use 'frame' to describe both the whole 'marriage and divorce' frame—that includes roles such as 'lover' and events such as 'flirting'. 'Frame' is a verb referring to the cognitive action of providing a script. Consider how the following description frames Barnier's attitude:

Whether the case or not, Barnier comes across as someone who doesn't really like the British and people are starting to notice it. He appears more as a *jilted spouse* than the leader of the EU negotiating team. The dashing Frenchman is seemingly unable to forgive *being jilted by his British wife. He moans and groans about perceived slights, he has outbursts of temper and he doesn't quite tell the truth about what has really been going on in the relationship.*[4]

Here the journalist frames Barnier, the leader of the EU negotiators, as a 'jilted spouse' and Britain as a 'wife', and the emotional reactions are all part of the script. There is embodied simulation of the actual sounds made by the jilted spouse. I propose that the journalists who had created and contributed to such a script for marriage in their reporting of Britain's relationship with the EU in the 1990s created the conditions (intentionally or otherwise) for conflict because they ignored the absence of the very first stage in the relationship script: sexual attraction and flirting. In an idealised script for lovers the early stages of romantic relationships are characterised by flirting—and it is the primal stage of sexual attraction that underlies *any* romantic relationship. However, when we look in how 'flirt' is used in the British press we find that Britain never 'flirted' with the 'European Union' but only with the idea of *leaving it:*

Eight ministers *flirt* with EU 'no' vote[5]
    Sir John Major has said it is wrong *to flirt* with leaving the European Union at a time when the world is coming together.[6]
    There are four main reasons why voters in Britain should think about Ireland and *not flirt* with a leave vote.[7]

If Britain had 'flirted' *only* with *leaving* little wonder that the effort to sustain the relationship was lacking.

In the 'marriage and divorce' script the Declaration of Article 50 served as a decree nisi and shifted the focus to negotiation of a 'divorce settlement'. Discussion of how much, if anything, Britain 'owed' the EU formed a heuristic in which moral intuitions about divorce could be applied in a political context—in a similar way to moral reasoning as the 'golf club' metaphor and based on the moral intuitions of Fairness/

Cheating and Loyalty/Betrayal. This was especially the case because of the unprecedented nature of the event: since no nation had ever previously sought to leave the EU there were no moral precedents. Was Britain a partner escaping a loveless marriage? Would she become an orphan or start a new family, or revive the Commonwealth family? Or was the period after Article 50 was declared simply an extended marriage guidance session prior to the couple getting back together again? The moral dimension implied by the various scripts for marriage and divorce had powerful framing effects so that it became almost impossible to reason morally about international relations in any other way than by emotionally driven moral intuition. There were potentially damaging, if not disastrous, effects at both the personal and social levels.

Not only did the divorce script imply the break-up of 'the European family', it also activated media discussions of divisions of opinion within *real* families—especially those of leading Brexiteers. Given that many younger people wanted to stay in the EU, some parents felt that they owed it to their children to vote against Brexit precisely because it risked being a messy divorce and they harked back to the earlier 'family of nations' that, as we saw in the last chapter, had motivated internationalist thought in the post-war period. Because of the nature of Brexit, the focus was very much on the broken marriage of the UK and the EU. As part of this painful process there were families who felt split as they had to declare their nationality for one country or another, even though they felt internationalist because they believed in the common 'European family'. The divorce script therefore created a painful mingling of personal and social experience with implications for interpersonal relationships.

For many the pain was too great and—in keeping with the claim of linguistic determinism that metaphors create the real world—the divorce metaphors of Brexit contributed to an increase in the actual divorce rate as families became politically divided. The tensions between the tribal emotions based on the 'nation as family' frame conflicted with the emotions and moral intuitions aroused by the internationalist idea of being part of a European family. We need *both* family frames to establish social relationships because at times we need the more reasoned approach of looking outwards beyond our tribal family, as if the nation were a person, while at others we rely on morally intuition by relying on the 'nation as a family'. What causes problems is when we cannot mediate between the frames of 'nation as person' and 'nation as family' in ways that ensure satisfaction of the need for a shared identity—a sense of 'community'. I will suggest that the 'marriage of convenience' script mediated between these two frames but that it did *not* do so in a way that created conditions for the survival of the metaphorical 'marriage'.

The 'Marriage of Convenience' Script in the Press

In the previous chapter we saw how, for many centuries, marriage between heads of states symbolised a close political alliance and therefore provided the basis for marriage to become the actual means for developing political relationships. Throughout history inter-marriage between powerful families created alliances and other mutually beneficial arrangements for the social elite—such as keeping wealth within the aristocracy. The concept of a 'marriage of convenience'—one based on judgements of self-interest—has therefore much longer origins than that of romantic marriage that only developed in the eleventh century from the courtly love described in fiction created for the French nobility. Political 'marriages of convenience' mediate between the inward looking 'nation as family' frame toward the outward prospecting 'family of nations' frame. Perhaps the most familiar historical illustrations of this were the marriages of undertaken by Henry VIII. When we speak of nations engaging in 'marriages of convenience' we really mean that it is their heads of state that are doing so.

The expression 'marriages of convenience' also had a literal sense meaning when an individual from outside the European Union sought to use marriage as a way of gaining legal entry into the European Union. In a judgement made on 4 August 2017 a removal order was issued against a European Union national who was resident in the UK, on the grounds that she had abused her right of residence by attempting to enter into a marriage of convenience with a non-EU national. In the UK this historically has been a problem in relation to some British Pakistanis who had used marriage to facilitate illegal immigration into the UK, often receiving payment in return. Another literal use of 'marriage of convenience' was to refer to the rapid increase in citizen applications based on marriage after the referendum result:

> The looming divorce between the EU the UK appears to have consolidated many continental relationships, with a sharp rise in EU nationals applying for citizenship through marriage. Numbers were more than double those recorded in each of the two years before the referendum...[8]

Of course, there were also citizenship applications the other way: in 2017 a total of 13,141 UK citizens obtained the nationality of another member state and this compared with only 1826 in 2015—although the majority of these were applications for dual citizenship on the grounds of ancestry rather than marriage.

There is some linguistic evidence showing that marriage is associated with very mixed emotional experience. When looking at the word 'marriage' in a 520-million word language sample the most frequent 'emotion' adjectives preceding 'marriage' are shown in Table 8.2.

I have only included adjectives that occurred more than 10 times and have excluded non-emotion adjectives such as: 'same-sex', 'traditional' etc. or numbers—'first', 'second' etc. as these don't indicate emotional experience. The linguistic evidence is that marriage is associated with intense and mixed emotions. Although it is reassuring that 'happy' is the most frequent description, there are significantly more negative word types associated with 'marriage': there are nearly twice as many negative words (16 as compared with 10). Metaphor is quite common in our way of talking about marriage problems, so it can be framed as a structure (stable, rocky, crumbling, disintegrating), as an inanimate thing (broken, shotgun) or a weather condition (stormy, turbulent). These metaphors describe problems in a marriage and create a script: each of us can think of a 'rocky marriage'—where the couple 'move apart' and then either 'return' or 'break up'.

As might be anticipated from the Fairness and Cheating moral foundation, the 'marriage of convenience' script has a powerful moral tone—which is probably why *The Express Online* foregrounded extracts from a speech by the EU negotiator Guy Verhofstadt:

Table 8.2   Emotion adjectives describing 'marriage' in COCA[a]

Positive		Negative	
Happy	272	Failed	127
Perfect	125	Bad	123
Successful	87	Unhappy	93
Wonderful	49	Troubled	83
Healthy	36	Forced	50
Stable	24	Loveless	45
Loving	20	Abusive	41
Ideal	20	Broken	36
Advantageous	13	Failing	35
Sacred	13	Shotgun	33
		Stormy	27
		Rocky	27
		Crumbling	20
		Disastrous	19
		Turbulent	13
		Disintegrating	10
Total	659		782

[a]The Corpus of Contemporary American English is a 520-million word corpus available at https://corpus.byu.edu/coca/

> The relationship between Britain and the EU was never easy, let's recognise that, it was never *a love affair*, certainly never *a wild passion*, it was *a marriage of convenience*..... During the start of the common market, Britain *walked away from the table* when we started that. In the early years of the union it was Macmillan who looked at the continent with *nothing less than suspicion*. What were they *cooking up in Brussels*, were they really discussing coal and steel or were they also talking politics in Brussels? *Plotting on* foreign policy, or god forbid, defence matters even?[9]

As well as the trust and betrayal frame, Verhofstadt draws primarily on the cognitive template offered by the 'marriage of convenience' metaphor to confirm the view suggested above that Britain flirted with the idea of *leaving* the EU more than it ever flirted *with* the EU. Margaret Thatcher's negotiation of a financial rebate reinforced the idea of a 'marriage of convenience' as did British rejection of the Maaschtrict euro 'child'. From then on, much of the British media behaved like a distant and gossipy aunt eager for news of possible break-ups elsewhere within the European family—until it realised that it was *Britain itself* that was no longer much loved in Europe. Somehow the British fell in love with Brexit, in a way that they never fell in love with the EU. Perhaps in order to feel the emotion of belonging to a family supporters of a hard Brexit had to rely on the moral intuitions of Fairness/Cheating and Loyalty/Betrayal, irrespective of considerations of social and economic harm.

It is not surprising that once the referendum became inevitable it got discussed in terms that cast marriage in a negative light. These metaphors have characterised debates about the European Union since its inception as has been illustrated by Andreas Musolff with reference to the notion of the bilateral Franco-German relationship in which the EU originated: 'France and Germany … are seen as a *married couple* and Britain is seen as the outside participant that *disturbs their marriage*', he goes on to point out that:

> …the assumption that the EU has been based mainly on the bilateral relationship between France and Germany, possibly complemented by Britain as a third partner. It exposes the notion of an egalitarian status for all members of the *EU family*, which features prominently in official discourse, as a diplomatic sham.[10]

He warns that the one of the dangers of viewing France and Germany as an established *couple* is that it condemns Britain to being the *lover* or *mistress* as in this Guardian piece:

> An adviser to Chirac says *the Franco–German marriage* remains fundamental to French European policy; many Germans agree. So long as they stick to *the marriage metaphor*, this makes Tony Blair either *lover or mistress*. That's a good reason for abandoning the metaphor, *not the threesome*.[11]

An implication of a marriage frame is that it captures bilateral arrangements because there are only two roles: the bride and the groom. The frame creates a division between those who are 'in' the relationship and those who are not—in this case the marriage between France and Germany excluded Britain. Unfortunately perhaps, the metaphor was not abandoned and in the media framing of Brexit, issues arising from the marriage and divorce script become salient: how much (if anything) was the EU owed and how long would the divorce take?

While I did not find many references to Britain as a lover, I found that the Franco-German relationship was described in the British press from the perspective of an outsider—a distant aunt—and always raised questions about the authenticity of the relationship. Looking in the period from 1990 onwards I found around 200 press articles that made some reference to 'France' and 'Germany' and the phrase 'marriage of convenience' somewhere in the text.[12] Therefore, even a long time before the Referendum, press articles framed France and Germany, as engaging in a 'marriage of convenience':

> A government source described the reforged Paris-Berlin axis as "*a marriage of convenience* rather than ideology" that was aimed at appealing to public opinion in both countries.[13]
>
> The *marriage of convenience* that is the Franco-German relationship celebrates its 40th anniversary this week in Versailles with a parliamentary party of bibulous bonhomie.[14]

But the relationship between France and Britain in their shared opposition to a federal Europe was also framed in this way:

> BRITAIN and France yesterday set their faces against a blueprint for a federal Europe drafted by Jacques Delors. An informal meeting of European Community foreign ministers here heard both the French and British ministers attack a proposal to put foreign policy and the criminal justice system under EC authority. The Anglo-French alliance on this issue is a *marriage of convenience*. Britain simply opposes many of the planned extensions of community power now under discussion.[15]

This suggests a relationship that is grounded in self-interest rather than in warmth or affection between the 'married couple'. In the first example there is a further impersonal effect conveyed by the use of a metonym CAPITAL CITY FOR GOVERNMENT (Paris for France) and the negative word 'axis' that was associated with Hitler's alliance with

Mussolini. Traditionally, whenever the metaphorical 'marriage' between France and Germany is discussed in the British press it is to highlight potential difficulties in the relationship:

> DESPITE publicly *renewing their marriage vows* and promising to see more of each other in future, the leaders of France and Germany emerged from crisis talks still divided yesterday on how to create a wider and more popular European Union.[16]
>
> After *decades of marriage*, he (Sarkosy) was planning *to divorce* Germany and run away with what his compatriots like to disparagingly call the "Anglo-Saxons".[17]

The metaphor was so common in describing the efforts made between Merkel and Sarkozy to save the euro it went viral according to one newspaper headline:

> Merkozy: *marriage of convenience* between French and German leaders becomes internet search term.[18]

Here the perspective is that of an outsider observing a relationship with what is called in German 'schadenfreud', the pleasure derived from another's misfortune. It is the viewpoint of a neighbour who after listening to years of noisy marital disputes is quietly relieved to hear that the couple is breaking up. It is quite rare to find a more neutral account of the relationship, although not impossible, as in the pro-European Guardian:

> Franco-German *pact*: Paris and Berlin feeling the 50-year itch: *It's not a marriage made in heaven*, but co-operation between the two nations has *underpinned* the European project, says Kate Connolly.[19]

While the author acknowledges that the relationship between France and Germany is not at crisis point, this is done somewhat reluctantly by framing it in a negative construction: it says what *it is not* rather than what *it is*—who, after all, thought that it was made in heaven? The use of 'pact'—while less hostile than 'axis'—is associated with a diplomatic power based alliance. As we have seen, it was not *only* the relationship between France and Germany that was framed as a 'marriage of convenience', in the following the French President attributes it to Germany and the UK:

> In a line later removed, Mr Hollande's party said: "The European project is *battered* by a *marriage of convenience* between the Thatcherite leanings of the British Prime Minister – who only conceives of a Europe *à la carte* and of rebates –and the selfish intransigence of Chancellor Merkel, who thinks of nothing but the deposits of German savers, the trade balance recorded by Berlin and her electoral future".[20]

The source for the quotation was a draft paper containing a socialist critique of European policy that was leaked to *Le Monde* and was not present in the final draft. Ironically, *The Financial Times* that was to become the strongest press supporter of Remain, was quite happy to draw attention to ideological differences between Hollande, May and Merkel. Potentially, therefore *any* bilateral alliance from which a third party felt excluded could be framed as a 'marriage of convenience':

> Mrs Merkel said that she would welcome Mr Hollande to Berlin "*with open arms*", though signs are that she would prefer *to strangle him*. For Mr Hollande, a man with no diplomatic, international or government experience, and who is not Mrs Merkel's *first choice of partner*, the meeting will be a *baptism of fire*. The political *marriage of convenience* between Mrs Merkel and Mr Sarkozy, two conservatives, worked.[21]

Once again the pro-Brexit newspaper is happy to highlight the potential for a fractious relationship between 'Mr Hollande' and 'Mrs Merkel'. The bilateral relationships of even quite distant nations from Britain were also evaluated using this metaphor:

> The conservative and Eurosceptic Czech President, Vaclav Klaus, has described his country's relationship with the EU as "*a marriage of convenience, not love*". The balance of power in the country is held by the left, which is likely to make gains.[22]

It is likely the 'marriage of convenience' script served the valuable purpose for the British press of creating the potential for highlighting divisions within Europe because of its rejection of a single federal European State. However, this was not the case for relationships within the United Kingdom. Here a contrast between a 'marriage of convenience' and a romantic union formed the argument for rejection of Scottish Independence. Although the British media emphasised the possibilities of their own national government's divorce or separation from the EU as *just the beginning* of a wider process of disintegration that would ultimately ensure a return to the fully sovereign nation state, the opposite argument was applied in relation to Scotland based on the frame THE UNITED KINGDOM IS A FAMILY:

> The Prime Minister (Theresa May) used a speech to the Scottish Conservative conference in Glasgow to deliver an impassioned case for the "enduring" benefits of the United Kingdom, arguing that unlike the EU it was not a *"marriage of convenience* or a *fair-weather friendship"*. ...'Ours is not *a marriage of convenience* but a true union, tested in adversity'.[23]

David Cameron continuously framed the Scottish referendum using the marriage and divorce frame and eventually it was fear of becoming a lonely and impoverished divorcee that pushed Scotland towards rejection of independence.

The 'Marriage of Convenience' Script on Twitter

Using the three hashtags #Vote Leave, #Vote Remain and #Brexit the phrase 'marriage of convenience' occurred 38 times on Twitter in the period 2016–2018. In some of these tweets the trope was not a metaphor at all but literally a request by someone looking for a marriage to gain European citizenship:

> Seeking cute European Union person for *marriage of convenience* to replace my UK citizenship #Brexit[24]
> So me and my gf are looking for a husband and wife respectively... mainly Canadian. Mainly a *marriage of convenience*... #Brexit[25]

Others were more ironic comments on those seeking such a marriage:

> Hey, liberal Brits? Need an EU *marriage of convenience*? Please send a photo and a recent bank statement. #brexit[26]

It was accompanied with an image of an Irish passport and referred to people who sought to guarantee citizenship rights through marriage. The tweeter, an Irish republican, is making an ironic moral comment on people who marry for convenience rather than love. It was retweeted 23 times and liked 69 times. Another tweet, also probably ironic, proposed a literal 'marriage of convenience':

> WLTM kind, liberal, educated citizen of EU country for *marriage of convenience* & passport. Am good with languages, cakes, & sarcasm. #Brexit[27]

But as a metaphor the idea of a loveless marriage, initiated by the British press, was echoed through social media among those supporting the Leave campaign. A popular tweet shared an article from *The Telegraph*[28] on the speech by Guy Verhofstadt that was referred to above:

> Chief #Brexit negotiator says UK-EU relationship was just a '*marriage of convenience*' and never a 'love affair'[29]

It was retweeted 29 times and received 22 likes, and a number of other accounts also referred to this event:

> "It was never a love affair, certainly no wild passion. It was a *marriage of convenience*," @GuyVerhofstadt setting tone in EP #Brexit debate[30]

The tweeter, DW Europe, is Germany's public international broadcaster: perhaps a curious source of support for a pro-Brexit tweet, though by this time the EU were taking a unified perspective. Some tweets highlighted financial reasons for a marriage of convenience:

> Guy Verhofstadt: EU relationship with UK 'was a *marriage of CONVENIENCE*'
> Yes, EU just NEEDED our MONEY
> #Brexit[31]

Others rejected the idea of mutual financial benefit implied by a 'marriage of convenience' and rejected the metaphor:

> It's certainly not a *marriage of convenience. We have been enslaved* by the EU and its time to leave as we want our freedom back *from the evil clutches* of Tusk and Juncker. #Brexit[32]

Others commented more explicitly on the absence of shared values or shared ideologies:

> Is #Brexit the biggest sign yet of the end of the 30-year *marriage of convenience* between economic neoliberalism and social conservatism?

Some queried the moral basis for the relationship between Britain and the EU on the grounds that it was established in secret:

> It was a *marriage arranged* on our behalf, *behind our backs.* Now we understand, we need to #VoteLeave[33]

And lacked real emotional warmth and sexual intimacy:

> UK and Europe consciously uncouple after lukewarm, sexless 40 year *marriage of convenience.* #Brexit[34]

Others were more oriented to the future and were prepared to put up with the difficulties of leaving the EU because of the unsatisfactory nature of the relationship:

> *A messy divorce is better than a broken and bankrupt marriage of convenience.* #Brexit[35]

It is worth noting that these were all posted using #Brexit and when I searched using only #Remain there was a single tweet containing the metaphor:

> More #Remain #StrongerIn #Joining the EU was a *marriage of convenience which has turned sour. Walking away* is the only sensible thing to do.[36]

This directs a pro-Brexit position towards Remain supporters and is what I describe as 'counter-messaging' because it is intended to influence opposing opinions. The message was not posted using #Brexit so it was *not* designed to reinforce the sender's own supporters, but strategically to influence those voting 'Remain'.

What all the Leave supporting tweets share is that they invoke either moral reasoning or moral intuition to support their position. We saw in the last chapter how Lakoff drew attention to metaphors that originated in parenting style to explain differences in the moral order of politics. Since typically children develop their sense of morality from their parents, so the family provides a model for all social relationships. Moral Politics Theory has been summarised as follows:

> ...people's beliefs about ideal family life serve as a conceptual anchor for their larger, moral belief systems about how society and its members should function, and these moral belief systems dictate people's political attitudes. The theory holds that the translation of family-level beliefs into nation-level attitudes occurs via the nation-as-family metaphor.[37]

The authors conduct empirical research that demonstrates that moral judgements about the family create conceptual templates that provide the basis for political judgements. The analysis of the 'marriage of convenience' metaphor in this section supports the view that it was used in moral reasoning about Brexit. The metaphor was initiated by journalists from 1990 onwards and then adopted by tweeters to express moral concerns about the nature of Britain's relationship with 'Europe'. Just as in life it is dishonest to continue in a relationship that lacks love, so many Brexit supporters resorted to Twitter to develop moral arguments about

Brexit. The 'marriage of convenience' metaphor provided a script for moral reasoning about various relationships within Europe—especially those from which Britain felt excluded. Initially the script described other European relationships, taking a third person 'marriage guidance' perspective, however the script soon shifted to Britain's own relationship with the European Union and therefore contributed to the cognitive conditions in which 'divorce' from Europe was morally necessary. Interestingly, and perhaps surprisingly, both pro-Brexit supporters and the European Union saw the rhetorical advantages to be gained for representing Britain's relationship with Europe as no more than a 'marriage of convenience': one in which—in line with the claims of linguistic determinism—divorce would happen sooner rather than later.

The 'Divorce' Script in the Press

Yet if marriage has always been was a way of forming international political relationships, then so was divorce. Henry VIII's desire to divorce his Spanish wife Catherine had symbolised a crucial political re-alignment away from Catholic Europe and contributed to the national identity of England as a sovereign state. Divorce metaphors satisfy both the purpose of engaging audiences, since divorce is an experience rarely forgotten, but also offers various scenarios for moral reasoning about Britain's decision to leave the EU. The divorce script had been quite commonly used in press discussions of Britain's troubled history with the EU:

> The possibility that Britain's *separation* from the European exchange rate mechanism will end in *divorce* may have increased yesterday [...].[38]

The processes involved in the negotiation of the UK's departure were communicated with reference to knowledge of the complex emotional and legal aspects that characterise divorce negotiations.

The word 'divorce' carries with it strongly negative associations arising from the 'break up' of a family: painful emotions and serious financial implications. If we look at the 520 million word corpus in which we examined 'marriage' earlier, we find the following adjectives are most commonly used to describe 'divorce': bitter (78)[39]; messy (72); nasty (47); painful (47); contentious (27); ugly (27); amicable (23); difficult (20); acrimonious (16). Apart from 'amicable' all the other adjectives have a negative semantic prosody with associations of unpleasant emotions and disagreement. I hope any readers who have had a divorce might describe it as 'amicable', but if so the linguistic evidence suggests that they are in a minority. It was probably for this reason that Leave politicians eventually realised that describing Britain's departure from the EU as a 'divorce' was unlikely to yield an attractive post-withdrawal 'deal'.

There were more than 3000 press articles with 'Brexit' and 'divorce' in their headlines in the period 2016–2018. Once the complex relationships between nations are represented as based only in self-interest, as implied by the 'marriage of convenience' metaphor, this creates the conditions for political relationships between nations to be framed as 'divorce'. I illustrated in chapter one how the payment that Britain was expected to make to the EU for its expenditure commitments became popularly referred to as the 'divorce bill'. Table 8.3 shows the frequency in press articles of headlines containing 'Brexit' and the pattern 'adjective + divorce' anywhere else in the article, so for example there were 87 articles on the topic of Brexit in the period 2016–2018 that included the phrase 'messy divorce'.

Readers may be puzzled by the high frequency of 'amicable' in the first half of 2016, nearly all of these occurred after the referendum result when the media quoted Jean-Claude Juncker, president of the European Commission: 'It's not an amicable divorce, but it was not exactly an intimate affair anyway', so 'amicable' is preceded by a negative form. Three quarters of the mentions of 'messy divorce' were from the pro-Remain press—*The Guardian, The Observer* and *The Independent* widely quoted George Osborne that it would be a "long, costly and messy divorce". Though *The Telegraph* and *The Times* reported Boris Johnson as saying: "Germany has the most to lose from a messy divorce." The phrase appeared again widely towards the end of 2018 in relation to Gibraltar quoting Tim Farron that: 'I worry that in this messy divorce we might be leaving one of the children behind'.

Table 8.3 Headlines with 'Brexit' and 'adjective+divorce': January 2016–December 2018

Adjectival premodifier of 'divorce'	January–June 2016	July–December 2016	January–June 2017	July–December 2017	January–June 2018	July–December 2018	Total
Amicable	81	18	3	8	1	5	116
Messy	31	3	5	14	2	32	87
Acrimonious	5	35	21	4	0	5	70
Bitter	37	5	12	3	0	1	58
Ugly	0	0	2	2	1	23	28
Nasty	4	3	4	0	0	0	11
Painful	1	2	4	4	0	0	11
Difficult	1	3	3	4	0	0	11

The divorce scenario was contested in terms of which side would lose most; the pro-Brexit press quoted those who claimed it would be the EU. For example, *The Express Online* quoted Jeremy Hunt's warning that the consequences of an "acrimonious, messy divorce" would be terrible for the European Union. The metaphor 'ugly divorce' was also attributed to Hunt: "It would be a mistake we would regret for generations, if we had a messy, ugly divorce, and would inevitably change British attitudes towards Europe".[40] A 'messy' divorce would presumably influence European attitudes to Britain as much as it would British attitudes toward Europe.

Not all references to 'divorce' are metaphors; most instances of 'acrimonious divorce' in the second part of 2016 refer to Gina Miller who successfully fought an action requiring a debate in Parliament prior to the declaration of Article 50 (that announced UK's intention to withdraw). *The Mail Online* launched a campaign against her with headlines such as: "The South American born former model who took on Theresa May and won: How millionaire married to 'Mr Hedge Fund' and said Brexit made her 'physically sick' has derailed British democracy".[41] The tenuous connection with divorce is that Mr. Miller, was involved in an acrimonious divorce from his ex-wife, Melissa after his 'childless marriage broke down after less than three years around the time he met Gina'. It is not easy to see the relevance of a divorce occurring several years previously, but the *MailOnline* was not slow to explore the negative associations of 'divorce' in its negative construal of Gina Miller.

In political contexts the divorce script was first introduced in relation to Scottish Independence and in June 2015 the metaphor was first used in relation to Brexit:

> Marc Boleat, effectively the political leader of the City of London Corporation, said an exit vote would lead to years of *"divorce" negotiations* during which London risked losing business.[42]

But once the Pandora's box of the 'divorce' metaphor was opened, journalists would not close it, and there were over 1000 uses of the metaphor in relation to Brexit in the period 2016–2018, peaking in December 2017 when concerns about the cost of leaving the EU were heightened.

Consider the following extracts from the historian Niall Ferguson in an article for *The Sunday Times*. The author establishes the divorce script at the outset, by highlighting the accuracy of his own prediction that leaving the EU would be much more difficult than Leave campaigners had admitted:

> I was wrong about Brexit - which I opposed - but I was right that it would be like a divorce. Last June, just two days before the referendum on Britain's EU membership, I made a prediction: getting a decree nisi after 43 years of marriage would take a lot longer and cost far more than anyone campaigning for the "leave" campaign wanted to admit.

He then developed the script by explaining how psychological factors obscured understanding of the practical difficulties involved in ending relationships:

> Most people contemplating divorce, I observed, are motivated by two things. First, they see only their spouse's defects. Second, they fantasise about an idealised alternative future. So powerful are these emotions that one is almost blind to the difficulty and expense of the divorce process. Only slowly does it become apparent that hell hath no fury like a spouse spurned - and that purgatory is staffed by lawyers.

Ferguson then provides evidence of this major argument of the complexities of Brexit and discusses the financial implications of Brexit:

> The EU side has dreamt up the hefty sum of (EURO)100bn as Britain's gross "Brexit bill" and stated flatly that there will be no discussion of future trade until this has been accepted. This is the equivalent of the spurned spouse demanding the family home, minus the mortgage, and refusing to discuss custody of the children until the deeds have been handed over.

He continued by comparing the moral implications of Brexit with its financial cost in order to arrive at a decision as to whether Brexit was, to use a moral accounting metaphor, 'worth it':

"The reason divorce is so expensive," a twice-wed American friend once explained to me, "is that it's really worth it." Will Brexit be worth it? Not in the ways that the "leave" campaign led voters to believe, no. All that money that was supposed to go to the health service? It will go on divorce bills. But it will ultimately be worth it if Britain can finally stop pretending that all its problems are the fault of Brussels. It will also be worth it for jilted Europe if it can now finally get on with fixing its institutions in ways that, as a member state, Britain always resisted.

He ended the article with a negative evaluation of a so-called 'soft Brexit' whereby Britain contributes to the EU budget without political representation:

You pay a contribution to the EU budget but you don't have a vote in any European institution. *Some divorce. It would be more like becoming a child bride under sharia.…*

Here a different aspect of the frame drawn from an alien culture is employed to argue for a hard Brexit. The divorce script provided Ferguson with an allegorical frame for moral reasoning about Brexit; unlike single one-off metaphors, the divorce script offers insight into the socio-psychological aspects of Brexit and explores how moral decisions faced by nation states can be understood and evaluated allegorically with reference to divorce. Given that many people have far more experience of divorce than they do of negotiating international relationships, this is a style of deliberation that is appropriate for an opinion article in an upmarket newspaper whose readership is primarily from people who can afford to get divorced. However, he selects those aspects of the script that most favoured an argument to continue with Brexit—whatever the cost.

An article that employed the divorce script in a more nuanced argument for a 'softer' Brexit was authored by the Labour MP Emily Thornbury, herself a barrister. In a style chosen for *The Daily Mirror* she initiated the divorce frame by profiling the emotional suffering it often entails:

"WE'RE getting a divorce." It's something we all dread hearing, whether from our children, siblings, best friends or parents.

It's not just the heartbreak of seeing their marriages end, it's also the gut-wrenching knowledge of the pain it will bring. Because while everyone starts out hoping to keep things friendly and civil, we all know it rarely ends that way. Ever since the Brexit result came through, I've thought of it in the same way. Both in terms of how complex it will be *to negotiate the divorce settlement*, and how challenging it will be to remain *amicable with our European partners* throughout the process. No one will benefit if it descends into a bitter row where success is judged not by whether we reach a sensible deal, but on which side comes out the winner and which side the loser.[43]

Her lexical choices emphasised the emotional suffering, the difficulties involved and rejected a 'winner' and 'loser' script that invited a frame for war. She highlighted the reliance of the 'Tory' opposition on the emotive war frame and contrasted this with the complexity of divorce script to develop an argument for independent negotiators to take emotions out of what is in reality a complex legal process:

The Tory Brexit team agree.... All three of them - and the hopeless Theresa May seem to be treating this divorce not as a complex, sensitive process of diplomacy, but as a battle in which - whatever they demand - they can expect to get it. But divorce proceedings rarely work out that way, and huge damage is often done in the process, as countless celebrity cases over recent years have proved.

She then created an analogy between the negotiating role of divorce lawyers and the civil service, arguing the need for 'cool heads' and emotional detachment. However, other newspapers employed the divorce script much more emotively in their moral accounting. Consider the following from *The MailOnline*:

Give us wine, art and property!: Britain's Brexit *divorce lawyers* will demand a share of the EU's vast assets - including Margaret Thatcher's old Tory party HQ.

In the article the author claims that Britain will 'battle' for a share of the EU's assets that include a £42,000 wine cellar, art works and £7.5 billion property holdings—including Margaret Thatcher's former Conservative Party HQ, 32 Smith Square in London. The articles then concludes:

> Given its history in UK politics, it (32 Smith Square) is believed to be seen as a prize asset to obtain in any Brexit *divorce proceedings.*

So here a pro-Brexit newspaper is attempting to reframe the issue of the 'divorce bill' on the basis of moral reciprocity away from the money owed by the UK and towards the assets that were commonly owned by Britain and the EU. One of these was a building that had previously been used by Margaret Thatcher. The author undertakes moral reasoning on the basis of reciprocity and knowing the symbolic significance of Margaret Thatcher to Mail readers. Drawing on the script that it is typical in the event of a marriage break-up for the assets to be divided fairly, the author argues that Britain deserves her fair share of these. The roles are those of a divorcing couple and the scenarios involve expensive lawyers wrangling over ownership of emotionally privileged assets. There is the self-righteous conviction implied by 'will demand', and the evaluation of a building as a 'prize asset'; identity is concealed by the use of the passive 'it is believed'. It is rightly believed by the *MailOnline* editor that this makes a good story because it arouses moral intuitions related to Fairness and Cheating.

But 'divorce bill' framing was not the most likely means for reaching a constructive outcome—the discourse of the TV or radio soap opera proves highly ineffective in solving real world problems. The use of the phrase declined during the period of the Salzberg meeting—for example in September 2017 there were 89 headlines using 'Divorce Bill' whereas in September 2018 the phrase only occurred in 16 headlines. The framing by the press of the financial settlement as a 'divorce bill' did not make it easy for those negotiating a settlement. The speechwriter Simon Lancaster did some research into this by asking 100 people via an online survey how much money they thought Britain should pay the European Union using two different question formats—one referred to it as a 'settlement' and the other as a 'divorce settlement'. When the second format was used the number of people who selected 'nothing' increased from 24 to 44% and the number with 'no opinion' decreased from 14 to 6%.[44] This shows that moral reasoning is influenced by metaphors based in moral intuitions as they heighten emotional involvement, this may have influenced May to avoid using the term 'divorce settlement' as it created higher expectations by the public of a lower payment and could interfere with negotiations with the European Union.

Some journalists explained how Brexit was *not* like a divorce:

> A divorce is between two equal partners. But the UK is to the EU what Belgium, Austria or Portugal are to Germany: an entity eight times as small. If the EU informs the UK that "no soft Brexit means no soft Brexit" then that is what it is.[45]

Other journalists rejected the whole divorce framing by evaluating the moral reasoning that it implied when used by journalists:

> Stop calling Brexit "a divorce" - we were never married to the idea of the EU. Why do so many political pundits use marital divorce as a like-for-like metaphor for Brexit? …Then in The Times, David Aaronovitch criticised attempts to do deals with Brussels saying: "It is as if a spouse sues for divorce, demands the house and then suggests popping round every now and then for a quickie." That sounds terribly clever but it is stupid. We wanted a trade deal 43 years ago with the European Community not till-death-do-us-part nuptials with declarations of undying love and confetti. There isn't a "divorce" and there was never a "love affair" or a "marriage" either.[46]

The author's metaphor arouses the moral intuition since most people would feel that it was degrading to expect sexual favours from a divorcing partner. Many articles discussed the impact of Brexit on personal relationships arguing that it was leading to an increase in the divorce rate—this supports linguistic determinism since once social issues are metaphorically framed as 'divorces', then 'real' divorces become more likely. A major theme of such articles was how differences of political opinion as regards Brexit had increased pressures on personal relationships; Nigel Shepherd, who is chair of an organisation of family lawyers, is quoted as saying:

We have come across a number of families in this country [who are splitting up] because one them voted differently [to the other] in the referendum. They fell out in a big way because one voted for remain and one for leave. I suspect that was unlikely to have been the sole reason [for divorce] but we have heard of cases from a number of our members. It was a really divisive campaign. It pushed some couples [over the edge]. It was the last straw that made them think 'we are really incompatible'.[47]

Developing a similar theme *Express Online* quotes a Relate counsellor Gurpreet Singh on the Brexit effect:

Arguments over Brexit, who to vote for and other topical debates can bring up underlying issues within the relationship as they highlight where couples have a lack of shared values... I've seen several clients in 2016 who have mentioned Brexit in counselling sessions. In some cases, Brexit is causing anxiety about the future and this is putting pressure on the relationship. ...In many cases Brexit has simply added fuel to an existing fire - couples will mention how their partner voted in the EU referendum as an example of how 'you never listen to me', 'I don't feel understood', 'you don't value my opinions', 'you always want to do your own thing'.[48]

The Times ran an article on the topic of divisions of family opinion within families that contained politicians who needed to declare their positions on Brexit.

The Johnsons are another family who do not see eye-to-eye over Europe. Boris and his mother, Charlotte, are in the Leave camp; Rachel, a journalist, Jo, the science minister, and their environmentalist father, Stanley, all wish to remain in the EU.[49]

The article went on to gossip about purported disputes within the Osborne and Corbyn familes. The actual divorce of Boris Johnson was considered highly newsworthy:

Boris Johnson's wife confronted him about being unfaithful months ago - but they agreed not to divorce until after Brexit. A source claims Marina Wheeler feared a public split would detract from her husband's role in the negotiations.[50]

While anecdotal in nature, for at least some families the divorce script provided insight into their own interpersonal relationships. It may be that the Referendum, with its high stakes binary choice, encouraged protagonists to employ binary metaphor choices—marriage or divorce—friend or enemy etc.—and that the interaction between memory and framing effects invited scenarios that entailed two 'sides'. This may, in turn, have impacted on their interpersonal relationships. This process of socio-emotional political cognition is illustrated in Fig. 8.1.

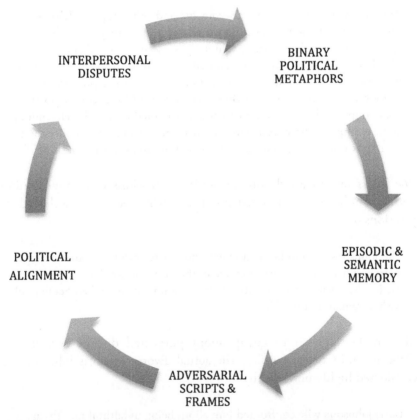

Fig. 8.1 Binary metaphors, adversarial scripts and their social effects

It seems plausible that the divorce script contributed to an adversarial climate in a similar way to the other adversarial frames we have looked at, such as war and invasion, and distrust and betrayal; framing influences both personal relationships and political alignments. Similarly moral intuitions are paired as opposites: Loyalty or Betrayal, Fairness or Cheating etc. Declarative memory is comprised of personal episodic memory, often based in emotionally charged experiences, and semantic memory or general factual knowledge. It may be that episodic and semantic memory mediates between binary metaphors and adversarial scripts, frames and moral intuitions. The mediating effect of personal episodic memories contributed to adversarial scripts, frames and moral intuitions that had been triggered by binary metaphors and were then imported into Brexit discourse. If this were the case then binary political metaphors contributed to adversarial metaphor frames and moral intuitions that then contributed to adversarial social and political alignments. The resulting negative effect on personal relationships may have had a detrimental effect on the political context. If this was the case then it is no wonder that some pubs banned Brexit related discussion on the assumption that its binary nature would lead to side taking and argument.

The 'Divorce' Script on Social Media

The divorce script was equally active on social media, especially by the LeaveEU campaign that was attracted by adversarial frames, as in the following posts from Aaron Banks' Leave.EU account:

> READ | All very well calling the spineless EU "discourteous". How about causing some real alarm by pulling out of negotiations and *withdrawing that treasonous divorce bill?*
> We're *dealing with bullies,* we need to treat them as such. (733 retweets)[51]

LeaveEU rejected the concept of paying money to the EU on ideological grounds—and in line with the Invaded Nation script. By contrast,

Vote Leave, following the 'Sovereign Nation' script, did not use the marriage and divorce frame in its tweets: neither 'marriage' nor 'divorce' occurs in any of them. Once again this reveals the range of rhetorical styles adopted by Brexiteers: they had the choice between the adversarial script of divorce based on Cheating and Betrayal or avoiding scripts that encouraged positive moral intuitions about international relations such as Fairness and Loyalty. The detailed profiling of voters by Cambridge Analytica using Facebook data allowed messages to be crafted in such a way that they could be targetted toward those who would respond more favourably to the script. For example, those whose profile revealed that they were divorced would be more likely to respond to a tweet employing the divorce script. It is for this reason that the LeaveEU campaign continually returned to the divorce script throughout the negotiating period as a method of arousing moral intuitions. There were three types of argument for the rejection of the the so-called 'divorce bill'; the first was that it was not something to which the UK was legally commited:

WATCH | Howard says the UK doesn't legally have to pay any EU *divorce bill.* These huge figures they use to scare us are nothing but hot air! (440 retweets)[52]

The second argument included an endorsement—either by an overseas politician, or a known national level supporter of Brexit:

"A world trade Brexit lets Britain set its own rules…No '*divorce bill*' whatsoever should be paid to Brussels," added the former Australian PM. Thriving Australia has an independent trade policy and controlled borders. This should be our future. (459 retweets)[53]

Some much needed #WednesdayWisdom from Wetherspoons boss and Brexit legend Tim Martin, whose new beer mats call for our leaders to wise up and *refuse to pay the EU's outrageous divorce bill* (+emoticon of clapping hands) (204 retweets)[54]

The third argument did not explicitly reject a 'divorce bill' in all circumstances but argued that it should be used as a bargaining tool in order to negotiate the best possible 'deal':

READ | "The time has come to say publicly that we are willing to walk away and withdraw our £39 billion *divorce settlement* if we aren't happy with the final deal," writes Andrea Jenkyns .. (1300 retweet)[55]

READ | "To have any real leverage in the Brexit endgame, the UK must reserve the right to walk away without a trade deal and take with it the £39billion it has offered to pay as part of a *divorce settlement.*" (551 retweets)[56]

LeaveEU strategists had identified a demographic of angry men some of whom were unhappy with their own divorce settlement and were attracted by the idea of 'walking away'. The number of retweets and likes for such messages suggests that episodic memories of personal experiences of divorce and moral intuitions regarding having been cheated could be activated through the divorce script and offered a form of pyscho-emotional gratification. There were also some Leave EU tweets that relied more generally on the divorce script:

Brexit Britain and the EU *have filed for divorce* at the WTO, paving the way for Britain to regain her independent seat at the top table of world trade. (492 retweets)[57]

READ | The Remainer strategy is emerging: use the grotesque *divorce* bill to push for a second referendum. Needless to say, they don't call themselves patriots. (277 retweets)[58]

The divorce script therefore provided a method for moral reasoning about what was financially fair in the event of divorce.

But what of the Remain campaign: how far did they employ the script of divorce in their framing of issues? To explore this question I compared 100 randomly selected tweets posted in the week before the Referendum and classified them by whether they supported Remain or Leave. There was no clear correlation between use of the divorce script and the position taken in the referendum: in this sample Remain supporters were slightly more likely to frame Brexit in terms of divorce: there were 38 Pro-Remain tweets; 32 Pro-Leave tweets and 30 neutral tweets and I illustrate a few in Table 8.4.

Remain supporters frame their tweets from the perspective of a part-ner (male?) who regrets divorce because of the negative circumstances in which he finds himself. Conversely, Leave supporters emphasise the

Table 8.4 Referendum week 'divorce tweets' by affiliation

Pro-Leave
Alastair Cambell uses marriage analogy to remain. Look at the divorce rate mate, people stuck in, dying to get out (Andy,22 Jun 2016)
#Brexit isn't the divorce, it's the reconciliation with the first wife, the real one, and the kids. The slut can go jump off the cliff. (Malapert Press, 22 Jun 2016)
#brexit=a divorce! The EX doesn't get to keep the keys and free access to the (EU) house after the split. Vote #Remain (Liz-anne, 22 Jun 2016)
The EU divorce papers are in the post. You can have the politics and we'll keep our house, car jobs and £££ #Brexit #VoteLeave (Benben, 21 Jun 2016)
Pro-Remain
Like Farage I'm married to someone Germanic from another EU member state. Unlike Farage, I don't want a divorce from the EU #VoteRemain (John Kolm Murray, 22 Jun 2016)
The EU is like a marriage. Getting a divorce will seem like a good idea until you're living in a rented bedsit eating microwave mash #Brexit (Hayley Jane, 22 Jun 2016)
Divorce also means sitting in your pants eating beans from a can wishing you hadn't fucked it up. #EUref #Brexit (Klaus Von Trapp, 21 Jun 2016)
Brace yourself for possibly the world's most expensive divorce! #Brexit #UKreferendum (Mubina Kapasi, 22 Jun 2016)
Neutral/Unclear
To all my English friends: even when you divorce (haha) from the EU: I love you. #Brexit (Wessel van Alphen, 22 Jun 2016)
Easy trade deals with Europe after quitting EU membership would be like a divorce where you can still have sex with your ex #brexit #remain (Edward Upton, 22 Jun 2016)

emotional benefits offered by divorce such as moving on to new relationships. Both sides raise the issue of cost, but while Remainers are afraid of the cost, Leavers prefer to contest the amount. An alternative strategy for Remain would have been to *reject the script of divorce* altogether, rather than to frame the debate in terms of something that invites an emotionally negative intuitive response.

Summary

From the very start the dominant presence of the 'marriage and divorce' frame in the traditional media provided a rhetorical frame that could readily be introduced into the Brexit debate online. Since marriage is often stalked by the shadow of divorce, and evokes moral intuitions based on Fairness/Cheating and Loyalty/Betrayal, understanding UK's relationship with the EU as a 'marriage of convenience' always meant that once there were difficulties, the divorce script was waiting in the wings. Just as in the discourse of relationship counsellors, events such as divorce can be reframed in terms of 'moving on', so I suggest that the departure of the UK from a particular institution could also be framed in terms of forming new relationships that avoid the negative associations of divorce.

If I might be permitted a historical analogy. Elizabeth 1st believed that the unity of the national family could only be ensured by keeping her suitors guessing and eventually by rejecting the marriage option. Dying heirless was deemed less of a risk than alienating Catholics or Protestants. I would suggest that Theresa May found herself in a similar position: she rejected a marriage with supporters of the European Research Group (strongly pro-Brexit) but also rejected those who sought to remain in the EU or wanted a second ballot. For both Elizabeth 1st and Theresa May 'the nation as family' frame predominated and the overriding consideration was to avoid splitting the family. For May the DUP in Northern Ireland was a crucial member of the family on which her government depended—this part of the family is more concerned with remaining a UK family member than with the UK's divorce from the EU. Ironically, therefore, May's efforts to get the best possible 'divorce' only succeeded in uniting the European family against her while simultaneously splitting her own national family, and leading to them divorcing her! That's the difference between being a sixteenth century Queen and a twenty-first century Prime Minister.

Notes

1. DK Matai @DKMatai, 18 Jun 2016.
2. *The Times*, 29 April 1994.
3. *The Independent*, 10 October 1994.
4. *The Telegraph*, 11 September 2017.
5. *Sunday Times*, 23 August 2015.

6. *The Guardian*, 31 May 2016.
7. *The Guardian*, 19 June 2016.
8. *The Guardian*, 14 March 2018.
9. *Express Online*, 5 April 2017.
10. Musolff, A. (2006), p. 34.
11. *The Guardian*, 19 February 2004.
12. 123 articles had 'marriage of convenience' and 'France' & 'Germany', a further 40 had 'Paris' and 'Berlin' and 23 had 'Franco-German' with 'marriage of convenience'.
13. *The Independent*, 1 January 2003.
14. *The Times*, 20 January 2003.
15. *The Times*, 4 June 1991.
16. *The Daily Telegraph*, 2 February 2001.
17. *The Telegraph*, 10 December 2011.
18. *The Telegraph*, 8 December 2011.
19. *The Guardian*, 23 January 2013.
20. *The Financial Times*, 26 April 2013.
21. *Sunday Telegraph*, 13 May 2013
22. *The Independent*, 10 June 2004.
23. *The Daily Telegraph*, 4 March 2017.
24. c thot" stone @mill_ionnaire, 1 Feb 2017. (Account since deleted)
25. Owen G. Bevan @TheBigOBowski, 9 Nov 2016.
26. Tim Brannigan @tim_brannigann, 24 Jun 2016.
27. Emily @Emily_Thomas73, 29 March 2017.
28. http://www.telegraph.co.uk/news/2017/04/05/britain-braced-rough-ride-strasbourg-eu-parliament-sets-brexit2/.
29. @Telegraph, 5 Apr 2017.
30. DW Europe, 5 Apr 2017.
31. Brexit #Leave #EU Go #WTO, 6 Apr 2017.
32. Yorkshire Hero, Sep 24.
33. Denmore 24 Jun 2016.
34. Teddy Bear.
35. tefan, 24 Jun 2016.
36. Gavin Hardy, 19 Apr 2016.
37. 13 Jun 2016.
38. https://journals.plos.org/plosone/article?id=10.1371/journal.pone.0193347.
39. *The Financial Times*, 4 January 1993.

40. The number of times in brackets.
41. *Daily Star*, 18 August 2018.
42. *MailOnline*, 3 November 2016.
43. *The Telegraph*, 12 June 2015.
44. *MailOnline*, 1 October 2016.
45. Lancaster, S. (2018), p. 225.
46. *The Times*, 21 May 2016.
47. *Express*, 30 July 2016.
48. *The Guardian*, 8 November 2016.
49. *Express Online*, 30 December 2016.
50. *The Times*, 21 May 2016.
51. *mirror.co.uk*, 15 September 2018.
52. Leave.EU, 8 Feb 2018.
53. 2 April 2017.
54. 25 Oct 2018.
55. 8 August 2018.
56. 6 June 2018.
57. 24 June 2018.
58. 25 Jul 2017.
59. 29 Nov 2017.

References

Lancaster, S. (2018). *How Words Kill: You Are Not Human*. London: Biteback Publishing.

Musolff, A. (2006). Metaphor Scenarios in Public Discourse. *Metaphor and Symbol* 21, 1: 23–38.

9
Animals: Moral Intuition and Moral Reasoning

Introduction

This chapter identifies animal-related metaphors that characterised online discussion of Brexit and drew on cultural models to arouse moral intuitions. I identify two different frames for animal metaphors: in the first humans are attributed characteristics that are conventionally associated with animals; I describe this as the 'Human-as-animal' frame and suggest it is allegorical in nature. A typical example of this is when idioms containing an animal term provide stereotypical ways of talking about human traits such as deception and greed. This frame has a stylistic tendency towards intensification and hyperbole. The second frame is the 'Animal-as-human' frame. This is a frame where people attribute their own views on Brexit to their pets. This reflects a contemporary style developed in social media that involves creating and circulating memes such as manga style images, animal emojis and photographs of a pet (usually a cat or a dog)—with embedded text metaphorically expressing the pet's 'opinion'. This is a stylistically novel blend of humour, allusion, multimodality and metaphor that protects the sender from direct personal attack since to criticise the views of a

© The Author(s) 2019
J. Charteris-Black, *Metaphors of Brexit*,
https://doi.org/10.1007/978-3-030-28768-9_9

pet would appear stupid. The pet serves as an emotional shield, though other platform users could respond by posting the views of their own pet. I take this as a face-saving strategy that engages through humour and encourages a 'light' response with a stylistic tendency toward understatement and euphemism.

In the last chapter we saw how the experience of marriage and divorce created a script that could be used in moral reasoning—arguing about rights and responsibilities—although in reality it was moral intuitions that were equally influential. Animal metaphors were also used in moral reasoning in the UK partly because many British people live in close proximity to domestic pets and invest them with intense and deeply felt emotions. Cats, dogs—and even snakes—become surrogate family members to be spoken to, cared for, and protected. They are given human names such as 'Charlie', 'Max' or 'Bella',[1] attributed human-like moods and considered as having rights for attention, food and walks. Special arrangements are made for family holidays, medical insurance is taken out and, on their demise, they are commemorated symbolically. When animal metaphors are invoked people's reasoning is often based on emotional intuitions about animals. The philosopher David Hume regarded morals as linked to a range of emotions and passions and therefore as not based on reason.

Animal metaphors are also persuasive because they contribute to moral intuition; this is where something is right because it feels right. We will recall that in moral reasoning a series of stages are gone through in arriving at a view about the right form of behaviour. For example, in moral reasoning the 'club' frame identified in Chapter 7 argued that Britain could not continue to receive the benefits of being in the EU if it left because membership involves costs such as paying a subscription. Similarly, the 'divorce bill' frame in Chapter 8 argued that because marriage incurred obligations there should be repayment if the couple divorced. Of course moral reasoning might also be involved in *rejecting* the appropriateness of the club frame or the divorce script as a model for understanding the obligations incurred when changing international relations with 27 other nations simultaneously. By contrast, moral intuition is instantaneous and somatic; when someone says that they 'smell a rat' or describes someone as 'a lone wolf' there is instinctive disapproval that may show in visual responses such as screwing up the eyelids or twirking the nose. It evokes the Sanctity/Degradation foundation based on the emotion of disgust. Moral intuition does not involve reflection and people do not know why they fear rats or wolves and idioms involving these animals trigger moral intuitions that someone is dishonest or dangerous without them knowing why.

Endearing domestic pets take their place alongside earlier linguistic forms in which animals had dangerous and sinister meanings referring to the worst type of human behaviour—just think of the 'lone wolf' metaphor to refer to someone who plans an act of terror without being part of a group. Fairy tales offer mythic roles for animals where children could be eaten by wolves, livelihoods threatened by foxes, rats and other pests that might steal the crop or kill the chickens. Then there are the exotic animals of the zoo and circus: elephants and giraffes, tigers and lions that allow more scope for fantasy and imagination. These offer different types of moral intuition that are often more favourable in British culture because they are more geographically distant. For these reasons it is not surprising that during the Brexit campaign animals played their role—especially on Twitter.

Animal frames are widely used in political language because of the rich potential they offer for activating pre-existing knowledge and associations derived from myths, fables and allegories. These originate in a rich vein of cultural resources including the Bible, The Great Chain of Being, fairy tales (e.g. Grimms and Hans Christian Anderson), fables (e.g. Aesop's) and myths (e.g. dragons, phoenixes and gryphens).[2] Although politicians sometimes refer to animals in their speeches, in the present study I found that they were much more commonly used in the Referendum debate on Twitter than in the press and so this chapter takes animal metaphors as an illustration of some characteristics of Twitter style—invective, resisting invective and conveying moral intuition. Consider the following:

> No longer will the British *roll over like dogs* for a self serving elite! Post #brexit there must be real reform at home, this is our house! (24 retweets)[3]

In this case the 'British' are described with reference to the familiar behaviour of a submissive dog. Relying on moral intuition the tweeter argues that the 'British' should reject the authority of an 'elite'. This populist argues that the British need 'reform at home' to regain control of 'our house'—with intuitions that the home and house must be protected at all costs: these are the symbols of the 'Englishman's castle' (though it looks as if the tweeter has Australian connections). On the Leave side animal metaphors could introduce an ad hominem attack on the figureheads of the Remain campaign:

> *Straight from the horses mouth* & @David_Cameron still lies that he will seek further change @ukleave_eu #Brexit. (14 retweets)[4]

The trustworthiness of the horse validates the appraisal of Cameron as a liar. Such tweets express moral intuition rather than moral reasoning, whereas other tweets involve moral reasoning:

> Remainers saying "Experts say we should stay." Look at those 'experts' again and say you don't *smell a rat*! #Brexit[5]

This tweet then displays a table showing various institutions such as The Institute for Fiscal Studies, the OECD and Friends of the Earth and the amount they receive in EU funding. The reasoning is that these institutions are lobby groups acting only on the basis of their own financial interests. Of course with an account name like 'Whistling Dixie' one assumes the author is a Republican supporter of Trump (Dixieland etc.).

Pet anthropomorphism, increase in vegetarianism and concern for species survival all argue for the growing importance of animals in moral reflection. Conventional stereotypes of animals—such as being deceptive or greedy—are anthropomorphic in their origins because they derive from projecting onto animals what were really human moral behaviours. Animals are not really being deceptive or greedy when they hunt or eat because they are following their instincts in satisfying their biological needs: hunger, sex etc. Humans negotiate their relationships with other humans through sharing or challenging the attitudes and behaviours towards animals practised by other humans. Our ideas and experiences of animals—both in direct experience and cultural knowledge—become embedded into frames that enable us to use and understand metaphors that include an animal term. But to understand both the 'Human-as-animal' and the 'Animal-as-human' frames for modelling human-animal relationships it is first necessary to explore their origins in the Great Chain of Being cultural model.

The Great Chain of Being and the Human-as-Animal Frame

The evaluation offered by animal metaphors takes its origin in a culturally based model known as the Great Chain of Being that provided a complete explanatory frame for the universe throughout the Middle Ages with roles for mankind, the animal and plant kingdom and the divine realm (God, a hierarchy of angels and Satan). The Great Chain of Being is a way of thinking about the world in which everything— humans, animals, plants and natural objects—has its place in a vertically organised hierarchy where each level is defined by its highest properties. It has been summarised as follows:

> The Great Chain of Being is a cultural model that concerns kinds of beings and their properties and places on a vertical scale with the "higher" beings and properties above "lower" beings and properties. …The Great Chain is a scale of forms of being – human, animal, plant and inanimate object – and consequently a scale of the properties that characterize forms of being – reason, instinctual behaviour, biological function, physical attributes, and so on.[6]

The model includes all things in existence (kinds of being) and is an account that integrates every known thing: from the heavens, the social ordering of society, animals, plant and inorganic matter. The Great Chain is hierarchical with animate entities on the upper levels and inanimate objects on the lower levels. On the basis of attributes, such as thought or morality, humans are positioned towards the top of the 'Chain'—nearer to the divine; inorganic matter is located at the bottom and animals somewhere in the middle—so the hierarchy looks like this:

Divine: Orders of Angels: Seraphims, Cherabims, Archangels etc.
Human: Higher-order attributes and behavior (e.g. thought, moral systems).
Animal: Instinctual attributes and behavior.
Plant: Biological attributes and behavior.
Complex object: Structural attributes and functional behavior.
Natural physical thing: Physical attributes and behavior.[7]

Each level is differentiated by qualities that are unique to this, and higher, levels. So only humans and higher levels (but not animals) have morality. But each level may share properties with lower levels, so though humans are moral they also have animal-like instincts such as a desire for food and sex. Since animals are lower down the hierarchy they are further from reason, aesthetics and morality, and exist in a subordinate relationship to mankind and they may be utilised for his benefit—as in animal husbandry, livestock and as beasts of burden.

Animal metaphors involve shifting the entity they refer to up and down the hierarchy. When a human is described as 'animal' this implies removing the characteristics that define them as human and defining them with the attributes of a lower level in the hierarchy. Similarly, when a human is described as 'angelic' this transfers attributes from a higher level to a lower one—humans. Interpreting a metaphor based on the 'Human-as-animal' frame activates a cultural model for the animal concerned through its stereotypical attributes. For example, describing a human as a pig implies the attribute of greed. The human referred to by such a metaphor is shifted down the hierarchy and adopts a lower status. As mentioned above, this mapping of animal traits onto humans relies on a cultural model in which human traits such as greed were *conventionally attributed* to animals. Cultural models originate from the influence of fables, idioms, allegories etc. As we will see in the next section, an allegory such as *Animal Farm* works by reversing roles and considering the sort of frames that *animal* experience of humans might entail such as enforcing power—often through cruelty (called 'brutality'). Allegorical use of animal metaphors therefore works by category shift based on the Great Chain of Being.

The 'Human-as-animal' frame also originated in cultural experience in which there is a distinction between dangerous and non-dangerous animals. The English language views animals from remote cultures—such as lions, tigers and elephants—as having positive human traits such as pride, strength and wisdom rather than as being dangerous; they may be viewed differently in their native culture. A metaphor such as 'beast' is ambiguous because while implying that the person is 'untamed' it is also impressive in size and instinctive. Politicians who are described as 'big beasts' have influence because they speak with 'natural' authority—and with a high level of assuredness; Ken Clarke was a 'big beast' and in the Brexit debates Boris Johnson was frequently described as a 'big beast'—usually complimenting his supposedly instinctive nature. For example:

> Brexit big *beast Boris* Johnson has the last laugh over treacherous Michael Gove as he is handed key Foreign Secretary job in Theresa May's new top team.[8]

His physical size, appetites (for food and women), and spontaneity provide the basis for a positive representation. In a survey of articles containing 'Boris' and 'beast' in their headlines I found that 80% were from the Pro-Leave press. So danger can be overridden by other qualities of entities lower on the hierarchy. Animals that are more culturally proximate such as wolves and rats can be attributed negative qualities such as deception and dirtiness evoking the Sanctity/Degradation moral foundation. Irrespective of cultural proximity, dangerous attributes and behaviours include long teeth (tigers); harming (snakes), preying on humans (crocodiles), stealing (foxes), devouring children and babies (wolves), or because of their association with dirt and disease (rats and other vermin). By contrast, non-dangerous stereotypes include docile and submissive animals: so human 'chickens' just run around headless but are not dangerous, though they can be cowardly; in September 2019 many pro-Brexit newspapers reported: 'The Tories have had a fresh dig at Jeremy Corbyn as a party handout depicts him as a big bird. It comes after PM Boris Johnson branded the Labour leader a "gigantic chlorinated chicken" for supposedly running away from an election',

(*Daily Star*, 7 Sept 2019). Calling someone 'chicken' is a familiar rebuke in the school playground.

Other cultural stereotypes abound: human 'dogs' are loyal and submissive assistants—while human 'female animals' are ubiquitously unpleasant displaying qualities of bad character ('bitch'), bad appearance ('cow'), or rampant sexuality ('cougar'). These ways of thinking about humans are originally based on anthropomorphic stereotypes of animals, so calling someone a 'cougar' on the basis of their sexual behaviour originates in thinking of cougars as demonstrating promiscuous behaviour. To describe a greedy human as a 'pig' implies that at an earlier point in time human greed was attributed to pigs. There is some basis in human experience of animal behaviour that creates the conditions for the 'Human-as-animal frame'; for example, the observation of the eating habits of pigs could lead to them being viewed as 'greedy' perhaps because pigs eat most things and consume them very quickly. But originally it was human behaviour that was projected on to animal behaviour on the grounds of observed similarity or equivalence. But over time this behaviour then became a defining feature of the animal—so that pigs were thought to be inherently greedy and donkeys, stupid. When animals became stereotyped metaphors based on these animals became conventional. Once this had happened these metaphors could then be transferred back to humans—so we could call a person a 'cougar', a 'pig' or a 'donkey' and rely on the stereotypes that had come originally from applying these human traits to animals!

The Human-as-animal frame is closely related to Darwin's theory of natural selection that views mankind as in a competitive struggle for survival with animals since they represent threats and dangers from which humans need to protect themselves. As Goatly notes: "… constructing activity as a competitive race relates to the question of Human-as-animal metaphor, through neo-Darwinians' and socio-biologists' construction of human society as inexorably competitive".[9] Social Darwinist views have predominated in the build up to wars between nation states, when overall concerns for the physical fitness and the health of the nation were closely related to the likelihood of its members being equipped to succeed in military conflict. These animal frames are particularly important when it is social categories such as ethnicity (Jews as 'parasites'), gender (women as 'bitches') or class (businessmen as 'fat cats') that are being profiled by the metaphor.

At a low level on the hierarchy of the Great Chain of Being are those life forms that are invisible and hence so dangerous to human life that they may better be described as 'death forms'; these include bacilli, other types of bacteria and parasites.[10] So when a human is described as a 'parasite' (as the Jews were by Hitler[11]), this entails pushing human down towards the plant level on the hierarchy. When applied to humans, metaphor frames deriving from sources of extreme danger to health have been associated with the political far right in arguments that support genocide. Generally, views based on the "naturalistic fallacy" draw on natural behaviour as a warrant to justify human behaviour. Following this argument, human aggression in fighting wars is sublimated by metaphor into the language of competitive sports. Metaphors that profile aggressive human behaviour as 'natural', species-driven or derived from the natural world constitute linguistic articulation of Social Darwinist ideology.

Of course there are also *physical* attributes of animals that are employed to refer simply to physical aspects of individual human beings. We saw this with 'beast' and 'brute' but other attributes include height (giraffes), size (elephants and mice), size of mouth (frogs), movement (cats, weasels and snakes), sight (eagles), scent (dogs). Other metaphors derive from culturally based sporting and gambling practices such as betting on the outcome of races (horses and dogs), betting on the outcome of fights (cocks, dogs and, in the case of gladiators, lions). We should also recall the extensive use of animal metaphors based on the transfer of physical or social attributes in the product branding of cars (speed: Jaguar), petrol (strength: tiger), or beer (friendship: Brewdog). When employed for commercial purposes animal metaphors are ubiquitously positive, and at times odd animals are invoked—such as the meerkat that became highly successful in branding an online web site for comparing markets. Here the behaviour that provided the basis for the metaphor was popping out of a concealed place to have a look around.

The Human-as-animal frame was employed in the Brexit campaign when conducted on Twitter. When a group, typically Leave, is representing *itself* it selects competitive animals that are associated with powerful instincts for survival. For Leave supporters the animal attributes of power and strength were used metaphorically to symbolise the group that the speaker identified with:

Young Eurosceptics Retweeted David Grossman
   When the British *lion roars* nobody can beat us. We support #VoteLeave (21 retweets)[12]

Great Artiste Retweeted

#LeaveEU #Brexit The British *Lion stood proud* for 1,000 years without dictators in Brussels. It will do so again. (7 retweets)[13]

But when a tweeter is representing the opposing side it selects animals whose attributes and behaviours are viewed as threatening to human survival. As mentioned above, these typically included 'rats' and 'wolves':

@Jonteinspain after #Brexit has won the vote, Cameron the *filthy lying rat* must be kicked out for his deceit.[14]
   Don't be #sheeple! #TakeBackControl from *the wolves of Brussels*! Now is your once chance to #BeLeave![15]

However, there are other types of animal behaviour that, though not directly threatening to humans, are threatening to the species itself and hence likely to jeopardise its survival. Remain supporters represented their opponents using these metaphors. These typically include sheep because of the attribute of following a leader without reflection and lemmings because of the attribute of throwing themselves off a cliff:

#brexit is such a joke. If the dumb brits vote for brexit they think things will immediately be better *#sheep* dont know better[16]
   @Scientists4EU Don't be a *lemming* and follow Boris' #Brexit roadmap *over the edge of a cliff*. Vote IN (8 retweets)[17]

'Sheep' metaphors were also used by Leavers to frame Remainers as docile and too willing to allow themselves to be dominated by others— whether the 'others' were the EU or those who accepted the necessity of immigration:

> #VoteLeave, Britain! Don't *stay as sheep to be pushed around by #EU dogs*. Reclaim your great country! #Brexit[18]

Overall Leave supporters employed keywords from the Human-as-animal frame much more than Remainers. They used the following animals to refer to Remainers:

fat cat
dog
monkey
pig
sheep
rat
dragon
goat
parasite
snakes

They referred to themselves as: 'lions', 'tigers' and 'dragon slayers'. Conversely, Remain tweets in the Referendum week only referred to Leavers as 'lemmings' and 'wolves' (usually 'in sheep's clothing'). The number of animal types alone shows that Leave supporters employed 'animal' metaphors much more extensively. A number of tweets involving two animals made an explicit contrast between a positive self-representation and a negative representation of opponents; for example some contrasted 'lions' and 'sheep':

> Better to *live a day as a Lion then 100 years as a Sheep* #VoteLeave #Brexit #Euref[19]
>   Latest EU dictate, three *lions* on English Royal Standard to be replaced by three *sheep* #FFSLeave #Brexit[20]

There were a few tweets that contrasted large courageous, roaring British 'lions' with cowardly little Remain 'mice' or 'kittens'. The general pattern of these tweets was to contrast two animals with reference to the semantic opposition of their stereotypical attributes. Many of the stereotypes and culturally embedded meanings found in such tweets originate in idioms, allegories and fables and it is to these that I now turn.

Allegorical Animal Idioms

An allegory is a short story that has a second order symbolic meaning beyond what the story is apparently about and this symbolic meaning is typically a moral one. Interpreting an allegory requires working out the nature of the moral comment that is being made on first order political actors and actions. Ray Gibbs argues that many political metaphors have an allegorical character and reminds us that George Orwell's *Animal Farm* provided an allegorical account of Stalin's Russia—one that was also highly satirical.[21] Many tweets posted on the topic of Brexit were of an idiom that included one or more animal terms; the interpretation of these tweets relied on knowledge of an allegory and I will refer to these as 'allegorical animal idioms'. Fables are a type of allegory that conclude with a very explicit moral point and in the most well known of these—Aesop's fables—the frame comments on human traits such as deception, greed or guile by reference to two contrasting animals such as 'The fox and the crow'. These culturally embedded narratives rely on stereotypes for typical animal traits that are transferred to human behaviour, for example the fox is viewed as 'cunning' and flatters the crow. Of course these fables, allegories and tweets all reinforce the stereotype. The stereotype becomes linguistically embedded in an *idiom* so that we know that idiomatically to refer to someone as a 'fox' implies that the person is cunning or that a 'wolf in sheep's clothing' is a stereotype for human deception. In this section I show how many Brexit tweets with animal idioms relied on these stereotypical cultural meanings to heighten the emotional force of moral intuitions about Brexit.

Idioms provide cognitive access to allegories by offering a set of culturally available scripts that can be employed in composing a tweet and therefore pass a moral judgement on political actions. For example, an allegorical idiom such as 'rats leaving a sinking ship' is one that is familiar to people through their knowledge of the conditions of British trading vessels and the behaviour of rats that lived alongside the seamen but passes moral judgement on human disloyalty. Similarly, the image of lemmings jumping off a cliff is a culturally familiar folk myth and passes moral comment on any form of excessively self-destructive, human behaviour. There is a great deal of social psychological evidence that people resist explicit attempts to change their attitudes. They are more likely to accept such a change when it confirms something that they already subscribe to (known as 'an anchor'). Animal allegories are difficult to resist when they occur in idioms; by definition the meaning of an idiom cannot just be worked out from its parts, so when an idiom includes an animal allegory the meaning is embedded both culturally and linguistically, and so takes on the character of a cultural meme, evidence for this is when a hashtag is formed using the idiom. All that can be challenged is *how* exactly the cultural meme corresponds with political reality. We all accept that there are 'wolves in sheep's clothing' (a hashtag) but *the identity of the wolves* was contested between Pro- and Anti-Brexiteers. These cultural memes are highly popular in a forum of public debate such as Twitter.

In this section I identify the allegorical animal idioms and cultural memes that were used on Twitter and illustrate similarities and differences in how and to what extent the Leave and Remain campaigns used allegorical animal idioms. I also illustrate the allegorical frames for these idioms by identifying groups of idioms that demonstrate a single underlying mental representation that structures the argument of a whole category of tweets. For example both 'wolf in sheep's clothing' and 'snake oil salesman' share the same type of argument that is based on an allegorical frame for human deception and disloyalty. An advantage of identifying allegorical frames is that it enables us to identify the premise, or warrant that underlies an argument. The premise is something that you hold to be true, for example that all wolves are deceptive and dangerous—just as humans can be. We will see that this allegorical frame is essentially nothing more than a tautology—*x* is deceptive because I say that *x* is deceptive. By doing this we reduce the extent to

Table 9.1 Allegorical frames of animal idioms

Frame	Sample idiom
Deception and disloyalty	Rats leaving a sinking ship
Disclosure and non-disclosure	Elephant in the room
Greed	Fat cat
Self-destructiveness	Lemmings jumping off a cliff
Impossibility	Pigs might fly
Insanity	Mad as a box of frogs

which the argument can be said to rely on moral reasoning, although moral intuitions coincide with strongly held beliefs.

I identified two dominant allegorical frames for animal idioms: 'Deception & Disloyalty' and 'Disclosure & Non-Disclosure'; the first is based very much on the Loyalty/Betrayal moral foundation, whereas the second is based on Fairness/Cheating; these and various other frames are summarised in Table 9.1.

Allegorical Frame for Deception and Disloyalty

I will focus the discussion on those allegorical frames and animal idioms that occurred most frequently in tweets posted during the week before the referendum using the hashtags #Brexit #Leave and #Remain by each side beginning with Deception and Disloyalty as in Table 9.2.

The first point to note is that some of these posts have been since deleted; the second is that Leave used allegorical idioms much more frequently than did Remain. In Chapter 3 I proposed that Brexit supporters on Twitter and social media employed a frame for Distrust and Betrayal to arouse suspicion and significant distrust of an outside group. A set of allegories originating from classical, biblical and other phraseological sources was based on iconographic stereotypes of animals that profiled deception and disloyalty. In all of these, the animal role is to represent some threat. The agent of deception and disloyalty is constructed as potentially life threatening—crocodiles etc. The evolutionary origins of this allegorical frame are that failure to identify the deception would have fatal consequences: the ability to know deceit is therefore a core survival trait. There is evidence of this evolutionary basis for the

Table 9.2 Allegorical idioms for the frame of deception and disloyalty on Twitter: January 2016–December 2018

Idiom	Pro-Leave	Pro-Remain
Trojan horse	19	7
Wolf in sheep's clothing	3	10
Smell a rat	13	2
Snake oil salesman	9	5
Crocodile tears	12	2
Rats leaving a sinking ship	10	0
Snake in the grass	2	1
Total	68	27

intuition in the reactions of six-month-old babies to pictures of spiders and snakes: their pupils dilate much more than they do when shown pictures of fish or flowers.

These animal idioms provide iconographic references that associate a stereotypical behaviour of an animal with the person or group to whom it refers and the allegory provides a highly negative value judgement of the referent. The role of the speaker is to reveal the 'true' nature of opponents' leaders so that readers are protected from their deception and disloyalty. Together the animal idiom, the allegory and the act of revelation constitute a form of emotionally invested moral reasoning and, or, intuition about the similarities between animal and human sources of danger. The framing of issues in moral terms is a style marked by hyperbole and intensification. While both sides drew on the allegorical frame of Deception and Disloyalty, Leave supporters used them over twice as frequently on Twitter and their hashtags led to some allegorical animal idioms becoming memes for example 'Trojan horse' and 'snake oil salesmen'—images and links to other media sources stimulated their circulation. I will now briefly discuss some of the most frequent.

Trojan Horse

A number of tweets supporting Leave referred to Sayeeda Warsi as a 'Trojan horse' after she deserted the Leave campaign in reaction to claims about its xenophobic character:

> Baroness Warsi was a *Trojan Horse planted* by the Remain campaign to
> destabilise the @vote_leave campaign. Strength in independence #Brexit[22]

Some Twitters seemed unsure of her gender:

> Warsi was an obvious *Trojan Horse, planted* by Dirty Dave. He lies lies
> lies. He supports Turkey in EU but denies it #Brexit #VoteLeave[23]

The 'Trojan horse' allegory alludes to the deception practiced on the
Greeks by the Trojans that lead to the recapture of Troy and is therefore consistent with the frame for Deception and Disloyalty because it
advises caution against traps. Generally these tweets frame whatever is
a 'Trojan horse' as under the control of an external and often unknown
agent. In this respect the idiom contributes to a conspiracy frame, in
which true intentions and motivations of actors are unknown—except
to the individual who is revealing his[24] insider knowledge. Tweeters vied
to demonstrate their insight into detecting things that were not apparent
to others—a major psychological motivation of the conspiracy theorist.
Many conspiracy theorists are probably harmless individuals who react
to complexity by adopting allegories as a form of psychological release
for their own fears and doubts. More importantly, individuals who share
a belief in a conspiracy on the basis of a moral intuition form an online
discourse community, marked by 'ambient affiliation'[25] that overcomes
the isolation they may otherwise experience. The confirmation and elaboration of a conspiracy becomes a form of shared meaning construction
that offers a relatively low threshold of entry, no membership fees and
the cloak of anonymity if desired.

A number of Remain tweets unified around the view that Brexit itself
was a Trojan horse as it deceived people into accepting a far right form
of government:

> #LeaveEu is just a *Trojan horse* for the far right. UKIP, BNP, Britain First
> all support Leave. #VoteRemain[26]

This view became widely circulated among active Remain campaigners
during the withdrawal period:

Only way to defeat #brexit is to expose #Ukip for what it is -a *trojan horse built* by billionaires to cut their taxes & privatise the NHS. (429 retweets)[27]

The *Trojan Horse* has revealed its contents. #Brexit is nothing more than a right-wing authoritarian opportunity for oppression. Angry yet?[28] (502 retweets)

The representation of Brexit as a Trojan horse was one of the rare instances of effective Remain counter-messaging. Although Leavers set the pace in the development of dominant allegorical frames on social media, Remainers occasionally drew on the powerful conspiratorial potential of counter-messaging to intensify their moral intuition. The allegory of the Trojan horse was sufficiently flexible to target individuals or whole political stances and, while primarily based on moral intuition, could also be elaborated as a form of moral reasoning, for example when issues such as NHS privatisation were introduced as likely outcomes of Brexit. These tweets do not offer genuine arguments because a genuine argument needs to provide data in support of a claim; however, the 'Trojan horse' meme evokes an emotional response for those who already share the belief that 'x is a Trojan horse' and reinforces an ideological viewpoint. Identifying the metaphorical nature of the argument warrant also allows us to query it by asking exactly why it is that this tweeter is trying to influence others by claiming that a political act is 'in reality' an act of deception and disloyalty. We can always ask "how do you know?" Or "where is your evidence?"

Wolf in Sheep's Clothing

This was the only idiom from the frame for Deception and Disloyalty that Remainers used more frequently than Leavers. Quite often the idiom was modified in some way, for example:

Gregory Fallica Retweeted Elena Cresci
    Case in point. The #VoteLeave's *wolf fur* is starting to show through the *sheep's clothing...* #StrongerIn #Brexit[29]

The tweet was accompanied by a link to UKIP's 'Breaking Point' poster. The moral reasoning of the idiom traces its origin to the Bible, and one tweet supplies a biblical citation:

> Bianca Jagger Retweeted Martin Shovel
> *"Beware of false prophets who come to you in sheep's clothing but inwardly are ravenous wolves"* Matthew 7:15 #Brexit (15 retweets)[30]

The biblical allusion adds authority and gravitas to the otherwise ephemeral nature of the tweet. The allegorical idiom is culturally embedded since—as well as its biblical origins—it has a discourse history in a fable that was first told by the twelveth-century Greek rhetorician Nikephoros Basilakis concerning a wolf that disguises itself in a sheep's skin, though several other versions developed in the Middle Ages. Linguistically, bringing the verb forward to the beginning and using an imperative form increases its illocutionary force as a warning by arguing that those who fail to 'beware' will end up inside the wolves! It is highly allegorical and arouses intellectual curiosity as its interpretation requires allocating identities to the 'false prophets' and so contributes to a conspiracy theory by triggering the moral intuitions of Cheating and Betrayal. The allegorical force of the image comes from the contrast between the docility and meekness attributed to sheep and the supposed predatory and deceptive nature of wolves.

Its culturally embedded nature relies on the reader inferring the identity of the 'wolves' and the 'sheep'. Following the rules of an allegory we allocate human identities to animals. In Bianca Jagger's tweet above the 'wolves' are Leave leaders who are concealing their true purposes but this is not made explicit and has to be inferred from knowledge that the celebrity tweeter supported Remain. The vagueness is deliberate and relies on the reader activating contextual knowledge: people don't like to be told what to think and prefer to work it out for themselves. Establishing intention is crucial in moral reasoning: the prophet is false precisely because he conceals his intention by disguising himself as one of his victims.

Although the Distrust and Betrayal frame was employed predominantly by the Leave social media campaign, 'the wolf in sheep's clothing' was an idiom that Remainers believed strengthened their argument that Brexit was not what it appeared to be: control would be taken by right-wingers who supported privatisation and other rightwing policies; following Boris Johnson's election as leader of the Conservative Party in July 2019 this did indeed appear to be the case. The moral reasoning involved in deciphering the allegory was one that would strengthen the pro-Remain argument that the political right could not be trusted because it had a history of deceit. To avoid ambiguity most of the Remain tweets made either a general or a specific reference that identified the 'wolves':

> #Brexit leaders in a nutshell - the establishment in anti-establishment *sheep's clothing* (23 retweets)[31]
> You're nothing more than a *wolf in sheep's clothing* @BorisJohnson. Don't be fooled Britain, we're better than that! #EUREF #VoteRemain[32]
> @vote_leave Murdoch's pal Gove cannot be trusted. He is a *wolf in sheep's clothing*. Look at his record at Education. Awful. #VoteRemain[33]

Remainers construed right wing politicians as deceptive because, and, after seeing the popularity enjoyed by Leave arguments in traditional working class areas, they decided to adopt 'sheep's clothing' themselves by declaring their pro-Remain position in populist language. The Remain argument was that after Brexit these 'wolves' would adopt policies damaging to working class interests—for example by reducing social support services. The third tweet invites reflection on the evidence for this argument. The political implication is that a post-Brexit Tory government would seek to end favourable European social legislation so that Britain could become a low wage economy with great profits being made off the backs of working people.

Some Leavers contested ownership of the allegory by reversing the roles and reasoned that it was the European Parliament who were the real wolves:

> "A nation of *sheep will beget a government of wolves*"
> It's time to take back control.
> Vote #LEAVE #BREXIT (42 retweets)[34]

The archaic 'beget' evokes the resonance of biblical language and the use of quotation marks, contributes to its prophetic style, adding to its authority. The identities of the 'sheep' and 'wolves' needs to be decoded and it is only the 'take back control' slogan that allows the reader to work out that the 'government of wolves' refers to the European Parliament. It invites puzzle-solving instincts reader and invites the reader to draw on their moral intuitions and participate in a game of playful decoding. Effective tweets often display a self-referential demonstration of cultural capital, and insight in claiming knowledge about what's really going on! Tweets that refer to 'wolves' and 'sheep' always display a high level of modality—that is a certainty about a real state of future affairs—and contribute towards speculative prophecy.

'Smell a Rat' and 'Rats Leaving a Sinking Ship'

Metaphorically rats are viewed as threatening and, paradoxically, since they are geographically and biologically proximate to humans, are construed as morally distant. This is because of their association with disease, and—when cornered—attack and aggression, though sometimes this can be directed towards others of their own species as in the phrase 'rats in a bag'. The rat is therefore an intensely negative 'other' representation that dehumanises opponents by positioning them far away from the speaker and activates morally intuitive judgements of danger and threat derived from the Sanctity/Degradation moral foundation. Both allegorical animal idioms 'smell a rat' and 'rats leaving a sinking ship' imply strong feelings of distrust and suspicion. The folk belief that rats leave a sinking ship has metonymic roots: in the sixteenth century rats were believed to know in advance when a rotten structure was about to collapse and in the seventeenth century were observed departing from burning houses and by the eighteenth century were believed to abandon sinking ships. This was probably because they inhabited the lowest parts of the ship that were the first to be affected by a leak. The rat comes low on the animal level of the Great Chain of Being—only just above the parasite to which it is metonymically related as a carrier of parasites. However, some current research suggests that rats have empathetic qualities and forgo personal gains to save another rat from drowning but this conflicts with the emotions of disgust that have evolved towards something potentially threatening to health. Both idioms were used primarily by Leave supporters to argue that their opponents were not to be trusted.

Along with 'Trojan Horse' and 'Wolves in sheep's clothing' they activate the frame of Deception and Disloyalty (closely related to Distrust and Betrayal) that I suggest underlies this group of animal allegories. Leavers viewed the Remain camp with distrust and—in line with a widespread strategy of populist right wing rhetoric—the rat symbolised the elite and the establishment who would do everything possible to deceive and betray the innocent and trusting people. A typical 'rat' in the pro-Leave frame was David Cameron:

> @David_Cameron *like a cage rat* at the minute! Time we remove any vermin from our house #Brexit[35]

This tweet contained an image of an actual rat in a cage and is at the extreme scale of animal metaphors since the association with danger and disease is used as an argument for 'removal' of this 'vermin'. A larger number of tweets explicitly referred to Bob Geldof as a 'rat' though this was also motivated by wordplay because of the name of his band—'Boomtown rats'; the humour also drew on the boat he had hired to counter the Farage flotilla, thereby eliciting the phrase 'rats leave a sinking ship':

> This *rat will desert the sinking ship* as soon as he gets his 40 pieces of silver #judasgeldof #Brexit + picture of Geldof flicking a V-sign at the Farage flotilla[36]

Bob Geldof was the most visually represented individual in 'rat' tweets and most of these were taken from the media on the clash with the Farage flottila. As well as individual 'rats' there were also distrusted groups, these included 'capitalists' and 'experts':

@dailymailuk @kthopkins @mailonline voter *smells the rat* Capitalist gains with #Remain Working class'll be better off with #Brexit[37]

The post showed the EU as the funding source for a range of bodies that supported Remain including the CBI, the TUC and the Institute for Fiscal Studies. As with 'Trojan horse' and 'Wolf in sheep's clothing' allegories, 'rat' tweets contributed to a conspiracy framing and some implied that the murder of Jo Cox was planned by Remain supporters:

> Lefties are mad at me for pointing out the #VoteRemain false flag shooting of #JoCox, *rats* knowing they've been caught out.[38]

Commonly the idiom 'smell a rat' was used to mean 'to detect a deception':

> Loner gunman (linked with CUA front Nazi group) kills #remain MP when #brexit is ahead in polls up to 10%. Anyone else *smell an almighty rat?*[39]

This idiom was also used by Remain but to refer to the leaders of Brexit:

> I was #Brexit but I *smell a rat*. Yes I want my country back from the liars who are trying to drag us out of Europe[40]

However, the derogatory and negative representation of the other was more typical of the Leave style of tweeting with some very limited contestation by Remain. 'Rat' idioms encapsulate a number of persuasive features of tweets: first through their use of the familiar phrases they imply an allegorical narrative: the crowd behaviour of a group of people who believe a situation is threatening. But they also incorporate humour through situation-triggered punning. Geldof appearance on a boat triggered a pun with 'Boomtown rats' thereby reinforcing the 'rat on a ship' allegorical allusion. More broadly, moral distancing contains a deontic argument that rats are not to be trusted and therefore expresses the moral intuition that the arguments of Remainers are inherently deceptive: it is phrased in intensely emotive and hyperbolic terms.

Reptilian Allegorical Idioms

Reptiles are more biologically distant from humans than mammals and because they are on a lower level of the Great Chain of Being they are morally more distant too. Describing an opponent as a 'snake' intensifies a negative representation because it arouses moral intuitions of Cheating, Betrayal and Degradation. Allegorical idioms such as 'snake oil sales-man' express a highly emotive negative judgement of morality through the Great Chain cultural model and as a culturally embedded religious symbol for Satan. The concept of 'snake oil' originally referred to a lini-ment derived from snakes that was purported to bring relief from a wide range of ailments. Originating in the United States, it originally referred to purveyors of fake medicines but has broadened to include any unrelia-ble or deceptive individual. The snake oil salesman therefore represents a morally repugnant social category that exploits the naivity of others while enriching themselves. In political contexts it refers to an untrustworthy politician who puts forward policies that will benefit themselves at the expense of others and therefore elicits moral intuitions as in the following:

> Remember the £350 million/wk for #NHS? According to recent research #brexit is COSTING US £300 million/week. *Snake oil salesmen* lied to us (118 retweets)[41]

The expression reinforces the dominant frame for Deception and Disloyalty and reflects a pervasive scepticism about politicians' motives that has come to typify western democracies and contributed to the rise of populism. It remains to be seen whether the relatively new brand of populist politician that is gaining ascendancy in many western coun-tries is any less fraudulent than those it stigmatises as a corrupt elite. A rhetoric that relies on labelling political opponents as deceptive and untrustworthy is often a strategy that seeks to pre-empt these same accusations from being applied to those who deliver anti-elite rhetoric. Often those who use the most derogatory frames do so as a form of pro-tection against those frames being applied to themselves: the invective and ad hominem attack was always the 'strike-first and ask questions later' strategy of the playground bully.

Both Leavers and Remainers referred to 'snake oil salesmen' although, as with other idioms in this allegorical frame, Leave employed them much more frequently in the Referendum week. The only difference concerns the identity of the 'snake oil salesman': in Remain tweets it was nearly always Boris Johnson, while in Leave tweets it was usually David Cameron:

And #BorisJohnson is a *snake-oil salesman*. Trust him at your peril. #VoteRemain[42]

@BorisJohnson has to be commended for being a very able *snake oil salesman*, a great hot-air balloonist. #Brexit #remain #leave #EU[43]

#voteleave Cameron still doing the country down. We aint' *buyin' his snake oil*. Will he never learn? @telegraph[44]

The expression 'snake in the grass' was also used, but less frequently, and mainly by Leave supporters, and a couple of other tweets used the rather expressive reference to a 'snake's belly':

The belly of the snake....THIS IS THE EUROPEAN UNION from top to bottom

Lies innuendos falsehoods #VoteLeave...[45]

Other reptiles occupying low levels on the Great Chain hierarchy were similarly used to express moral intuitions about opponents:

@George_Osborne But you are a lying *toad*, trying to scare sensible people to death with your #ProjectFear crap. I'll #VoteLeave to escape EU[46]

'Frogs' were commonly referred to and a few saw a resemblance between this reptile and Farage:

Let's hope we never have to *Kermit frog face Farage* again #VoteRemain[47]

While there were 13 tweets that used 'frog' as the relatively mild colloquial term for "French people":

I bet *the frogs* would bail out quick if the Germans did a #Gexit.[48]

The *french frogs* will come into our bedroom and onto our bed #Brexit[49]

Curiously, this more biologically distant reptile is applied to people who are geographically the closest neighbours to Britain—although the term has become almost playground talk.

The expression 'Crocodile tears' originates in a folk belief that crocodiles weep while devouring their prey; this is partly based in biological fact since crocodiles have lachrymal glands that generate lubricating tears. The allegorical meaning is that since the crocodile appears to be crying—like the wolf in sheep's clothing—it no longer presents any danger, whereas in reality since these 'tears' do not originate in a genuine emotion it is preparing to consume its prey. In political contexts it is used as a mild form of criticism of opponents on the grounds that they are deceptive and manipulative because they feign an emotion that they do not really experience. The idiom was generally used by Leave supporters to reinforce the widespread populist stereotype of politicians as untrustworthy and hypocritical and so contributes to the moral intuition of Betrayal and to moral reasoning. For example, there were six tweets implying that Remain supporters who expressed remorse at the death of Jo Cox were only feigning grief because they were pleased about the positive effect it would have on their campaign:

> Never mind the crocodile tears, am campaigning all weekend.this is how they act while we still have a modicum of control over them #Brexit[50]

'Crocodile tears' invites moral intuitions in a political context by invoking a culturally embedded narrative, or allegory. Along with other forms of revelatory tweet it implies that their authors have superior moral intuitions because they are able to identify the deceptions and hypocrisies of others. Though predominantly a 'Leave' allegorical idiom, Remainers had accused Farage of shedding crocodile tears for the murder of Jo Cox:

> @Nigel_Farage blood on your hands, Farage.Your odious #Brexit campaign brought country to this. Your crocodile tears won't bring back #JoCox[51]

Table 9.3 Idioms for the frame of disclosure and non-disclosure on Twitter: January 2016–December 2018

Idiom	Pro-Leave	Pro-Remain
Elephant in the room	12	9
Cat out of the bag	6	7
From the horse's mouth	10	5
Total	28	21

Allegorical Frame for Disclosure and Non-disclosure

There were another group of allegorical animal idioms concerned with whether or not a topic was discussed openly or avoided—for example if you 'let the cat out of the bag' something that was concealed is now revealed. There are different reasons why something may be kept secret: people often avoid topics likely to disrupt relationships, or it might be to keep others ignorant. What such allegorical idioms share is that they comment on topic avoidance and argue for greater honesty. I will refer to this allegorical frame as the 'Disclosure and Non-disclosure frame' and it is summarised in Table 9.3.

Unlike allegorical idioms for the frame of Deception and Disloyalty, idioms in this frame were used fairly equally by each side. This is what we might expect as the Fairness/Cheating moral foundation was found to be common to the political left and the political right. A non-indigenous animal that features in an allegorical idiom is the expression 'elephant in the room' referring to a topic that everybody knows is being deliberately avoided. An elephant is too big to ignore and the idiom argues that the topic is too significant not to be discussed. 'Elephant in the room' proved attractive to tweeters on both sides as it invited a cognitive response to work out what the 'elephant' referred to. For Leavers metaphoric 'elephants' included: immigration, TTIP, and neoliberalism, while for Remainers 'elephants' included: the murder of Jo Cox, Northern Ireland and farming subsidies. Some seemed to be unsure of what the 'elephant' was or simply enjoyed using the expression:

There is a huge undeniable *elephant in the room* that needs to be addressed irrespective of the #Brexit result[52]

This tweet simply leaves it up to the reader to supply the elephant's identity!

The expression to 'let the cat out of the bag' was used by Leavers to refer to information that was being withheld by Remainers about the possible effects of a Remain win. The main 'cat' that was potentially 'let out of the bag' was based on a statement by Michael Heseltine that Britain would join the euro if Remain won:

> The *cat is out of the bag*. Heseltine says if we 'remain' we WILL join €. Please RT the hell out of this. Link to article claiming UK will join Euro. (214 retweets)[53]

The phrase fitted well with a conspiracy outlook motivated by fear and distrust of the Remain position and was exploited to stimulate any fear that might motivate Leave supporters:

> The *cat is out of the bag*. Fatal blow to #VoteRemain (link to article about Turkish immigration) (49 retweets)[54]

At least in these tweets there was some evidence in the form of links to press articles that could be examined for the quality of their evidence. The allegory offers a narrative in which cats are put in bags but really the 'cat' symbolises a secret and implies an agent who has intentionally put the cat in a bag. The moral reasoning is based on the idea that a cat would need to be put in a bag deliberately so it implies that someone is concealing a significant fact, which, as part of the broader conspiracy framing, the tweeter is now (like a journalist) revealing.

Closely related to claims of insider knowledge is the idiom 'From the horse's mouth', which, without revealing the source, has the moral claim to truth on the basis of reliable sources. It originates in betting myth that horses can actually tell humans who is going to win a race. Among Leavers this widely circulated tweet often had a link to a quotation from Juncker the President of the European Union:

From the horse's mouth so forget about there ever being a reformed EU #Brexit + quote from Juncker: "British voters have to know there will be no kind of any negotiation. We have concluded a deal with the prime minister. He got the maximum he could receive, and we gave the maximum we could give, so there will be no kind of renegotiation." (168 retweets)[55]

The claim that something is 'from the horse's mouth' is a way of fixing and intensifying the truth status of a theory so that it is now considered incontrovertible.

Other Allegorical Frames

There were a number of other allegorical frames that were one-shot idioms as summarised in Table 9.4.

Allegorical animal frames contribute a conceptually dense image or symbol for particular animals, so for Leavers 'fat cat' became a *symbol* for the greed of the rich. A measure of such symbolism was the multimodal representation—and there were many images posted of the 'fat cat' cultural meme. 'Fat cat' became a code word for those who were represented as having benefited financially from EU membership. Popular mythology, encouraged by Nigel Farage, had identified these as members of the European Parliament who were colloquially known to the Leave-supporting press as 'Brussels fat cats':

How *Brussels fat cats* spend YOUR money as if it grows on trees http://shr.gs/2jsSmHR #Brexit. #EUref #LeaveEU + link to *Daily Express* article with this title. (31 retweets)[56]

Stinking wealth and hypocrisy of those *Brussels fat cats* the Kinnocks #brexit #voteleave (8 retweets)[57]

Table 9.4 Other allegorical idioms on Twitter: January 2016–December 2018

Idiom	Frame	Pro-Leave	Pro-Remain
Fat cats	Greed	70	0
Lemmings (jumping off a cliff)	Self-inflicted harm	6	31
Pigs might fly	Impossibility	9	3

Han Solo Retweeted Lord Sugar
And I find it strange that *unelected fat cats* in the EU tell us British
what to do… ALL the time. #VoteLeave (8 retweets)[58]

Closely related to this allegorical idiom for exploitation was the idea of
parasitical animals that live off the labour of others. 'Parasite' was an
even more derogatory term than 'fat cat':

The EU is the very definition of a *parasite*.
#VoteLeave #Brexit[59]
Lord Parasite, Soros threatening us. The man who caused Black
Wednesday in 1992. All the more reason to #VoteLeave[60]

Although cats carry parasites, the 'fat cat' can be considered as more
euphemistic in tone, since the cat is generally a much-loved pet but the
adjective 'fat' de-emphasises the positive characteristics of 'cat'. 'Fat cat'
was extensively and exclusively used by Leavers and is indicative of a
common populist strategy that characterised pro-Europeans as elitist.
This cultural meme unites people by rejecting despised others who lack
principles and are only interested in money: it was therefore a phrase
that appealed to the moral intuition of Fairness and Cheating. It shows
good character and judgement to be able to identify those who exploit
others by making easy money through their affiliations with Europe.
But potentially *any* politician could be represented as 'elite' because, in
any elected democracy, the politician has already established himself as
part of a governing class—so populist rhetoric can label *all* opponents
as 'elites' and claim to be the prophetic voice of a single unified people:
they, and only they, are *the voice of the people*. References to 'parasites'
evoke the moral intuitions of Degradation that originate in evolutionary
based fears of threats to human health and life.

One exception to the general argument that Leave made greater use
of allegorical animal idioms were Remain tweets arguing that support
for Brexit was like lemmings jumping off a cliff. Some were humorous:

There's truth in satire. #VoteRemain ≫
Majority of *lemmings in favour of jumping off cliff* (+ link to an article
with this headline).[61]

However, there was not great take-up of these tweets—perhaps because there was not an established 'lemmings' idiom. As a result there were low retweet volumes and no strategy to develop the *idea* of lemmings jumping off a cliff into a meme. The only 'lemming' tweet that was retweeted included a political reason for the claim that Brexit would lead to social harm:

> The Tories will make a bonfire of workers rights if there's a #Brexit yet working people are *rushing like lemmings* to vote leave (8 retweets)[62]

If we compare 'lemming' iconography with 'pig' iconography we find a much higher level of emotional engagement in relation to pigs. The pig metaphor was employed as a form of ad hominem argument against the politician it referred to, with the purpose of associating them with benefitting from the European Union or from globalisation, as is pointed out by this American supporter of Donald Trump:

> Rockin Robin MAGA Retweeted Kristin Billitere
> #Brexit do not be bullied by these *globalist pigs* who want world domination. Save yourselves while you still can. (22 retweets)[63]

A number of tweets were specifically directed at David Cameron to trigger a political allegory that had partly undermined his ethos in the build up to the Referendum; this was a story alluding to the claim that as part of an initiation ritual for the Bullingham Club at the University of Oxford, he was purported to have inserted his penis into the mouth of a dead pig; several tweets alluded to this allegory:

> Remember if you vote to leave the EU, you'll be giving more power to a party which is led by someone who *had oral from a pig* #brexit[64]
> I'd say Cameron is at home shitting himself and *cuddling his pig* right now #brexit[65]
> PM David Cameron has warned that if we #Brexit the price of *pigs heads* will …[66]

Seeking to establish a cultural meme one image showed a picture of Cameron holding a young pig. Clearly this ad hominem argument was the source of much amusement among Leave tweeters, however it also aroused the moral intuition of Degradation since this form of sexual behaviour between humans and animals triggers the powerful emotion of disgust.

The most common allegorical 'pig' idiom was the phrase 'pigs might fly' implying that, since pigs cannot fly, a proposition should be evaluated as absurd. In the following a Leave supporter dismisses arguments from *The Times* that the EU could reform itself:

PoliticsSense Retweeted Emma Tucker
 The Times *'pigs might fly'* argument by coming out for #Remain arguing for reform & trade not politics. #Brexit[67]

However there was some counter-messaging with this allegory to dismiss Brexit arguments as irrational:

#Brexit basic stance:
1) All immigration is evil (except our ancestors)
2) #Brexit will stop all immigration.
Also, *pigs will fly.*[68]

This tweet is structured as a syllogism with a major premise followed by a minor premise and a conclusion that contains the idiom. But the impossibility of pigs flying undermines the logical connection between the two premises and so implies that Brexit will not stop all immigration. The allegorical idiom therefore questions the validity of Brexit claims regarding immigration and makes its arguments appear absurd.

The Animal-as-Human Frame: Cat Memes

However, there is another frame for animal metaphors that emphasises co-operation and symbiosis: in this frame animals from different species exist in relationships of mutual interdependence and show the capacity for love and affection. This frame incorporates a wide range of positive experiences that derive from nurturing young animals by keeping them as pets, naming them, giving them presents and providing the type of love, car and affection that would ideally be provided for a young human (were they so lucky!). It rejects the neo-Darwinist view that man is inherently in competition with the natural world as this more utopian frame views man *as part of* nature: just as humans can possess animal characteristics—the need for sustenance, sex and sleep—so animals can possess human ones—a need for sociability, a role in a group and altruism. It is clearly based on the moral foundation of Care/Harm. This is also an anthropomorphic frame and can be represented as Animal-as-human (rather than Human-as-animal).

The animal that has been the most productive source for Internet memes has been the cat. An illustration of this is 'lolcat'; this is a text with a macro image of one or more cats combined with quirky, grammatically incorrect text intended to mimic how a cat might be imagined as speaking and for which the term *lolspeak* has developed. The combination of cuteness and humour has appealed to Internet users seeking escape from the toxic discourse of many social media platforms. Sometimes politicians alluded to *lolspeak* as when French Europe Minister, Nathalie Loiseau (well-named![69]) commenting satirically on British positions on Brexit said that she would call her cat 'Brexit' because: "It wakes me up miaowing because it wants to go out, when I open the door, it sits there, undecided. Then it looks daggers at me when I put it out".

Although the cat meme was quite rare for politicians, it was developed on Twitter in the "Cats Against Brexit" hashtag that attributed political outlooks such as 'I am worried about Brexit' to the tweeter's pet—alongside a picture of the pet. This euphemistic style for using animal frames reflects a stylistic preference for some Twitter users. There is certainly no reason why metaphors deriving from the neo-Darwinian Human-as-animal frame should be any more persuasive, or contribute more to social identity than those based on the Animal-as-human frame. In Aristotelian terms both frames combine ethos with pathos but Human-as-animal profiles distrust, deception and danger and relies primarily on moral intuitions of Harm and Degradation to arouse emotions such as disgust or fear and in hierarchies derived from the Great Chain model. Conversely, the Animal-as-human frame combines moral reasoning based on notions such as concern and compassion with the moral intuitions of Care and Loyalty based on feelings of love and affection for animals, and the possibility of these being transferred to humans.

From the point of view of persuasive political language, animal frames therefore reflect two contrasting tendencies: animals can either be viewed as rivals in a struggle for survival in which loyalty to one's own species must always predominate, or as fellow members of the natural kingdom living in co-existence with human beings: on species loyalty or trans species affinity. In terms of moral reasoning these two different perspectives represent important contrasting worldviews of man's place in the natural world. From the second point of view, animals share with us many characteristics including a range of bodily functions, the need for exercise, food, sleep etc. and even the desire for affection. When the Animal-as-human predominates in political rhetoric, animals are framed as allies in a common cause, and as sharing the views of their owners. There were a number of cases where supporters of both sides attributed a political opinion to their pet, and in particular to their cats. Two contrasting hashtags emerged: initially #catsagainstbrexit and then a counter-hashtag #CatsForBrexit:

> My cat is sad because #Brexit. If you agree RT w your cat. #CatsAgainstBrexit. Come on guys, viral time!!! (100 retweets)[70]
> @lilianedwards this cat is worried that the price of cat biscuits might go up if UK votes #brexit #catsagainstbrexit (25 retweets)[71]
> My cat is praying for #Brexit #CatsForBrexit @vote_leave (18 retweets)[72]
> I'm sorry but cats are independent creatures not given to being herded around. Truth is all of them would #VoteLeave #CatsForBrexit (12 retweets)[73]

These hashtags went viral attracting many thousands of posts in the Referendum week. For example on the 18th of June there were only two multi-tweeted posts under #catsagainstbrexit; but on the 19th of June there were 32 posts of which 13 were multi-tweets. However by the 20th of June there were over 200 posts and over the following days there tens of thousands of posts. The contested cat meme was even debated in the International Press as the NYT reported:

> Last week, Lilian Edwards, a law professor in Scotland, posted a picture of her cat on Twitter, curled up on a pillow and looking slightly sad, and added the hashtag #CatsAgainstBrexit, asking other cat owners to join her. Soon thousands of cat owners who support British membership in the blog posted pictures of their cats in a purportedly resentful or irritated state, attributing their dark mood to Brexit-induced depression. ...So far, the cats opposed to leaving the European Union are winning the battle, with nearly 60,800 tweets in the last seven days, according to Dataminr, a monitoring service. Cat tweets in favor of leaving the European Union numbered around 2,700, with the dog tweets split 3,475 against to 1,360 for leaving, Dataminr showed.[74]

These tweets typically took the structure of a political statement followed by a picture of the cat. There is a distinction between tweets that relied entirely on the named cat to evoke an emotion based on moral intuition and those that offered a reason for the political stance attributed to the pet, and therefore demonstrate moral reasoning; examples of each type are shown in Table 9.5.

#CatsForBrexit emerged as a counter-messaging strategy as the first posts under this hashtag were two days later on June 20th, and the majority were not retweeted, but when they were argued for unity rather than confrontation:

> Harry is still on the fence and has a paw in both camps #CatsForBrexit #CatsAgainstBrexit (38 retweets)[75]

A similar tweet format was employed offering a pet dog's view on Brexit with the accompanying photograph of the dog. However, on Twitter it was more common for the dog to symbolise oppression and this formed an allegory for the relationship between Britain and the European Union:

> @David_Cameron We threatened to leave EU and couldnt sort it out
>   If we stay we're *like the beaten dog* that goes back to its owner. #VoteLeave (14 retweets)[76]

Table 9.5   Pro-Remain #CatsAgainst Brexit

Moral intuition	Rosie wants to stretch her arms around Europe
	(Care + Emotion = pleasure from affection)
	Shona and Jenny think we're better together. Don't forget to vote!
	(Care + Emotion = pleasure from togetherness)
	Nala was completely shocked when she heard people wanted to leave the EU
	(Care + Emotion = pain from surprise)
	Augustine is relaxed because he's sure it will be a Remain victory tomorrow
	(Care + Emotion = pleasure from confidence)
Moral reasoning	Terry and Malcom are #CatsAgainstBrexit bc they love immigrants and freedom of movement (especially through the catflap)
	(Reason = benefits of being in Europe)
	Rusty is worried about the increase in cost of food if we leave the EU
	(Reason = food prices may increase)
	Ripley looks out at a cold dark world where we no longer have status or influence in Europe
	(Reason = loss of influence in Europe)
	Stinson is a Siberian cat with a Slovenian mum living in Scotland. He hates Nigel Farage
	(Reason: mixing of DNA is natural)

The moral intuitions associated with dogs were largely negative and were used exclusively by Leave:

> EU has made a *dogs dinner* of agriculture, fish, money, & borders.
>   Now it wants to control our armed forces and your taxes.
>   #VoteLeave (91 retweets)[77]

Sometimes the 'dog' frame was used with a more positive evaluation as a symbol of freedom:

> Are you a dog lover? If so *unleash the lead* and let our beloved Britain *run free of EU shackles.* #Brexit #VoteLeave (10 retweets)[78]

Cat and, to a lesser extent, dog memes are interesting because they show how conflict can be negotiated: many people have pets, and even if you don't like the owner it is unlikely that you dislike their pet to the same extent. The domestic pet symbolises peaceful coexistence of humans with animals and by metaphoric transfer it argues for peaceful coexistence of humans with each other deriving from the moral intuitions of Care and Loyalty. Pet memes avoided the confrontational and aggressively, hyperbolic style that typified much interaction that the binary 'Leave' or 'Remain' choice had invited; this was because attributing a political opinion to a cat or dog constituted a whimsical style that downplayed the emotional intensity that dominated such a 'high-stakes' decision. This mimetic style reminds me of the imaginative exploration of possible worlds that children enjoy when they make their toy animals speak by miming their voices. A mimetic world avoids a face threatening reaction because it would be absurd to be annoyed by the views of a cat: so the cat meme offered a mask that protected the face of the tweeter.

There are potential criticisms of the anthropomorphism implied by the cat meme: it is a form of deception as it attributes human emotions to animals that in reality rely on instincts rather than morality. However, it is an example of how an animal frame can enhance the quality of human-to-human interaction by drawing attention to shared feelings of empathy for cats or dogs among pet owners. Once an empathetic frame is established through the mimetic 'animal is human' frame, online conflict and hate speech becomes less feasible because it would infringe the interactional rules established by the frame.

According to one Cabinet source David Gauke's told colleagues that a "managed" no deal would be like a "unicorn that needs to be slaughtered"… "A managed no-deal is not a viable option," he said. "It's not on offer from the EU and the responsibility of Cabinet ministers is not to propagate unicorns but to slay them."[79] Perhaps such mythical animals offered a better insight into the nature of Brexit than actual animals; with this in mind I will consider in the final chapter some metaphors for the whole Brexit experience.

Notes

1. These were the most common dog names in 2018.
2. In a previous study of British politicians I found that over 4% of the metaphors their speeches derived from animals (Charteris-Black 2011).
3. David Peterson @Australiaunwra6, 19 Jun 2016.
4. Dagenham Man @ktf1965, 22 Jun 2016.
5. Whistling Dixie @DixieBelmont, 21 Jun 2016.
6. Lakoff & Turner (1989), pp. 166–67.
7. Lakoff & Turner (1989), pp. 170–71.
8. *MailOnline*, 13 July 2017.
9. Goatly (2007), p. 54.
10. See Lancaster (2018) for a discussion of many of these.
11. See Musolff (2010) for a detailed discussion of Nazi metaphors.
12. Young Eurosceptics @Y_Eurosceptics, 22 Jun 2016.
13. Great Artiste @GreatArtiste45, 21 Jun 2016.
14. Marty@CrazyGman2013, Jun 19.
15. Alice Smith @TheAliceSmith, 22 Jun 2016.
16. Wade Y @wy3134, 22 Jun 2016.
17. Frances Williams @FranJWilliams, 21 Jun 2016.
18. Lois Rogers@lois_rogers, Jun 22.
19. Brexit Alarmism @BrexitAlarmism, 21 Jun 2016.
20. Fred @fastfredi, 21 Jun 2016.
21. Gibbs (2015).
22. Natasha Lauren Hart @LaurenHart1975, 20 Jun 2016.
23. @DaveBallTiger, 20 Jun 2016.
24. Some research suggests that a higher proportion of Twitter users are men, so I have used the male pronoun.
25. This phrase was used by Zappavinga (2012).
26. Trevor Stables @trevdick, 21 Jun 2016.
27. Around My Dad, Harry Leslie Smith @Harryslaststand, 28 Nov 2016.
28. SpaceAngel #StopBrexit & #GTTO @spaceangel1964, 11 Sep 2017.
29. Gregory Fallica @gregoryfallica, 16 Jun 2016.
30. Bianca Jagger@BiancaJagger, 22 Jun 2016.
31. Martin Shovel @MartinShovel, 19 Jun 2016.
32. Lee Neal @leeneal321, 21 Jun 2016.
33. Helen @HelenMagi, 19 Jun 2016.
34. Alex Powell @PowellPolitics, 21 Jun 2016.

35. David Peterson @Australiaunwra6, 17 Jun 2016.
36. sean mac ruairí @seanmac65, 16 Jun 2016.
37. NonStateActor @ActorNon, 19 Jun 2016.
38. Dan Quixote @Fash_UK, 16 Jun 2016.
39. A Nice Cup of Tea? @gareth_hurley, 20 Jun 2016.
40. Our world @artyartist4, 20 Jun 2016.
41. Jacky Davis @DrJackyDavis, 2 Dec 2017.
42. David Head @DavidHeadViews, 22 Jun 2016.
43. Revo @arbolioto, 19 Jun 2016.
44. Malcolm Burton @Freeas4bird, 18 Jun 2016.
45. Dennis Bache @DennisBache1, 16 Jun 2016.
46. The Grey Haired Dude @QPR4Me, 19 Jun 2016.
47. Brad Walker #FBPE #IamEuropean @bradrw123, 22 Jun 2016.
48. Daniel Jeffries @thankfulchav, 16 Jun 2016.
49. barababor @fleuteu, 21 Jun 2016.
50. Frederick Clark @kirktoun, 17 Jun 2016.
51. Mistress 9 danke @catsinbelfry, 16 Jun 2016.
52. Kev @NotBabbling, 21 Jun 2016.
53. Ann Sheridan @bernerlap, 21 Jun 2016.
54. NOT Diane Abbott MP@hackneyabbatt, 21 Jun 2016.
55. Carol McGiffin @McGiff, 22 Jun 2016.
56. Vicky @2tweetaboutit, 20 Jun 2016.
57. Ko Barclay @KoBarclay, 17 Jun 2016.
58. Han Solo @WeirdLittleHen, 21 Jun 2016.
59. Stu@TheHanz1976, Jun 19.
60. Andrew Deane@LongshanksNA, Jun 20.
61. Ludwig IV @Ludwig_IV, 21 Jun 2016.
62. Trish1878 + @Azzurri1878, 2 Jun 2016.
63. Rockin Robin MAGA @greeneyes0084, 21 Jun 2016.
64. Seraphina @RainbeauBae, 22 Jun 2016.
65. Stephanie Lord@stephie08, Jun 22.
66. pele@pele1888, Jun 22.
67. PoliticsSense @PoliticsSense, 18 Jun 2016.
68. Anarchic Teapot @anarchic_teapot, 15 Jun 2016.
69. l'oiseau means 'bird' in French.
70. Lilian Edwards @lilianedwards, 18 Jun 2016.
71. Liz Probert @greysquirrel300, 19 Jun 2016.
72. Maria Caulfield MP @mariacaulfield, 20 Jun 2016.

73. ukipwebmaster@ukipwebmaster, 20 Jun 2016.
74. https://www.nytimes.com/2016/06/23/world/europe/on-twitter-even-cats-and-dogs-are-divided-over-brexit.html?smid=tw-share.
75. Colin @theabingdontaxi, 20 Jun 2016.
76. @g_a_zz, 21 Jun 2016.
77. RedPill @LNACurrie, 18 Jun 2016.
78. Bryan Eastwood @BryanEastwood2, 18 Jun 2016.
79. *Daily Telegraph*, 19 December 2018.

References

Charteris-Black, J. (2011). *Politicians and Rhetoric: The Persuasive Power of Metaphor*, 2nd edn. Basingstoke and New York: Palgrave Macmillan.

Gibbs, R.W. (2015). The Allegorical Characters of Political Metaphors in Discourse. *Metaphor and the Social World* 5, 2: 264–82.

Goatly, A. (2007). *Washing the Brain: Metaphor and Hidden Ideology*. Amsterdam: Benjamins.

Lakoff, G. and Turner, M. (1989). *More than Cool Reason: A Field Guide to Poetic Metaphor*. Chicago and London: University of Chicago Press.

Lancaster, S. (2018). *How Words Kill: You Are Not Human*. London: Biteback Publishing.

Musolff, A. (2010). *Metaphor, Nation and the Holocaust: The Concept of the Body Politic*. Abingdon, UK and New York: Routledge.

Zappavigna, M. (2012). *Discourse of Twitter and Social Media*. London: Bloomsbury.

10

Metaphors for Brexit

Introduction

Over the previous chapters I have outlined many of the metaphors *of* Brexit that featured in press articles, online debates and political arguments across various genres. In this final chapter, I will discuss whether there is a master metaphor *for* Brexit? Of course the choice of metaphor is strongly influenced by ideological affiliation, the stage in the withdrawal process and the speaker's, or writer's, rhetorical purpose in a specific discourse context. First I consider some of the master metaphors for Brexit proposed in the press and then offer some personal reflections.

Master Metaphors for Brexit in the Press

The master metaphor for Brexit proposed by the press during the withdrawal period was incompetence. *The Times* reported on the plight of David Davis, Britain's chief Brexit negotiator on forgetting his coat when visiting Moscow:

© The Author(s) 2019
J. Charteris-Black, *Metaphors of Brexit*,
https://doi.org/10.1007/978-3-030-28768-9_10

David Davis has been struggling with what he calls the Single European Cold. Perhaps the Brexit secretary picked it up on a recent trip to Warsaw where he attended an outdoor ceremony in conditions approaching zero degrees with only a suit jacket to keep the chill off his back. The Politico website reports that Davis *had left his coat in London and stubbornly refused a loan from his chief of staff.* It's almost a metaphor for the Brexit negotiations: no proper planning, we'll just muddle through any setback without showing the foreigners that we're in trouble. (Patrick Kidd, *The Times*, 15 December 2017)

The pro-Remain *Times* framed the negotiations in an allegory for government incompetence. As the negotiations continued pro-Remain metaphors increased in their negative evaluation. In the following Chris Grayling was criticised for framing the future faced by British citizens in terms of rescuing the victims of a bankrupt airline:

Grayling. "When I stood in front of you a year ago, I had just returned from Manchester Airport where I met the first flight bringing passengers back after the collapse of Monarch Airlines," he said. "In the following days we brought back nearly 100,000 people. And when I say we, this was a huge team effort involving other UK airlines, the Civil Aviation Authority and ten government departments. We all worked together to get people home and I am proud of the swift response. It was a tribute to what this country can do in times of change. That ladies and gentlemen is what will happen to this country after Brexit, regardless of the outcome of negotiations." ...And here he was, likening the very thing he'd campaign and voted for, to *the emergency repatriation of passengers left stranded by a stricken airline.* It's an analogy that invites a whole range of questions: Would Monarch's passengers, who in this scenario take the role of the people of the United Kingdom, have had a better or worse holiday if the airline they had booked with had not gone bankrupt? (Tom Peck, *The Independent*, 2 October 2018)

Grayling's analogy was intended to frame the government's role in enabling people to come 'home' as heroic—but Tom Peck's interpretation raises the possibility that it was Brexit that was contributing to the bankruptcy that had led to repatriation being necessary. By the end of 2018 even the pro-Brexit press saw the apparent incompetence of British ministers in performing their daily affairs as symbolic of the whole Brexit negotiations:

> The Prime Minister *was locked in the car as bumbling aides made a number of attempts to open her passenger door* while the German Chancellor waited to greet her in Berlin. Ms Anderson said: *"Did you see Theresa May not being able to get out of her car while Merkel was waiting outside?"* That's the best metaphor for Brexit. (Joe Barnes, *Express*, 19 December 2018)

Not only does this indicate incompetence but it also evokes the CONTAINERS ARE BOUNDED SPACES concept that implies imprisonment as well. There were no positive evaluations by the press of the government's performance during the negotiation period. These metaphors emphasised national powerlessness and vulnerability— almost the antithesis of the taking back of control that had been promised during the Referendum campaign:

> That is why the UK has capitulated to almost all the EU's demands, including ceding our right to determine our own fishing policy until December 2020..... It could almost be a metaphor for Brexit itself: *a fringe group packed on a small boat without any firepower and at the mercy of outside elements.* (Jason Beattie, *Mirror*, 21 March 2018)

Here Jason Beattie combines THE NATION IS A SHIP with CIRCUMSTANCES ARE WEATHER but the ship has now become a 'boat' and its occupants are framed as potential victims of inclement weather. In the following there is ironic comment on the increasing difficulty that fruit farmers had in obtaining pickers from Eastern Europe:

> If you're grasping for a metaphor for Brexit as national decay, you couldn't do much better than *an English strawberry, slowly turning to mulch in a field.* Seasonal migrant workers from the EU are giving Britain a miss this summer, leaving summer fruit unpicked. (Simon Childs, *The Independent*, 28 June 2018)

Simon Child's 'mulching' metaphor is an image of decay arising from lack of care and attention. There was a general feeling that progress was not being made and so traffic congestion became a readily available frame that had already been primed by Boris Johnson in his image of entrapment in the back of a taxi, or the boot of a car and was echoed by Patrick Kidd:

> The roads in Westminster were gummed up yesterday as dozens of black cabs crawled round Parliament Square, honking their horns all the way, in protest at Uber offering a cheaper, more convenient taxi service. Or perhaps this *slow-moving cacophony going round and round without getting anywhere was just a metaphor for the Brexit debate.* (Patrick Kidd, *The Times*, 11 February 2016)

Increasingly, the quest for freedom and liberty from the constraints of EU membership became trapped within a web of endless negotiations and the conceptual metaphor CONTAINERS ARE BOUNDED SPACES became the master metaphor for Brexit.

Some master metaphors for Brexit were more fanciful and writing for the strongly pro-Brexit *Telegraph*, Stanley Johnson (Boris Johnson's father) aroused images of Britain's vulnerability in a post-Brexit world in comparison with a relatively stable European Union:

> In a room full of magnificent Bruegels, we saw Pieter Breugel *the Elder's Fall of Icarus* and I was at once reminded of W H Auden's poem, inspired by the paintings and entitled "The Musée des Beaux Arts". Icarus falls from the sky but, as Auden puts it, the torturer's horse goes on "scratching its innocent behind on a tree," while the *"expensive delicate ship that must have seen something amazing, a boy falling, had somewhere to get to and sailed calmly o*n". Was this a metaphor for Brexit, too, I wondered, as I stood there. Would the *EU ship of state "sail calmly on"*, barely noticing if Britain left? (Stanley Johnson, *The Telegraph*, 17 June 2016)

Here the metaphor of Icarus is one of hubris, and it is reinforced by harnessing the solid and stable ship of state metaphor to the EU rather than the UK—a reversal of the roles that we saw in chapter one in relation to the Titanic. There was indeed an element of pride and crowing in Nigel Farage's address to the European Parliament following the Referendum result, and increasingly during the withdrawal period the EU became more intent on resolving its own issues and leaving the UK to get on with sorting out its own Brexit-related difficulties. This was a case where the orphan had left its parents rather than been abandoned by them and was it also an ironic comment on his son's aspirations?

Another group of metaphors from *The Times* was more philosophical and questioned the futility of the whole enterprise. These gradually increased in their level of intensity so that what was initially just complex, a lot of red tape, increasingly became a dark night of the soul. David Davis was usually quite light-hearted about the complexity of Brexit reflecting whimsically on the metaphors that he might use in discussions with the opposing negotiator Michel Barnier:

> Monday I'm in Brussels for the start of Brexit negotiations with my EU counterpart Michel Barnier.
> "This is going to be the most difficult thing we've ever done," I tell him, cheerfully. "One might as well *build a meringue igloo on the moon!*"
> "A what?" says Barnier.
> "Or *shave a tiger with a toothbrush*," I say. "Or *eat 470 pies made of steel*." Barnier sighs. Then he says there's some concern in Brussels that I've spent the past year mainly thinking up weird and jovial metaphors for Brexit. Rather than doing any actual work on it. (David Davis, *The Times*, 22 July 2017)

But a year later Brexit had shifted to something more tragic and existential, as Ann Treneman noted—a black hole that sucked all political energies into it:

> Even Samuel Beckett's *Waiting for Godot, in which two men spend hours waiting for something that never happens,* quite early on began to feel uncomfortably like a metaphor for Brexit negotiations. (Ann Treneman, *The Times*, 20 August 2018)

Some, noted Carly Read, were less polite when discussing Theresa May's deal:

> Tory MP Steve Double said he was unsure how to vote on the Prime Minister's deal, describing the deal as a *"polished turd"*. He said: "The choices before us are two wrongs, they are two things I don't want to

happen, they are two impossible choices to make. I will make a decision and I will vote tonight. But it's a choice I do not want to have to make between *a turd of a deal* which has been taken away and *polished* and is now a *polished turd*, but it might be the *best turd* we've got before us, or the alternative, which is those who want to stop Brexit altogether and the risk of that happening is very real." (Carly Read, *Express*, 12 March 2019)

Here the metaphor is an exercise in moral reasoning aloud, as the MP searches for an allegory to describe the emotional frustration he experiences when faced with a situation where he is compelled to make one of 'two impossible choices'. The dark humour was in keeping with the style of political communication of the time—serving as the only anasthesia from the pain of Brexit.

The patience and moderation in the language of the EU negotiators was significant as their framing of Brexit emphasised progress in overcoming difficulties:

The hiking theme harked back to a speech Mr Barnier gave last month, when he used his love of walking as a metaphor for Brexit. He said: "If you like walking in the mountains you have to learn a number of rules. You have to learn to put one foot in front of the other, because sometimes you are on a steep and rocky path. You also have to look what accidents might befall you - falling rocks. You have to be very careful to keep your breath, you have to have stamina, because it could be a lengthy path and you have to keep looking at the summit." (Reiss Smith, *Express*, 19 June 2017)

Ultimately, this more philosophical framing of Brexit was one that lead to a shift in opinion in the UK as the image of the EU as a brutal or abusive partner seemed to match less and less with the reality; though much of this was due to the close attention it now gave to the framing of Brexit.

Writing for the Remain supporting *Observer*, Nick Cohen framed Brexit with the master metaphor of 'original sin':

The *original sin* of the authors of Brexit was to refuse to admit that it must either bring a shuddering dislocation as Britain tore itself out of an integrated European economy or turn Britain into an EU vassal state that obeyed EU rules but had no say in their formulation. The greater dishonesty was that the EU referendum was never just about the EU. It was a howl of rage from Thatcherites, who cannot accept that their ideology failed, from the old against the young, and from all who could not make their peace with the sexual revolution of the 1960s, the environment science of the 1980s and the multiculturalism of the 2000s. Their leaders see the chance to abolish a modern world they neither like nor comprehend. Hence their fanaticism. Hence their determination to go for broke and tolerate no compromises. (Nick Cohen, *The Observer*, 13 October 2018)

So here the metaphoric 'original sin' was a failure to accept social change in which Brexit symbolised right-wing rejection of all the social and cultural changes that had emerged from the 1960s onwards and represented a backward looking nostalgia for a pseudo golden age when children respected their elders and got a short back and sides haircut. The tabloid press also offered the 'original sin' metaphor as a theological frame for Brexit:

Perhaps it won't work and despite our best efforts we'd carry with us the seeds of our own destruction, an *original sin* of stupidity that can never be wiped clean however many well-meaning people get themselves nailed to a tree, and we'll infest planets with idiocy until a wiser race of beings eradicates us. (Fleet Street Fox, *Mirror*, 14 April 2017)

Here the original sin is causing unnecessary self-inflicted damage. It argues that supporters of Brexit are lacking in intelligence because they are bent on self-inflicted pain and is closely related to the frames and moral intuitions that have been discussed in earlier chapters. Finton O'Toole employed a similar master metaphor when he described Brexit as 'sadopopulism'—a situation 'in which people are willing to inflict pain on themselves so long as they can believe that, in the same moment, they are making their enemies hurt more'.[1] Rather than attributing this to stupidity he puts it down to the sadomasochistic influence of British boarding schools, such as Eton, in which many Brexit leaders were educated. As a master metaphor pain works well—but rather than the release of physical pain, it is more like the prolonged psychological trauma of a long awaited operation, that is unlikely to have any better outcome than amputation—with the possibility of subsequent phantom limb syndrome.

Reflections on a Master Metaphor for Brexit

Leavers had always felt ensnared by the EU and sought to throw off its shackles so that Britain could emerge reborn like a butterfly from a chrysalis. Immediately after the Referendum supporters of Brexit celebrated victory over European 'colonisation' as if it were VE Day. The referendum result symbolised fighting for freedom from oppression and escape from domination by an alien power. So for Leavers, at this point in time, the metaphor for Brexit was simply 'Liberation' or as they themselves put it: 'Independence Day'. But the euphoria of decolonisation gradually dissipated once divisions emerged as to the nature of the departure and disputes over the model for the future relationship with the EU. The EU was not going to let the UK have their cake and eat it and refused to engage in any discussion of future trading relationships until the issues of the UK's responsibilities and obligations incurred by EU membership had been resolved. So while for Brexiteers the referendum result was an occasion for liberty and freedom, by late 2017 metaphors for ensnarement returned. The negotiations reinforced the frame of conflict and struggle that permeated all language and thought about Brexit—whether it was 'ground campaigns' or 'cyberwars'. So the dominant metaphor for these contested worldviews became Guerilla Warfare and those Conservative opponents of a No-Deal Brexit were referred to as 'saboteurs' who had 'cut the legs off' Boris Johnson's negotiating position. Boris Johnson would 'take a chainsaw to' anything that stood in the way of leaving the EU. The violence of the language corresponded with the polarisation of political positions. When Boris Johnson said in Parliament on 5th September 2019 that he would rather be "dead in a ditch" than ask the European Union for a further extension he was using a metaphor that was far removed from the language of hope and freedom that had characterised Leavers' reception to the referendum result.

As far as the EU were concerned, Brexit opposition to the European federal State and its various projects, such as European Army, needed to be eliminated by moral reasoning as to the UK's obligations from being a club member for many years: why should they be loyal to a traitor who had betrayed the EU? While grounded in the moral intuitions of Care and Fairness their negotiators were sufficiently skilled to use restraint in language—whatever they might have used behind closed doors—and were aware that such language would be viewed as retaliatory and counter-productive by reinforcing the Brexiteers' War frame. So for the EU metaphor was substituted by the language of reason and ethics with concepts such as 'Fairness', 'Values' and 'Responsibility'. Metaphors often get lost in translation and become risky in conveying different frames from the intended ones. There were attempts by Brexiteers to revive earlier symbols for national celebration as when in September 2018 Theresa May announced that a Festival of Great Britain and Northern Ireland would be held in 2022. This evoked memories of its precursor of 1950 that celebrated Britain as a forward-looking post-war nation. This national blossoming would set off a chain reaction across Europe in which nation states would be restored to their prelapsarian glories. Meanwhile the massive Joint Research Centre of the EU Commission explored why it was not always getting its message across. When asked for professional advice, I suggested they consider the EU as a grandparent, building on the moral framing offered by the family metaphor. I suggested that since the family is the social unit for the instilling and learning of moral values so then the EU could be framed as a kindly grandparent who would appear to:

1. Plan for the future prosperity and success by getting in place an inheritance plan.
2. Think of the long-term future by showing concern for the crucial issue of the environment that the national government may overlook in its more immediate concerns.
3. Provide for the cultural, spiritual and intellectual growth of its grandchildren as means of helping them to grow as fulfilled individuals.
4. Keep the different branches of the family in touch with each other.

This role of the EU-as-grandparent contrasts with an alternative 'STRICT FATHER' frame that was conveyed by opponents such as Boris Johnson who uses the 'Nanny Brussels' metaphor to refer to the EU Commission as an over-controlling authoritarean force.

For Remainers the Referendum result was a shock to the system, an unexpected and unprepared return to a darker age of myth dominated by ignorance, tribalism, populism and a resurgent racism that threatened to overwhelm the social-democratic values, and the institutions that had enshrined these, since the Second World War. Like the collapse of the Roman Empire, Brexit would take us into a post-Darwinian nightmare as tribes across Europe engaged in atavistic, internecine struggles. Those who had enjoyed the benefits of easy and cheap travel to the European mainland, who delighted in the ready availability and convenience of Polish cleaners, Czech nannies or Romanian architects feared a decline in the quality of their lives as these services faded, or became more expensive as sterling fell. For Remainers Brexit was a sort of collective psychosis in which the imagined dangers arising from EU membership were a smokescreen for real major social issues such as poor levels of education in deprived areas, ever-lengthening waiting lists for routine operations and increased levels of knife crime. For them the metaphor for Brexit was perhaps a colonisation of the soul which was carrying the nation down in spiraling vortex from which it was increasingly impossible to find an exit: 'Exit from Brexit', became a slogan adopted by Remainers.

In the week when Britain was originally scheduled to leave the European Union (29 March 2019) there were very different metaphors corresponding with the two competing worldviews. Brexiteers, sensed betrayal and treachery in the air leading to a resurgence of the Distrust and Betrayal frame that had characterised their longstanding view of 'Europe'. Quislings and traitors were again everywhere—and often among those who were previously the most strident bearers of the flame. When switching to support Theresa May's withdrawal agreement even the arch-Brexiteer Jacob Rees-Mogg remarked that some would find his behavior 'treacherous'. For both sides the failure to find a political solution has created a language of shame and humiliation. For Remainers Brexit had become a scapegoat for the sins of the nation. Like a rotting albatross they carried Brexit around their national neck as a mark of dishonor symbolising the outrageous hubris that would exact its own tragic revenge. Like a serious and incurable illness, it became an increasingly taboo topic that was best avoided in polite circles. If Brexit had opened a Pandora's box, then there was remarkably little sign of hope alongside famine, fire and plague, let alone the option of closing it.

Why had Brexit proved so unfathomable? We cannot forget that opponents of the European Union project had always had a wellspring of nationalism on which to draw—especially after the creation of the euro and the formationof the Schengen area set Europe on two different courses. There was a fast track in which a shared currency the removal of national borders and the diminution of the authority of national government were all milestones on a journey to fully federal union. And there was a slow track for nations that sought to keep their own sense of national identity by retaining borders, with armies to protect them and were unconvinced of the value of a single uniform currency. The Greek financial crisis had shown the need for the type of microeconomic policy that was no longer possible in a single currency. The frame of Distrust and Betrayal reflected a deep suspicion embedded in historical national identities and settled happily alongside the Patriotism and the Nation frame—through celebrations of local monarchy, national football teams or regional gastronomies. But, like good and evil, one could not exist without the other, and the tide of historical events would lead to endless oscillation between celebration of the in-group and demonisation of the out-group.

Philosophically, perhaps a metaphor for Brexit could be the human condition: complex, nuanced, and dependent on circumstantial influence? Is there not always a tension between love of those who we know and fear of others who we don't know? The moral foundations are all themselves framed as opposites: Care and Harm, Fairness and Cheating etc. If this is the case, then Brexit becomes more like the human spirit: an intermingling of desire for social enhancement and selflessness with fears of loss of what is valued because of incursions by outsiders. Or at a more metaphysical level perhaps, taking the media framing of Original Sin, Brexit enabled the opportunity for indulging in several of the Deadly Sins including:

Greed—rejecting net contributions to the EU budget when these contributed to greater economic equality across Europe;

Pride—the idea that it was feasible to reject an economic union on which nearly half British trade relied and go it alone in international markets;

Envy—of the salaries and working conditions of those employed in Civil Servant jobs at the EU Commission in Brussels;

Sloth—the behaviour of MEPs who don't do any real work.

If, as in the much quoted tautology 'Brexit means Brexit', then perhaps Brexit itself is a metaphor for travelling back in time to the 1950s or 60s, a time when life was purported to be less complex, less driven by technology, social media and online hate videos. Support for this claim was in the 2011 poll showing that 62% agreed with the statement: "Britain has changed in recent times beyond recognition, it sometimes feels like a foreign country and this makes me uncomfortable". It is as if Leave voters wanted a return to the time when the world was thought to be simpler and kinder, when neighbours knew neighbours, and people left the backdoor unlocked because there was no danger of a thief creeping in; when a sense of community and a friendly face was always available down at the local pub. Was online contact with strangers really a satisfactory substitute for real people? In this case the best metaphor for Brexit was the Myth of a Golden Age. But perhaps this is grasping at straws or snatching at dragon flies? Since a reason why some Labour Party supporters voted Leave was to escape an institution that encouraged neoliberalism—yet without fully considering the social cost of the disruptions it entailed.

The argument put forward by Leavers is that Britain would be open to the rest of the world ready to embrace opportunities to trade anywhere. But what might such a globalised Britain look like—other than a more extreme form of liberalised economy where workers no longer had the protections offered by the European Social Contract? If we are competing with the BRICS countries, costs including labour costs, will need to be kept down to a level as low as these competitors. That will exert downward pressure on wage and salary levels; and while we will be able to control immigration we may only be able to pay wages that will attract immigrants from outside of Europe. If this argument is accepted then Brexit has always been an illusion—a chimera, a golden city on a hill—that has promised more than it could ever offer in reality. But if this is not the case, and there remains a vision of a future Britain independent of the EU, then this New Jerusalem still needs to be revealed.

Note

1. O'Toole (2018), p. 133.

Reference

O'Toole, F. (2018). *Heroic Failure: Brexit and the Politics of Pain*. London: Zeus.

Metaphor Brexicon

B

Backstop* (Neutral)	Leaving the UK inside a customs union with the EU to avoid a hard border in Ireland
Blind Brexit (Neutral)	Not known what will happen on withdrawal from the EU
Body politic (Neutral)	The institutions of the state
Breaking point (poster) (Leave perspective)	A UKIP poster showing masses of non-European migrants that would be entering Britain because of EU membership
Bremorse (Remain perspective)	Feelings of regret about the referendum result
Brexhausted	Feeling exhausted by the topic of Brexit
Brexitgeddon (Remain perspective)	The disastrous consequence of leaving the EU without a withdrawal deal
Brexit means Brexit (Leave perspective)	A form of circular argument used by Theresa May known as 'tautology' in which the evidence is the same as the claim that is being made
Brexodus (Neutral)	Leaving Britain because of Brexit

C

Cat out of the bag (Both sides)	Revealing what was previously a deliberately concealed secret
Cherry picking (EU perspective)	Choosing only the benefits of EU membership with any costs (see also 'having your cake and eating it')

© The Editor(s) (if applicable) and The Author(s) 2019
J. Charteris-Black, *Metaphors of Brexit*,
https://doi.org/10.1007/978-3-030-28768-9

Cliff edge (Also 'crashing out' Remain perspective)	Economic disruption caused by leaving the EU, its single market and customs union without a future trade deal lined up
Crocodile tears (Leave perspective)	Untrustworthy politicians who feign false emotions

D

Diktat (Leave perspective)	Order from the European Commission
Divorce bill (Leave perspective)	The amount to be paid by the UK when leaving the EU for outstanding financial commitments made under the current budget

E

Trying to take the eggs out of an omelette (EU perspective)	Pascal Lamy's metaphor to describe the complexity of negotiating Brexit
Elephant in the room	A topic that everyone knows is being deliberately avoided
Emergency break	A limit on in-work benefits for new immigrants from other EU countries
Enemies of the people (Leave perspective)	*Daily Mail* term for the judges who ruled that Parliament should decide on when Article 50 (notice of EU withdrawal) should be triggered

F

Fat cat (Leave perspective)	Someone who benefits financially from EU membership
Father of Brexit (Neutral)	The person most responsible for the vote to Leave—usually attributed to Nigel Farage or Tony Benn (see Chapter 7)
Four freedoms (Neutral)	The basic trade principles of the EU's single market: free movement of goods, capital, services and people
Frictionless trade (Neutral)	Trade without customs delays at borders

G

Gammon (Remain perspective)	Older white man, who supported Brexit, and appeared pink faced when emotional
Gravy train (Leave perspective)	Corrupt practice of MEP'S benefiting from expense claims
Grexit (Neutral)	Coined by Willem Buiter in 2012 to refer to the possibility of Greece exiting the eurozone

H

Hard Brexit (Neutral)	Leaving the EU's single market and customs union; ending its obligations to respect the four freedoms, and ending EU budget payments and the jurisdiction of the ECJ

Having your cake and eating it
(EU perspective)

Having tariff free access to the single market without accepting the four freedoms or making payments (see also 'cherry picking')

At the heart of Europe
(Neutral)

At the centre of European politics

From the horse's mouth
(Neutral)

Something that is true because it is from a highly reliable source

I

Independence day
(Leave perspective)

Day when Britain would withdraw from the EU

K

Kicking the can down the road (Leave perspective)

Delaying making a decision until the withdrawal date

King Arthur
(Leave perspective)

Usually Nigel Farage or Boris Johnson

L

Lemmings
(Remain perspective)

Brexit supporers who are inflicting self-harm on the nation

M

Marriage of convenience
(Leave perspective)

Political arrangement made on the basis of pragmaticism rather than affection

O

One-size-fits-all
(Leave perspective)

A standard policy across the EU that does not take into account the individual needs of each nation

P

Parasite
(Leave perspective)

Someone benefiting from EU membership

Pigs might fly
(Neutral)

An irresponsible position that shows a lack of grasp of reality

Project Fear
(Leave perspective)

Campaign policy to deliberately exaggerate the dangers of leaving the EU to encourage people to vote Remain

R

Rats leaving a sinking sheep
(Leave perspective)

The establishment who sought to betray the people

Red lines
(Neutral)

Non-negotiable positions

Red tape
(Leave perspective)

Unnecessary bureaucracy associated with the EU

Regrexit (Remain perspective)	Feeling of regret about voting to Leave
Remoaners (Leave perspective)	Those who supported staying in the EU and com- plained about the Referendum result

S

Sclerotic (Leave perspective)	Failing (usually applied to the EU)
Sinking ship (Both sides)	Institution facing disaster, typically the EU though possibly also the UK
Smell a rat (Both sides)	Detect a deception
Snake oil salesmen (Both sides)	Someone that exploits others while enriching themselves
Soft Brexit (Neutral)	Leaving the EU but staying economically close to the EU by remaining in either the single market or the Customs Union, or both
Sunlit Uplands (Leave perspective)	An imagined ideal future state after Brexit when the UK arranges its own trade deals. (Allusion to Martin Luther King)

T

Take back control (Leave perspective)	Regain complete sovereignty
The Titanic (Both sides)	For Leave it refers to the EU while for Remain it refers to Britain after withdrawal
Trojan horse (Both sides)	A conspiracy frame, in which true intentions and motivations of actors are concealed

V

Vassalage/ vassal state (Leave perspective)	The UK as a member of the Single market/ custome Union but without voting rights or influence on policy

W

Wolves in sheep's clothing (Remain perspective)	Leave campaign leaders who are concealing their true purposes

*Where a word indicates a particular ideology ('Leave' or 'Remain') I have indicated this. 'Both sides' means that it is a metaphor with an ideological perspective that was used by Leave and Remain. 'Neutral' means that the metaphor does not express a particular ideology

References

Banks, A. (2017). *The Bad Boys of Brexit* (Oakeshott, I. ed.). London: Biteback.

Barsalou, L.W. (2008). Grounded Cognition. *Annual Review of Psychology* 59: 617–645.

Bennett, S. (2019). Values as Tools of Legitimation in EU and UK Brexit Discourses. In V. Koller, S. Kopf, and M. Miglbauer (Eds.), *Discourses of Brexit* (pp. 17–31). London: Routledge.

Buckledee, S. (2018). *The Language of Brexit: How Britian Talked Its Way Out of the European Union.* London: Bloomsbury.

Burgers. C., Konijn, E.A., and Steen, G.J. (2016). Figurative Framing: Shaping Public Discourse Through Metaphor, Hyperbole, and Irony. *Communication Theory* 26, 4: 410–430.

Charteris-Black, J. (2004). *Corpus Approaches to Critical Metaphor Analysis.* Basingstoke and New York: Palgrave Macmillan.

Charteris-Black, J. (2006). Britain as a Container: Immigration Metaphors in the 2005 Election Campaign. *Discourse & Society* 17, 6: 563–582.

Charteris-Black, J. (2011). *Politicians and Rhetoric: The Persuasive Power of Metaphor*, 2nd edn. Basingstoke and New York: Palgrave Macmillan.

Charteris-Black, J. (2016). The 'Dull Roar' and the 'Burning Barbed Wire Pantyhose: Complex Metaphor in Accounts of Chronic Pain'. In R. Gibbs (Ed.), *Mixing Metaphor* (pp. 155–178). Amsterdam: Benjamins.

© The Editor(s) (if applicable) and The Author(s) 2019
J. Charteris-Black, *Metaphors of Brexit*,
https://doi.org/10.1007/978-3-030-28768-9

Charteris-Black, J. (2017). Competition Metaphors & Ideology: Life as a Race. In R. Wodak and B. Forchtner (Eds.), *The Routledge Handbook of Language and Politics* (pp. 202–217). London and New York: Routledge.

Charteris-Black, J. (2018). *Analysing Political Speeches: Rhetoric, Discourse and Metaphor*, 2nd edn. London: Palgrave.

Chilton, P. (2004). *Analysing Political Discourse*. London and New York: Routledge.

Clarke, H.D., Goodwin, M., and Whiteley, P. (2017). *Brexit: Why Britian Voted to Leave the European Union*. Cambridge: Cambridge University Press.

Edelman, M. (1988). *Constructing the Political Spectacle*. Chicago: Chicago University Press.

El Refaie, E. (2009). Metaphor in Political Cartoons: Exploring Audience Responses. In C.J. Forceville and E. Urios-Aparisi (Eds.), *Multimodal Metaphor* (pp. 173–196). Berlin: Mouton de Gruyter.

Entman, R.M. (1993). Framing: Toward Clarification of a Fractured Paradigm. *Journal of Communication* 43, 4: 51–58.

Gibbs, R.W.J. (2006a). *Embodiment and Cognitive Science*. New York: Cambridge University Press.

Gibbs, R.W.J. (2006b). Metaphor Interpretation as Embodied Simulation. *Mind & Language* 21: 434–458.

Gibbs, R.W. (2015). The Allegorical Characters of Political Metaphors in Discourse. *Metaphor and the Social World* 5, 2: 264–282.

Goatly, A. (2007). *Washing the Brain: Metaphor and Hidden Ideology*. Amsterdam: John Benjamins.

Goodhart, D. (2017). *The Road to Somewhere: The Populist Revolt and the Future of Politics*. London: C. Hurst.

Graham, J., Haidt, J., and Nosek, B.A. (2009). Liberals and Conservatives Rely on Different Sets of Moral Foundations. *Journal of Personal and Social Pyschology* 96, 5: 1029–1046.

Haidt, J. (2001). The Emotional Dog and Its Rational Tail: A Social Intuitionist Approach to Moral Judgment. *Psychological Review* 108, 4, October: 814–834.

Haidt, J. (2012). *The Righteous Mind: Why Good People are Divided by Politics and Religion*. London: Penguin.

Heywood. (1546). *Dialogue of Proverbs*.

Koller, V., Kopf, S., and Miglbauer, M. *Discourses of Brexit*. London and New York: Routledge.

Lakoff, G. (2002). *Moral Politics*, 2nd edn. Chicago and London: University of Chicago Press.

Lakoff, G. and Johnson, M. (1980). *Metaphors We Live By*. Chicago, IL: University of Chicago Press.

Lakoff, G. and Turner, M. (1989). *More than Cool Reason: A Field Guide to Poetic Metaphor*. Chicago and London: University of Chicago Press.

Lakoff, G. and Wehling, E. (2012). *The Little Blue Book: The Essential Guide to Thinking and Talking Democratic*. New York: Simon and Schuster.

Lalic-Krstin, G. and Silaski, N. (2019). Don't Go Brexin' My Heart: The Ludic Aspects of Brexit-Induced Neologisms. In V. Koller, S. Kopf, and M. Miglbauer (Eds.), *Discourses of Brexit* (pp. 222–236). London and New York: Routledge.

Lancaster, S. (2018). *How Words Kill: You Are Not Human*. London: Biteback Publishing.

Measuring Effects of Metaphor. https://www.ncbi.nlm.nih.gov/pmc/articles/PMC4517745/.

Müller, J. (2017). *What Is Populism?* London: Penguin.

Musolff, A. (2006). Metaphor Scenarios in Public Discourse. *Metaphor and Symbol* 21, 1: 23–38.

Musolff, A. (2010). *Metaphor, Nation and the Holocaust: The Concept of the Body Politic*. Abingdon, UK and New York: Routledge.

Musolff, A. (2014). The Metaphor of the "Body Politic" Across Languages and Cultures. In F. Polzenhagen, Z. Kövecses, S. Vogelbacher, and S. Kleinke (Eds.), *Cognitive Explorations into Metaphor and Metonymy* (pp. 85–99). Frankfurt: Peter Lang.

Musolff, A. (2016). *Political Metaphor Analysis: Discourse and Scenarios*. London: Bloomsbury Academic.

O'Rourke, K. (2018). *A Short History of Brexit*. London: Pelican.

O'Toole, F. (2018). *Heroic Failure: Brexit and the Politics of Pain*. London: Zeus.

Orwell, G. (1945). *Notes on Nationalism*. http://www.resort.com/~prime8/Orwell/nationalism.html.

Purnell, S. (2011). *Just Boris: The Irresistible Rise of a Political Celebrity*. London: Aurum Press.

Reddy, M.J. (1979). The Conduit Metaphor: A Case of Frame Conflict in Our Language About Language. In A. Ortony (Ed.), *Metaphor and Thought* (pp. 284–310). Cambridge: Cambridge University Press.

Schank, R. and Abelson, R. (1977). *Scripts, Plans, Goals and Understanding*. Hillsdale, NJ: Lawrence Erlbaum.

Semino, E. (2010). Descriptions of Pain, Metaphor, and Embodied Simulation. *Metaphor and Symbol* 25, 4: 205–226.

Shipman, T. (2016). *All Out War*. London: Collins.

Thibodeau, P.H., Boroditsky, L. (2011). Metaphors We Think With: The Role of Metaphor in Reasoning. *PLoS One* 6: e16782. https://doi.org/10.1371/journal.pone.0016782 [PMC Free Article] [PubMed].

Thibodeau, P.H., Boroditsky, L. (2015). *PLoS One* 10, 7: e0133939.

Thompson, M. (2016). *Enough Said: What's Gone Wrong with the Langauge of Politics?* London: Penguin.

van Dijk, T. (1998). *Ideology.* London: Sage.

Zappavigna, M. (2012). *Discourse of Twitter and Social Media.* London: Bloomsbury.

Zappavigna, M. (2019). Ambient Affiliation and Brexit. In V. Koller, S. Kopf, and M. Miglbauer (Eds.), *Discourses of Brexit* (pp. 48–68). London: Routledge.

Index

CPI Antony Rowe
Eastbourne, UK
November 15, 2019